First Published as a Ferrington Historical Monograph

THE SEEDS OF EVIL

Robin Blick lectures in Politics and History at South Thames College, London. His published works include two books (under the pen-name Robert Black): STALINISM IN BRITAIN (1970) and FASCISM IN GERMANY (two volumes, 1975); and numerous essays and articles on modern history and contemporary political issues.

This book is dedicated to the memory of Adam Westoby; friend, educator, writer and political campaigner; born October 19, 1944, died November 27, 1994.

THE SEEDS OF EVIL

Second Revised Edition

Lenin and the Origins of Bolshevik Élitism

Robin Blick

One ought, I believe, to admit that all the seeds of evil were there from the start.
George Orwell

STEYNE PUBLICATIONS, LONDON
1995

First published by Ferrington, 1993

ISBN 09503571-1-1

Second Impression

Typeset by Saxon Graphics Ltd, Derby
Printed and bound in Great Britain by
Biddles Ltd, Guildford

CONTENTS

FOREWORD

Few would dispute that, as we approach the new century, the one we are leaving behind has dashed more hopes than it has realised. Whether it is the individualist gospel of free market capitalism, the collectivist creed of Leninist state socialism or the quest, by means of fascism and national socialism, to synthesise the supposed virtues of both, the truth is that even when judged by their own goals, each attempt to re-organise human society has, either partially or totally, failed. When the time comes to draw up the balance sheet of this century, among its greatest outrages must surely be the relentless and unceasing devouring of countless millions of human beings, either by design in the death and slave camps of Nazi and Bolshevik totalitarianism, or as an inevitable (even if unintended) consequence of the appetites of unrestrained capitalism. And for those who are tempted to argue, in support of whatever cause, that the end can justify the means, it needs to be pointed out that even if this was in some perverse way true, the goals have not been realised; that, just as our century began, so it will surely end with the vast majority of the human race living in conditions that condemn it to an expectation of life in some cases little more than half of that enjoyed by the remainder. In the Netherlands, men can expect to die at seventy-four, women at eighty, compared with thirty-nine for men and forty-three for women in Ethiopia. And poverty is not only bad in itself. It is, as Dr Johnson once said, bad for liberty. So, inevitably and tragically, what also prevails is a malnutrition of the spirit, a pattern of repression throughout entire continents where an enduring respect for human rights is as rare as a well-balanced diet, where arms dealers from East and West vie for the privilege of equipping well-fed and grandly uniformed tyrants to wage war on their own people. And the results, it must be agreed, are often spectacular. The 'Marxist-Leninist' rulers of famine-ravaged Ethiopia still managed to mobilise in their defence an army (fruitlessly as it proved) of 315,000 men – the largest in Africa, and approximately tenth in the world – whilst 'socialist' Iraq, with a total population of 17 million, could afford to conscript no less than one million of them for Saddam's wars of conquest against Iran and Kuwait, and of repression against Kurds and Shi'ahs. Not to be outdone, Saddam's Ba'athist rivals in the no less fraudulently 'socialist' Syria devote twelve per cent of its GDP to 'defence' while maintaining an income differential of 16 to 1 between the richest twenty per cent and the poorest.

But these conditions are not unique to the third world. Ravaged, polluted, demoralised and de-politicised by decades of totalitarian rule, many of the states of the former Soviet empire totter towards a similar fate. By 1992, the per capita GDP in eastern Europe (excluding the former states of the USSR) had sunk to thirteen per cent of those in the west. Here, too, there is being unleashed a surfeit of military muscle amidst galloping poverty, while national and tribal hatreds rage unchecked by any serious tradition or experience of political freedom, toleration and civic responsibility.

Only in the countries of established and advanced capitalism can we, like Marx in his day, discern the contours of a better world. Yet even here, for all its undoubted (though unevenly shared) prosperity, and broadranging political freedoms (habitually denied in the past to its colonies) capitalism has, in various ways, grown rich partly by visiting poverty on others. And yet, despite its many and immense advantages, advanced capitalism has, thus far, found it impossible to escape from the wearisome and debilitating cycle of boom and slump, has been unable to counter the social and cultural as well as economic consequences of technological change, industrial decay and acute structural imbalances. For all capitalism's sophistications, it cannot make work the mechanisms it has devised to harmonise and regulate world trade and economic performance. Capitalism desires stability, but everywhere generates tension and, on occasions, even chaos. It would dearly love to establish a universal and ever-expanding market, but, in a world where India, typical of its kind, has a per capita GDP only five per cent that of the United States, and runs up a foreign debt amounting to twenty one per cent of its annual national income, the advanced national capitalisms find themselves driven towards a self-denying and stultifying protectionism. There is much talk of the peace dividend, and yet East and West continue to re-stock their arsenals as if the cold war still raged, not so much for fear of each other, but of yet more unemployment should arms production decline.

A kind of creeping paralysis has gripped the world economy. Third world and former 'communist' poverty abroad, with its attendant lack of markets, drives up unemployment at home. Stagnation, rather than expansion, threatens to become the rule. And so, for all the cultural, technological and scientific achievements of capitalism, gross, and even accentuating, social and economic inequality still prevails. As in the third world and the former Soviet bloc, so in the first, the gap between rich and poor widens. The economic as well as moral case against capitalism is overwhelming. The human race deserves, and surely wants, something better.

Like so many educated young Russians of his day, Lenin thought so too. After all, his country was more afflicted than any other in Europe by the injustices of a class-divided society and a repressive political system. His elder brother, Alexander, had already died on the gallows in a failed attempt to rid Russia of its evil and antiquated autocracy by assassinating its personification, Tsar Alexander III. It was to the same end, and with the same determination, that the young Lenin selflessly devoted his life to the development and implementation of a doctrine and system of political organisation that could answer the challenge of our times – how to advance from a world of exploitation, war and tyranny to a new order of economic well-being, international harmony and political liberty. But that was not all. As he grew to a young man, broadening his experiences and deepening his studies, Lenin looked beyond the insular populist doctrines that guided the tragically misconceived actions of his brother. By the time of his arrival in St Petersburg in the autumn of 1893, Lenin had become totally convinced that he had found the answer in Marxism. Henceforth he would always claim, as do his followers to this day, that the movement which he, more than any other, helped create (and which, after 1903, became known as Bolshevism) stood entirely within the traditions and upon the principles established by Marx and Engels, and that his opponents (initially the Mensheviks, but later, all other tendencies within socialism, Marxist or otherwise) were invariably acting, wittingly or not, as the accomplices of capitalism. There was only one road to emancipation, not only in Russia, but throughout the world, and that was Bolshevism.

The purpose of this work is to examine the truth of this claim, not least because its unquestioning acceptance has led generations of selfless and courageous individuals – their number runs into millions – to embark, like Lenin, upon a path of political action which, far from bringing the desired goals nearer, has helped erect yet more obstacles to their achievement. Tragically, what Leninism regards as its greatest triumphs – namely, the discrediting, defeat and, where this proved feasible, destruction of all other socialist tendencies, and carrying through of what was claimed to be the world's first socialist revolution – have largely convinced friend and foe alike that Bolshevism is indeed the only genuine revolutionary alternative to capitalism. Yet what Leninism still sees as a victory has proved to be a catastrophe for Marxism in particular, and the cause of socialism in general. How ironic that now, with the world confronted with the spectacle of the collapse of Soviet rule in eastern Europe, and the eruption of the misery and bitterness engendered by its wretched legacy, Leninism in its death agony should be proving such a godsend to a capitalism only too anxious to convince us that, for all its difficulties and shortcomings, it is the best that we can hope for. And, but for a handful of Leninist zealots (and they have invariably seen themselves better suited to the role of scientist than guinea pig in the Bolshevik experiment), who could fail to agree that if the only alternative to capitalism were indeed life (and quite possibly a premature death) under totalitarian state socialism, then capitalism it must be?

This argument has considerable force, and has undoubtedly played a part in persuading many to reject the socialist alternative to capitalism. It is surely reasonable to doubt, especially in the light of the Russian experience, that any future order of society, socialist or otherwise, even supposing it were realisable, would *inevitably* surpass the achievements of the one we live under now. Even so, this should not prevent those of us who find our present order of things seriously wanting from trying to devise another that can be better, and, with the consent and active participation of the majority, from attempting (cautiously) to achieve its realisation. But it is not enough to reject the present, or even to devise alternatives that might replace it. There inevitably arises the question of means, of how to organise the forces that will accomplish the desired transformation. Marx and Engels, in their time, advanced one solution. Lenin, in his time, proposed and attempted another. The many and radical divergences between these solutions, and their significance for modern socialism, comprise a large part of the subject matter of this book.

It is one of the intellectual conundrums of our times that Marx and Engels (and in this they were emulated by their followers) spent one part of their lives seeking to prove theoretically that communism would inevitably succeed and surpass capitalism, and another part in various activities which suggested that communism was anything but inevitable, and that even the successful overthrow of capitalism would not guarantee the establishment of a higher form of society. That is why in the thought of Marx and Engels there is an unacknowledged, but nevertheless real, tension between the would-be scientific component, with its attendant quest for economic laws and historical certainty, and the 'activist' element, which comes to the fore in their search for the most effective forms of working class organisation to achieve the goal of a socialist revolution. And, most puzzling of all, it is hard (if not impossible) to discern any obvious, let alone inevitable, progression that leads on from conclusions arrived at in the first realm of inquiry (for example, the labour theory of value) to the kinds of answers developed in response to the problems of the second. That is why it is reasonable, for the purposes in hand, to treat the organisational ideas of Marx and Engels as if they were largely a self-contained and self-sustaining entity. For similar reasons, the same approach has been adopted with the organisational theories of Lenin. Although differing in almost every detail, they, likewise, comprise a very distinct part of his thinking, and also like those of Marx and Engels, owe very little to his general analysis of society, which, in most respects (again, for example, the labour theory of value) he derived from Marx and Engels.

The divergence is profound. Believing that it is from the working class itself, 'a class which forms the majority of all members of society', that there 'emanates the consciousness of the necessity of a fundamental revolution',[1] Marx and Engels, from the very outset of their political collaboration, insisted that 'the proletariat can and must emancipate itself'.[2] Lenin argued from the opposite premise. Given that 'class political consciousness' could be 'brought to the workers only from without'[3] and that 'talented leaders' were 'not born by the hundreds',[4] he advocated the creation of an 'organisation of revolutionaries' consisting 'first and foremost of people who make revolutionary activity their profession',[5] and directed by 'a dozen wise men'.[6]

One final word. Wisdom after the event is better than none at all, and wisdom during the event, better again. But the most valuable (and rarest) wisdom of all is that which precedes the event and (although this is an obvious paradox) by so doing, tries to prevent it from happening. Predictions as to where the organisational methods proposed and practised by Lenin might lead were indeed made, but too few either heard or heeded them. Yet they could not so easily be dismissed as the carpings of doubters since, in every instance, they came from Marxists, in the first place from his own Party comrades – Vladimir Akimov, Yuri Martov, Paul Axelrod, Rosa Luxemburg, George Plekhanov and Leon Trotsky. All, in their different ways, did what they could to alert Russian and international social democrats to the dangers of Lenin's organisational methods and political amoralism. But, amongst them, special tribute needs to be paid to the founder of Menshevism, Yuri Martov, who, until the split of 1903, was Lenin's closest friend as well as most trusted comrade. Because he knew and understood Lenin better than anyone (perhaps better even than Lenin himself), Martov was able to predict, with Lenin's casting of the Bolshevik die at the Second Party Congress, that 'here is a man fatally compelled to roll down that plane on which he chose to stand, and which leads him on straight to the complete political perversion and fragmentation of social democracy.'[7] Tragically, they proved prophetic words, far more so, as we can now see, than Trotsky's arrogant quip, on the night of the Bolshevik seizure of power in Petrograd, that Lenin's *coup* had consigned Martov and his fellow Mensheviks to the 'dustbin of history'.[8] It is, to be sure, deservedly one of the most famous, and frequently invoked, of ripostes in revolutionary history. Martov's reply, that 'one day you will understand the crime in which you are taking part'[9] understandably, given the circumstances and the audience, fell largely on deaf ears, and was quickly forgotten. Yet the same muse invoked by Trotsky has, with the passage of time, passed its verdict on just who it was, on the fateful night of November 7-8, 1917, came closer to the truth. Trotsky's *bon mot* has finally been turned against him as, first in eastern Europe, then in the Soviet Union itself, anti-Leninist revolutions tossed onto the same dustbin of history the system created by the Petrograd *putsch* of November 1917. No more should we forget that it was Martov, already sick with and soon to die of tuberculosis, who rallied with courage and integrity the democratic socialist resistance to emergent Bolshevik tyranny. With Plekhanov and Rosa Luxemburg gone, and Trotsky now Lenin's second-in-command, Martov was supported in his struggle to understand and combat Leninism by some of the finest minds of European Marxism, most notably the theoretician Karl Kautsky and the economist Rudolf Hilferding. While Kautsky regarded the Bolshevik regime as 'Tartar socialism',[10] being a unique modern variant of 'oriental despotism',[11] Hilferding saw the USSR in entirely European terms, the 'first totalitarian state in modern history' that heralded the subsequent emergence of similar regimes in Fascist Italy and Nazi Germany.[12] Even so, unlike many leftist thinkers of their time and ours, they were at one in refusing to accept that the system created by Lenin's *putsch* shared anything in common with the ideals and methods of traditional democratic socialism, or that it was in any sense a 'workers' state', however 'degenerated'.

Others, of the left but not Marxists, also resisted the prevalent and, amongst radical intellectuals, fashionable, tendency to ignore or even deny the repressive features of the Bolshevik 'experiment', like the philosopher Bertrand Russell and the writer and essayist George Orwell. Those who now, as in the past, try to annex the author of *Animal Farm* to the cause of an undefiled, pristine and pre-Stalinist Bolshevism would do well to remember that in Orwell's judgment, 'the seeds of a totalitarian society were plainly there [that is, in the USSR] well before 1923', and that Lenin and Trotsky were as capable of employing methods 'as barbarous, or nearly as barbarous as Stalin' to remain in power.[13] Orwell, Russell, Martov, Kautsky – each in his own way saw the system created by Lenin for what it was: one that far from liberating the oppressed, had created new chains for their enslavement.

By contrast, Bernard Shaw set a trend amongst the radical intelligentsia of his day in idealising, from their very inception, the methods of Bolshevik rule. As a mark of his esteem, in 1921, Shaw dispatched to Lenin a signed copy of his play 'Back to Methuselah' (aptly, for it is a plea for government by the wise) with a dedication to 'the only European ruler who is displaying the ability, character and knowledge proper to his responsible position'.[14] What had so captivated Shaw was the 'terrific energy' with which Lenin's 'ruthless dictatorship' had set about proving that 'socialism must be effected not by discussion and vote, but by those who actively desired killing those who actively objected to it'.[15] Soon, and for the same reasons, Lenin was joined in the Shavian pantheon by, first Mussolini, then the 'heroically public spirited' Stalin[16] and finally, Hitler. Emulating Lenin, *Il Duce* had also demonstrated that the people 'wanted not liberty' but 'hard work, hard discipline, and positive and rapid state activity'.[16] If this was true, where was the sense in protesting at fascist atrocities? Instead, and with obvious relish, Shaw proclaimed the 'democratic idealism of the nineteenth century' to be as 'dead as a door nail'.[17] The choice was either to 'get the socialist movement out of its old democratic grooves' or 'wait paralysed' until its measures were 'understood and sanctioned and approved by a majority of the proletariat', ninety per cent of whom, in Shaw's judgment, were 'unable to make a living without direction'.[18] Predictably, when Hitler destroyed the last remnants of Weimar democracy, and outlawed all its working class organisations, Shaw heralded the ensuing Nazi militarisation of labour, as he had Lenin's, as 'essentially communist'.[19] Shaw was not, it is quite true, typical of his kind in embracing simultaneously all the varieties of modern despotism. But in his undisguised contempt for all individual liberties save his own, he most certainly was. He had grasped, in his own idiosyncratic fashion, the core of Leninist theory: namely, that socialism only could be realised under the leadership of a self-selecting *élite*. The origin of that doctrine is the subject of this book.

INTRODUCTION

The ignominious collapse, in the land of its birth, of the system established by the Bolshevik revolution of November 1917, should surely have compelled at least some of its adherents to question the principles and methods by which Lenin's Party came to power and set about the creation of a new, supposedly socialist, order of society. After all, they would have us believe they are scientific socialists, and what remains of science if it ignores facts? Yet in their quest to square the Leninist circle, to renounce or disclaim the historical consequences of Bolshevism, whilst preserving the doctrine itself, all the contending schools of Leninism still continue either to ignore or deny the most compelling and incontestable fact of all, namely, that the doctrine of Leninism, once applied in Russia to the task of seizing power and realising its vision of a collectivised society, has, whatever the original intention, culminated in the tyranny that goes by the name of Stalinism. Take, for example, the many public pronouncements on this subject by the architect of 'perestroika', the former Soviet President and Communist Party General Secretary, Mikhail Gorbachev. On the occasion of the seventy-fifth anniversary of the Bolshevik revolution, he called upon fellow Party members, just as in days of yore, to develop 'the ideas and practices of Leninism and the October Revolution' and exalted, entirely in the spirit of his predecessors, the 'great party of Lenin' which had 'roused the forces of the nation' for 'an assault on the old world'. Then, after Lenin's death, 'relying on his doctrine and his behests, the party leadership was to find the optimum solutions that would consolidate the gains of the revolution and lead the country to socialism.' Combating various oppositional tendencies, in the first place that of Trotsky, 'the party's leading nucleus, headed by Joseph Stalin... safeguarded Leninism in an ideological struggle.'[1] Other pronouncements, all in a similarly 'orthodox' vein, were made right up to the eve of the abortive August 1991 coup. The Party leadership was said to be 'verifying' its efforts 'with the help of lofty fundamental ideas set forth by Vladimir Ilyich Lenin, his methods, and style of work, his immortal theoretical and moral [!] heritage.'[2] And so the Lenin cult continued until the very end, with Gorbachev officiating as its high priest. There was to be no 'retreat', not 'even a step' from 'Marxism-Leninism'. And why should there be when 'democratism suits the very essence of the Leninist conception of socialism'?[3] Any past failings in the Soviet system were attributed, predictably, to Stalin's 'crude political blunders' and the 'arbitrary rule perpetrated by him and his entourage'.[4] There was, therefore, no question of any re-examination of Leninism. 'We do not give up Lenin's concept of the Party as society's political vanguard.' On the contrary, 'at the stage of perestroika the Party's role further grows in the perfection of socialist society.'[5] And this, we were invited to believe, was to constitute the Soviet Union's march to genuine pluralism and democracy!

Even as late as November 1989, with the entire Soviet bloc about to crash around his ears, Professor Yuri Krasin, Rector of the Social Science Institute of the Communist Party of the Soviet Union, could still be heard protesting that 'if the intelligent, flexible policies outlined in later years by Lenin had been followed', the prospects of socialism would have been 'transformed'.[6] As the crisis of the Soviet bloc reached its climax in the ultra-Stalinist coup of August 1991, this response amongst Leninists became universal. At all costs (including the dispensing of an at best fanciful history of Bolshevism: see Appendix One) Lenin had to be rescued from drowning in what was held to be exclusively Stalin's dirty bathwater. Mike Hicks, General Secretary of the Stalinist rump of the Communist Party of Great Britain was no more prepared than was Prof. Krasin to re-consider fundamentals. It was not Bolshevism's attempt to build socialism that had failed, 'but the capitalist system'. Socialism was still 'the only system that can solve the problems.'[7] Andrew Rothstein, veteran Stalin-apologist and re-writer of Soviet history, insisted, with more hope than reason, that the entire past of Bolshevism, from its birth in 1903, was a guarantee that the Party created by Lenin 'can and shall withstand even these cruel blows'.[8] As for the Trotskyist tendencies of Leninism, they had nothing new to say either, chiefly because they have always conducted themselves as if the crises of the Soviet bloc had no fresh lessons to teach them. Each new turn of events (some totally confounding earlier predictions) has for decades now been routinely passed off as one more confirmation of the infallibility of ideas inherited, in a bowdlerised form, from an admittedly highly gifted politician who died more than half a century ago. For, despite their many other differences, Trotsky's epigones all agree, with more vigour than consistency, that authentic Bolshevism ceased to guide the destinies of the USSR after the death of Lenin and Stalin's removal of Trotsky from the leadership of the Soviet communist Party. So what we are witnessing, they assure us, is not a crisis of Leninism, which is, we are always reminded, alive and well in the activities of the various Trotskyist sects, but the death agony of Stalinism.

It is easy to appreciate the appeal (if not sophistication) of this argument. It rests upon the assumption, which is challenged in this book, that there exist no essential continuities between the Bolshevism of Lenin and the political methods of Stalin, and between the way the Soviet Union was ruled up to (say) 1923, and the way it was ruled afterwards. But the Trotskyists do not have a monopoly on this argument. Even Tony Chater, the editor of the 'Panzerkommunismus' *Morning Star*, is willing to concede that from the 'late twenties onwards we can now[!] see that decisions began[!] to be taken which took Soviet society down a road which violated socialism and democratic principles in important respects.'[9] And did not Khrushchev tell us, as long ago as 1956, that it was all Stalin's fault? And yet, incredibly, some even now still wish to give the tyrant what they claim is his due. Former Greater London Council leader and Labour M.P. Ken Livingstone would like to persuade us that we owe the welfare reforms of the 1945 Labour government not, principally, to the pressure, struggle, votes and demands of the British labour movement, but 'largely' (yes, 'largely') to 'the presence of post-war developments in eastern Europe', just as the peoples of the third world supposedly owe any improvement in their fortunes to the existence of the USSR as an 'anti-capitalist force'.[10] Despite its Stalinist undertones, this argument is nevertheless deeply rooted in Trotskyist Leninism. It is therefore, perhaps, of significance that Livingstone has not only spoken of his 'respect that surpassed friendship' for Gerry Healy, the notoriously brutal, amoral, disgraced, expelled and now deceased one-time leader of what was, for some years, reputedly the largest of Britain's many Trotskyist sects, the Workers' Revolutionary Party. He has revealed that he 'never met Gerry Healy without learning something from each and every meeting.'[11] What special wisdom could Healy have possibly imparted to such a well-informed and experienced politician? Quite apart from his several unique qualities, Healy shared with all other 'orthodox' Trotskyists (including those who eventually expelled him) the unshakeable conviction that, for all the crimes, betrayals and atrocities of its ruling *élite*, the USSR remained (until its collapse in 1991) an intrinsically higher form of society than even the most advanced and liberal capitalist states, a belief shared by numerous personalities in the labour movement ranging from prominent trade union leaders to former cabinet ministers. In an often vulgarised form, this belief derives from Trotsky's conviction, sustained to his dying day, that, even at the height of the Stalin terror (when the USSR was effectively ruled by one man, and a mass murderer at that), by virtue of state ownership of the means of production – that and nothing more – 'the nature of the Soviet Union as a proletarian state is for us basically defined'.[12] And here Trotsky was simply echoing in his turn Lenin's definition of socialism as 'merely state-capitalist monopoly which serves the interests of the whole people',[13] a society 'in which the land is socialised and the factories nationalised'.[14]

Contemporary Leninism has not advanced an inch beyond the limits of this mode of thinking, which is statist and *élitist* to the core, demonstrating how little today's Bourbons of the left are either able or prepared to learn from history, even when it unfolds before their eyes in the most spectacular fashion imaginable. And in case these tumultuous events encourage a questioning of the axioms of Leninist theory and practice, the faithful will be advised not to heed 'those who slander October' by suggesting that 'Stalinism was the inevitable outcome of Leninism'.[15] To dissuade true believers from even entertaining such a thought, the flock must be warned of its Satanic origin and motivation. Those who doubt the integrity of Bolshevism are not, as they would have us believe, honest (even if misguided) seekers after truth. Their real, and only, intention is to 'undermine the confidence of the working class in its own strength' and to 'head off a revolutionary solution to the growing calamity [!?] ... of capitalist crisis'.[16] In his zeal to defend the threatened dogmas, our Trotskyist Grand Inquisitor (in this instance, Peter Fryer of the WRP) forgets exactly what they are. Was is it not Lenin himself who once denounced advocates of 'more faith in the forces of the working class' as 'accomplices of the bourgeoisie and the landowners'?[17] But what does it matter? It will be presumed – and usually rightly – that as in the age of medieval piety, the flock will be blissfully unaware of these inconsistencies. For them, the message is clear: "Believers – on your guard! The devil is amongst us!" As for those who doubt, indeed those who dare to think rather than simply believe, they are already lost. They have become Satan's accomplices. Shun them for the apostates and traitors that they are. And, like all thought crimes, this particular heresy will be suppressed and the Bolshevik church saved – though not by debate, for that will serve only to lend credence to the heresy – but with the well-tried Jesuitical methods of misrepresentation, excommunication, quarantine and the incantation of 'eternal verities'. To this end, our high priest of Leninism promises us the 'tireless explanation [not examination or discussion] of what did in fact happen in Russia 75 years ago and the true [!] nature of the Bolshevik revolution.'[18]

The delusion that Bolshevism did not give rise to Stalinism is encountered well beyond the confines of organisations which describe themselves as Leninist. The late Labour M.P. Eric Heffer was just such a case, arguing that it was 'under Stalin' that the Soviet trade unions 'lost their independence, becoming "transmission belts" for the bureaucratic party and state machine'.[19] Now, while it is perfectly true that Stalin once defined the Bolshevised Soviet trade unions as 'transmission belts which link the Party with the [working] class',[20] he did so not only in the lifetime of Lenin (April 1923), but in accordance with Lenin's own earlier description of the Bolshevik regime as an 'arrangement of cogwheels' or 'complicated transmission system'.[21] Similar examples, too numerous to cite here, turn up in all manner of places, from history textbooks to television documentaries. All have the effect, and usually the purpose, of conjuring up a supposed 'golden age' of pre-Stalinist Bolshevism, and belong to the *genre* of historical mythologising that, adapting Robert Blatchford, we can best describe as 'Merrie Leninism'. And, like all myths, it crumbles at the first contact with the world of reality, of facts, evidence, proofs. That is why the Leninst hierarchy, just like its Roman Catholic counterpart at the time of the Reformation, has always preferred to assert rather than reconsider and debate. As long as it remained in power (and, within its organisations, even in countries where it was not), Leninism deployed all the means necessary to ensure that its views prevailed no less surely than those of the counter-reformation Popes. But now the game is up. Shuffle their beads and cross themselves as they may, the dreaded discussion of the 'true nature of the Bolshevik tradition' cannot be avoided. It has already started. In fact, for some, it began nine decades ago. This essay is intended to be both a contribution to, and a continuation of, the debate that was initiated by the emergence of Bolshevism and Menshevism at the Second Congress of the Russian Social-Democratic Labour Party in the summer of 1903. It will argue for the following heresies:

a) that Leninism's claims to Marxist 'orthodoxy' are bogus;

b) that Leninism (in whatever of its versions or mutations) was and remains, by virtue of its assumptions and ethos, an *élitist* and totalitarian doctrine, capable of creating, whatever its subjective intentions, only *élitist* and totalitarian societies, in which the proletariat either becomes or remains a politically repressed and economically exploited class;

c) that, consequently, Leninism constitutes a monumental and tragic hoax perpetrated on countless millions of oppressed and exploited human beings, not only in Russia, but throughout the world;

d) finally, that to understand how and why this came about, it is essential to examine, in all their aspects, the events preceding and surrounding the Party Congress at which Lenin first made his bid (initially abortive) for leadership of the Russian revolutionary movement.

The significance of the Second Party Congress (the first, largely symbolic, was held at Minsk, west Russia, in 1898) is, surely, beyond dispute. For the hitherto smouldering antagonisms which erupted during the August of 1903, did not remain the private concern of its participants for very long. Witnessed by sixty or so delegates gathered in a church hall in the leafy suburbs of North London, the simultaneous births of 'hard' Bolshevism (literally, those of the majority) and of 'soft' minority Menshevism (or, as Lenin once put it, interestingly, the 'female line'[22]) had, by 1917, become events transcending and erasing not only the bonds of personal friendship, as was the case with the founders of the two tendencies, Martov and Lenin, but the loyalties of party and the frontiers of nation and continent. However one views Bolshevism, it seems hard to contest the proposition, shared by adherents and opponents alike, that even though the leading participants in the drama of the Second Congress numbered no more than a dozen or so men and women, the rupture of 1903 proved to be a moment of decision and destiny for not only the subsequent history of Russia, but, by virtue of that country's role in world affairs, and of the impact of Leninism on the international workers' movement, for humanity as a whole. For what was involved in the rift at the Second Congress was something far more substantial than the wording of a clause in the party rules, or who was to wield what Lenin described, revealingly, as the 'conductor's baton'.[23] It foreshadowed a conflict between two utterly incompatible views of socialism and the means for its realisation, a contest between a Bolshevism which, belying its name, conceived of the revolution and the order it established as the work of a small and self-selecting minority, and a Menshevism which, for all its many errors of judgment and internal inconsistencies, remained true to the tradition that genuine socialism must and can only be the goal and creation of what Marx and Engels described as the 'immense majority'. Tragically,

Lenin's *élitist* and coercive 'blood and iron' state socialism triumphed over Martov's unwavering vision of a society that was both collectivist and democratic, a world where individual liberty and humanistic values would not be sacrificed, as they were under Bolshevism, to the supremacy of a single party and (vainly as it proved) the conquest of global power. Today, it is evident to all but unthinking zealots that the Bolshevik victory of 1917 has proved a defeat for not only Russian, but for world socialism, discrediting, and possibly damaging beyond repair, a movement and ideal that began with such promise and hope.

What follows is an inquiry into two aspects of the question: namely the origins of the split of 1903, and the nature of the movement and doctrine to which it gave birth – Leninism.

CHAPTER ONE
BOLSHEVISM AND MENSHEVISM

One of the more intriguing aspects to the traditional Leninist explanation of the split at the Second Congress is that, nuances apart, it is shared by trends as antagonistic in other respects as Stalinism and Trotskyism. This is the view which, following Lenin's own assessment, sees the split of 1903 as 'the anticipation' of the great historical events which followed it. First advanced by Lenin, and subsequently endorsed without exception (though sometimes with nuances) by his followers, this conception seeks to explain the emergence and evolution of both Bolshevism and Menshevism as a series of distinct though intimately linked stages, each phase constituting, in the case of Menshevism a progressive unfolding of an inherent counter-revolutionary essence, and in that of Bolshevism, of Menshevism's polar opposite. According to this explanation of the split, what Lenin initially perceived only as Martov's 'opportunism in organisational questions'[1] (the argument over clause one of the Party rules), or what Trotsky understood as the contrasting psychological chemistry of the two principal contestants, had by the Russian revolution of 1905 proved itself to be an anticipation of a more general Menshevik opportunism in strategy and tactics, one that in and after 1917 allegedly culminated in its desertion to capitalist counter-revolution. The bench-mark for this treatment of the subject was definitively set by Lenin himself in 1920 with the allegation that the Menshevik's 'role as bourgeois agents in the working class movement was clearly realised by the entire bourgeoisie after 1905.'[2] Faithfully echoing this approach, Stalin's own fantasy Party history, the 'Short Course' of 1938, avers that while at the Second Congress 'the opportunism of the Mensheviks revealed itself in questions of organisation'[3], and during the 1905 revolution had evolved into 'differences over tactical questions',[4] by 1907 Menshevism had fully emerged as the 'virtual agent of the bourgeoisie within the working class.'[5] More recent official Soviet Party histories, while adjusting their stance on other questions (for example the role of Stalin and even certain of his victims), have continued to appraise Menshevism in identical fashion:

> The Mensheviks slipped lower and lower, revealing themselves more and more as agents of the bourgeoisie in the working class movement.[6]

This is a typical and constantly recycled product of the Leninist school of falsification. Yet, like so many others, it can be refuted by reference to Lenin's own writings. They show that it was not Bolshevism, but left tendencies within and close to Menshevism, that projected the most radical (even if mistaken) perspectives for the revolution of 1905. The truth of the matter is that while the journal *Nachalo*, edited jointly by Martov and Trotsky, advocated a direct transition to a workers' government in accordance with the latter's theory of 'permanent revolution',[7] Lenin remained firmly wedded (albeit with certain novel modulations) to the more traditional Marxist conception of the 'two-stage' revolution, rejecting the idea of the conquest of power by the workers as 'absurd' and 'semi-anarchist'.[8] Refuting by anticipation his own subsequent assessment of 1905 Menshevism as an agency of the bourgeoisie, Lenin initially accused *Nachalo* not of collaboration with the bourgeoisie, but of excessive leftism, of 'gallop[ing] from democratic dictatorship [Lenin's formula] to socialist dictatorship'[9] and 'inclin[ing] towards the dictatorship of the proletariat'.[10] As for the Bolsheviks, the truth of the matter is that in the revolution of 1905, they cut rather a poor figure in comparison with the Mensheviks, resolutely resisting the temptation to participate, without any prior conditions, in the first open and in many instances legal class actions of the Russian workers. Taught by Lenin to mistrust working class spontaneity and generally all movements that did not defer to their leadership, the Bolsheviks preserved their purity by conducting a series of noisy but largely sterile boycott campaigns. These included abstention from the Gapon movement in St Petersburg, which culminated in the famous 300,000-strong 'March on the Winter Palace' and its ambush by Tsarist troops (so-called 'Bloody Sunday'); and boycotting the ensuing concession of factory elections to the government-sponsored Shidlovsky Commission inquiry into the working conditions of the St Petersburg labour force. The Bolsheviks next boycotted, in the autumn, even more absurdly, the St Petersburg Soviet and finally, in early 1906, the elections to Russia's first parliament, the Duma. For their part, the 'opportunist' Mensheviks energetically participated in all these actions of the Russian proletariat, winning, as they did so, a level of support from the workers that by the time of the Fourth Party Congress of 1906, enabled the so-called 'minorityists' to command a clear lead over Lenin's self-styled 'majorityists'. Finding himself thus outflanked (partly as a consequence of his own tactics) by the Mensheviks, Lenin attempted to make up the lost ground by adopting methods which owed more to Blanquist *putschism* than they did to traditional Marxism. Urged on from afar by Lenin, then staying in Finland, the Bolshevik leaders, even after the revolution's ebb, chose to hurl small groups of poorly armed Moscow workers into an ill-prepared insurrection against the might of the Tsarist state machine, a tactic not only doomed to failure as its Menshevik critics pointed out, but certain to inflict terrible casualties on the workers involved, even if its instigators managed to avoid sharing the same fate. One account reveals that 'while fighting continued [in Moscow] on December 17 and 18, [Bolshevik] party leaders hid and waited, finally managing to escaspe out of Presnia [the centre of the fighting] into the city,' while at the Prokhorov factory, which held out to the last, 410 workers were arrested.[11]

Given that the bulk of the Bolshevik 'committee men' in Russia (like, for example, Stalin) had been selected and reared on the basis of Lenin's mistrust of spontaneous movements that lay outside the control of the Party machine – a prejudice codified, as we shall see, in his 'What Is To Be Done?' of 1902 – these tactics were hardly a surprise. That is why Stalin's writings for the year 1905 contain not one reference to the existence of the workers' Soviets spontaneously created during that year of revolutionary struggle, let alone a positive evaluation of their role. They do, however, as we shall see, include lengthy endorsements and embellishments of Lenin's book.

Although these facts have always been known by those responsible for fabricating the 'official' history of the Communist Party of the Soviet Union, it is not hard to see why they were never allowed to intrude into any of its approved versions so long as Stalin lived. Yet, despite the emergence, following Stalin's death in 1953, of a more flexible attitude amongst Soviet historians towards other aspects of their Party's past, the official line on the split of 1903 has, if anything, become even more harshly anti-Menshevik. While all post-Stalin Party histories continued to ascribe the same historical and political significance to the schism of 1903, one, in its zeal for orthodoxy, even went beyond Lenin by projecting the existence of Menshevism back to a period before the Second Congress:

> The division of the RSDLP into "majority" and "minority", Lenin showed, was a direct and inevitable continuation [n.b.] of the division of the Social-Democrats into a revolutionary and an opportunist wing.[12]

Lenin, of course, 'showed' no such thing, nor could he have done. His account of the origins of Menshevism is, as we would expect, highly coloured by factional bias. But, in its own partisan way, Lenin's is, unlike later Stalinist versions, relatively honest. He was always ready to acknowledge that up to the Congress, and even for the first half of its proceedings, those who comprised the inner core of the '*Iskra*' tendency (after the journal of that name founded by Lenin and Plekhanov in 1900) and who after the Congress divided into Bolsheviks and Mensheviks, were united on all the political questions of the day, small as well as big. We can also be sure that when the Congress began it had not occurred to Lenin that before its conclusion, he and Martov would be the leaders of two separate factions, or that afterwards these two factions would crystallise out into two antagonistic political parties each claiming the true legacy of the same parent Party, the RSDLP. Least of all could Lenin have suspected that his quarrel with Martov over the wording of one party rule (for that is how it began) would culminate, as it did, in the slandering, arrest, execution and hounding into illegality and exile of those who were once the most respected of his comrades and the loyalist of his friends. Truly, the history of Bolshevism and Menshevism has all the ingredients of a Greek tragedy.

There is another aspect to what we might call the 'original sin' explanation of Menshevism. What all accounts of its origins and nature (not least Lenin's) fail to explain is how the Bolsheviks remained in the same party with 'agents of the bourgeoisie' up until almost the eve of the October Revolution, only finally constituting themselves as a separate party in the course of the events of 1917. That is why Trotsky's treatment of the split is particularly interesting, not least by virtue of his own personal role in the events he later describes. Trotsky began the 1903 Congress as a fervent partisan of Lenin (thereby earning, from his opponents, the soubriquet 'Lenin's cudgel'), only to end it as a no less vehement supporter of Martov. It was as a Menshevik that he then wrote, over the next year, his two trenchant critiques of proto-Leninism, 'Report of the Siberian Delegation' and the oft-cited 'Our Political Tasks', wherein he develops his prescient theory of Bolshevik 'substitutionism'. Then, repelled by what he saw as the too-accommodating attitude of most of the Menshevik leaders towards Russian liberalism, he evolved his theory of 'permanent revolution', spending the period from 1905 until the beginning of 1917 as a persistent (but largely unheeded) advocate of unity between the two factions, only finally joining the Bolsheviks, with a small but gifted group of co-thinkers (the so-called 'Interdistrict' organisation) at the Bolshevik Party Congress of August 1917.

Trotsky's political peregrinations explain why he undertook two contrasting assessments of the Second Congress, the first (in 1903-4) as a Menshevik, and the second, after the October Revolution, as a Bolshevik. Recalling, many years later, his own role in the events of 1903 (he chaired the final caucus meeting that precipitated the split) Trotsky subsequently presented the 'anticipation' hypothesis in a highly personalised form, insisting (in his tribute to Lenin after his death in 1924) that even 'before the split and before the Congress, Lenin was 'hard' and Martov 'soft','[13] terms used initially by Lenin before being supplanted by 'Bolshevik' and 'Menshevik'. As such, they conveyed (quite accurately) what was, initially, a difference of style rather than of policy. And it was this aspect of the split that in later years especially intrigued Trotsky, who during his pre-war stay in Vienna, developed a serious interest in the new discipline of psychoanalysis. This approach is nowhere more evident (and natural) than in his autobiography, written after his deportation from the USSR in 1929. Discussing the difficulty Martov experienced in focusing his thoughts during the revolution of 1905, a problem which the Menshevik leader put down to a medical condition, Trotsky offers the following alternative diagnosis:

> Martov did not know what to call his illness. But it has quite a definite name: "Menshevism". In an epoch of revolution, opportunism means, first of all, vacillation and inability to "gather one's thoughts".[14]

Here, too, Menshevism (in its early years at least) supposedly manifests itself principally as a mood, a way of thinking or, rather, of avoiding or being unable to draw practical conclusions from certain generally agreed premises.

So, despite their nuances, all schools of Leninism attribute a profoundly teleological and providential significance to the supposed causal connections between Martov's behaviour in 1903 and how he and his adherents allegedly conducted themselves in subsequent years of revolution and Bolshevik rule. According to the Leninist thesis, an initial and apparently trifling Menshevik 'opportunism in organisational questions', or what Trotsky understood as Martov's supposed lack of revolutionary will-power, not only did lead to the eventual adoption by the Mensheviks of supposedly 'counter-revolutionary' (a synonym for non- or anti-Bolshevik) policies on every question – they were fated to. And the proof was as simple as it was fallacious: *post hoc ergo propter hoc*. By the very nature of things, totalitarian or absolutist doctrines, and Leninism is one such, establish grounds for the condemnation, purging and punishment of apostasy by adopting a form of argumentation that usually works very well for the true believers. Unlike a secular movement founded on the acceptance of broadly-shared methods of discourse and argumentation, Leninist organisations and states governed by them, consider doubt or opposition as its own condemnation. Guilt thus established (aided invariably by distorting almost out of all recognition the real beliefs and actions of the dissenter) then serves to re-inforce the infallibility of the traduced doctrine and the continued loyalty of its true believers. So it was with the Jesuit crusade against Luther the anti-Christ, and with Stalin's against Trotsky, supposedly Hitler's accomplice. And thus it has been with Bolshevism's nine decades long campaign of slander and misrepresentation of Menshevism, the 'agent of the bourgeoisie within the working class'.

If we reject the methods of Leninist demonology, we must accept that the truth of these accusations can only be evaluated in the light of the available documentary evidence, and the testimonies of the leading participants in the formation of and conflict between Bolshevism and Menshevism. And where better to begin such an inquiry than at the Second Congress?

CHAPTER TWO
LENIN PREPARES

To begin with, there is the question of the legitimacy of the Second Party Congress. Was this gathering, as Lenin afterwards claimed, convened 'on the basis of the fullest representation';[1] or was it, as some insisted at the time and subsequently, an assembly rigged by the political tendency represented by the journal *Iskra* (and therefore chiefly by Lenin, with the connivance of its other editors) to rubber stamp Lenin's planned re-structuring of the party and domination of its leading institutions? Or was it rather something between the two? As to its representative nature, this much is certain. The Congress was convened, and the delegations invited, by a body designated the Organising Committee, or O.C. In turn, this committee worked under the constant and personal supervision of Lenin, who with his wife, Krupskaya, comprised two of its five members. Moreover, one of the remaining three committee members was also an 'Iskraist', ensuring that Lenin's proposals would carry the day against opposition from whatever quarter it might come. Grigori Zinoviev, later to become one of Lenin's closest collaborators, recounted after the revolution of 1917 just how tight was Lenin's grip on all the pre-Congress arrangements:

> Comrade Lenin placed himself [*sic*] at the head of this practical work, and formed the Organisation Committee attached to *Iskra*. And Comrade Lenin, who bore the chief brunt of the literary labour in the *Iskra* and in the theoretical journal *Zarya*, at the same time became the soul of the Organisation Committee. The wife of Comrade Lenin [Krupskaya]... was the secretary of *Iskra*, and the secretary of the Organising Committee... All written intercourse fell upon her. At one time she carried on a correspondence with the whole of Russia.[2]

Summing up (in 1918) Lenin's activities in this period Zinoviev concluded that 'Lenin sedulously, step by step, collected [*sic*] the underground organisation'[3] – so assiduously, in fact, that he provoked the normally affable Martov to protest against what he saw as the undue political influence exerted (on Lenin's behalf) by his wife, whom he described as 'the secretary of the super-centre, Lenin'.[4]

Even allowing for exaggeration on the part of the sycophantic Zinoviev, it is still reasonable to assume that, on the eve of the Congress, Lenin not only controlled the key posts in *Iskra*'s political and literary apparatus (and here we should include its *émigré* organisation, the League of Russian Social Democrats) and held in his hands all the threads that connected the *émigré* centres with the committees in Russia; Lenin was also, as the leading figure on the Organising Committee, in the ideal strategic position to win any battles that might arise over the composition, organisational aspects and the agenda of the Congress itself. How successful Lenin was in this respect can be ascertained from the following:
a) forty-three voting delegates attended the Congress, eight having two votes, giving a total of fifty-one mandates;
b) fourteen others attended with consultative voices but no votes;
c) of the political tendencies represented, *Iskra* was, at the outset, in a clear majority, casting on most issues (until the split over the rules) thirty-three votes out of a total of fifty-one;
d) the consistent anti-*Iskra* minority, usually comprising 8 votes, was made up as follows:

1) the Jewish workers' organisation, the Bund, with five votes and
2) the so-called 'Economist' tendency, with three votes, being those of the Union of Russian Social Democrats Abroad, with two votes, plus one other vote (not always cast with the other two) from a single delegate from the St Petersburg Workers' Organisation;
e) the remainder of the votes, about ten in number, belonged to delegates whom Lenin described (subsequently) as the centre, or 'marsh', being mostly from south Russian regional committees of the RSDLP.[5]

So much for the groupings and their representation.

The tactics that Lenin adopted towards each of the non- or anti-'Iskraist' delegations provide us with several fascinating insights into his approach to the problems of revolutionary organisation, and, at the same time, help to explain why, with varying degrees of support from his *Iskra* comrades, he had felt the need to declare a permanent 'state of siege' within the party in the period leading up to the Congress itself. Take, for example, Lenin's attitude towards and treatment of the southern delegates. Broadly, they sympathised with *Iskra*, supporting its general political line, but they resented Lenin's intention to use them as voting fodder. Justifiably fearing that this group might adopt a too-independent stand at the Congress, Lenin sent instructions to Russia that 'our own [i.e. *Iskra*'s] *reliable people*' should 'try to undermine the Southern Central Committee of the southern committees' [emphasis in the original]. Lenin even threw out a hint, perhaps intended for factional use, that the southerners were being 'manipulated' by a possible 'agent provocateur', a suspicion which proved to be groundless. Just how precarious Lenin felt *Iskra*'s situation to be is indicated by his injunction to 'subordinate everything to this task' (the nomination of pro-*Iskra* delegates) and to 'bear in mind the significance of the Second Congress'. Otherwise, warned Lenin, 'we shall inevitably be ousted'.[6] It seems that, in this instance at least, these tactics failed, because nearly a year later Lenin was still complaining that *Iskra*'s agents in Russia should be 'more actively preparing [*sic*] the committees', in particular those of Nikolayev and Odessa in the South.[7]

Then there is the crucial matter of the balance of representation at the Congress of the various political tendencies active in the Russian working class. Was it really, as Lenin afterwards claimed, in any way an accurate reflection of their influence within Russia? And if not, was this imbalance the intended result of a deliberate policy on the part of Lenin? It is at this point that we enter the terrain of unavoidable controversy, though even here, certain facts are not in dispute. The Jewish Bund, for example, was not only by far the largest of all the organisations affiliated to the RSDLP. Its membership, which at the time of the Congress probably stood at something in the region of ten thousand or so, was, unlike the rest of the Party, overwhelmingly proletarian in its class composition, and was probably numerically larger than all the party's other sections taken together. At all events, Lenin's Organising Committee saw to it that the Bund's representation was cut down to a number grossly disproportionate to its size, standing and influence in the broader Russian workers' movement.

Having seen how Lenin reacted to the challenge presented by the basically (but nevertheless insufficiently) docile 'Iskraist' Southerners, it is not so difficult to understand his utterly implacable hostility to the Bund, an attitude frequently reflected in private correspondence concerned with preparations for the Congress. As early as May 23, 1902, Lenin was advising F. V. Lengnik in Samara to 'turn himself into a committee [*sic*] for preparing the congress' and, once having accomplished this metamorphosis, to 'accept the Bundist into this committee after assessing him *from every angle*'[8] [emphasis in the original].

Then, on July 16, 1902, Lenin advised I. I. Radchenko in St Petersburg not to allow the Bund to 'stick its nose into Russian affairs', a remark which, in view of *Iskra*'s intention to stick its own Russian nose into the Bund's Jewish affairs, was perhaps a little tasteless. Lenin proposed that the Bund should be treated at best as an 'unreliable friend' and, at worst, as 'an enemy'.[9] In another letter, dated November 11, 1902, to P. A. Krasikov (already a valued and notorious 'hard' whom he later chose to be his principle faction organiser at the Second Congress after the break with Martov and who, after the revolution, served first Lenin and then Stalin as a dispenser of Bolshevik 'justice'), Lenin demanded that the Organising Committee be 'stricter with the Bund' and to reduce its function in the pre-Congress arrangements 'to such a minimum that in any case it cannot be of importance.'[10] Then, with the Congress less than four months off, and all the tendencies counting heads, Lenin wrote directly to the Organising Committee on March 31, 1903:

> ... (privately) we earnestly request you everywhere and among everyone to prepare the ground for a struggle against the Bund at the Congress. Without a stubborn struggle the Bund will not surrender its position. And we cannot accept its position. Only firm determination on our part to go through to the end, to the expulsion of the Bund from the Party, will undoubtedly compel it to give way.[11]

In other words, the Bund was to be 'set up'. The 'position' in dispute was, of course, the Bund's insistence on retaining its hitherto recognised status, agreed by the First Party Congress in 1898, as the sole representative of the Jewish proletariat within the RSDLP. Lenin, with the support of the entire *Iskra* organisation, including the Jews Martov (who, ironically, was himself a pioneer of the Bund), Trotsky and Paul Axelrod, was determined to end that agreement and to bring about what would amount to the virtual disbanding of the Bund and the absorption of its considerable membership into the ranks of the Party. Given Lenin's expected victory at the Congress, this would involve the entire Bund organisation placing itself under the 'Russian' tutelage of *Iskra*. Little wonder the Bund refused to yield.

Rightly anticipating the Bund's intransigence, and mindful of the possibility that it might find allies for its independent stand among other delegates equally resentful of *Iskra*'s over-zealous stewardship, Lenin wrote to G. M. Krzhizhanovsky in Samara on April 3, 1903, urging him to 'make every effort to expedite the Congress and ensure a majority of intelligent (and "our") delegates.' Lenin suggested that one way to 'get the maximum number of our people adopted' was to exploit 'the system of two votes from each committee' – clear evidence that by this time, Lenin was actively engaged in packing the Congress in preparation for a show-down with his opponents. Lenin's sense of urgency is all too obvious:

> We must make everyone understand, simply 'ram it into every head', that it is necessary to prepare for war against the Bund... War at the Congress, war even to the extent of a split – whatever the cost.[12]

War it proved to be. And anticipating events, it was, ironically, the Bund's walking out of the Congress over Lenin's ultimatum, together with the withdrawal from its proceedings by the Economists, that enabled Lenin, in the closing sessions, to turn the tables on Martov's 'softs'. They, the future Mensheviks, had only managed to defeat Lenin over the party rules with the (unsolicited) support of the five Bund and two Economist delegates, giving Martov's draft a majority of six votes over the *Iskra* 'hards'. Now deprived of eight potential votes, the 'softs' lost their grip on the Congress. Lenin's moment had arrived. With the support of Plekhanov and the 'hards', Lenin now used his narrow majority (no more than two) to purge the leading bodies of the party of Martov's supporters, and to replace them with his own creatures.

The other anticipated source of opposition to *Iskra*, as the voting over the rules confirmed, was the so-called 'Economist' tendency. Like the Bund, the Economists had secured for their organisation a far broader and deeper base in the Russian working class than *Iskra*, which remained predominantly a grouping of *émigrés*, intellectuals and 'hard' professional revolutionaries of the Stalin-Krasikov type. Lenin's sensitivities concerning the social composition of 'Iskraism' reveal themselves in several letters which he wrote at about this time, just as his 'What Is To Be Done?' had focused on the dominant role he believed should be played by the intelligentsia in the formation and development of what Lenin called, somewhat perversely for a supposed Marxist, 'socialist ideology'. The mud then thrown at the Economists by *Iskra* in general, and Lenin in particular, still sticks to this day, despite ample evidence that they did not hold the anti-political views attributed to them by their critics. This is especially evident from their contributions to the debates at the Congress, as well as their publications. Contrary to Lenin's claims, Vladimir Akimov's *Robochia Delo* consistently emphasised the necessity of the struggle for political liberty against the Tsarist autocracy, and opposed restricting the working class to purely 'economic' campaigns and issues.[13] The real 'Economist' heresy (as is evident from a careful reading of 'What Is To Be Done?') was to oppose the leading role of the intelligentsia in the party, and not only to advocate but, where conditions permitted, to practise the election of workers to party committees. And since the Bund also followed the same procedure, it was only natural that they should join forces at the Congress, each feeling menaced by Lenin's plan to impose a hyper-centralist regime upon the party. By contrast with the Economists and the Bund, *Iskra*'s local groups in Russia were managed by self-appointed committees of intellectuals turned 'professional revolutionaries', an arrangement which provoked repeated conflicts with rank-and-file workers. The same was true of their respective publications. 'Economist' papers were not only written for workers but by them. Sometimes as many as half the articles in an issue came from the pens of proletarian correspondents. *Iskra* on the other hand was not only written almost exclusively by intellectuals, but also largely for them.[14]

Given these substantial divergences between the two tendencies, it was only to be expected that Lenin would confide to George Plekhanov, as early as December 20, 1901, that 'this is the time to crush them'.[15] But first it was necessary to ensure that, as in the case of the Bund, the Congress majority would comply with Lenin's wishes. The difficulty was, that while *Iskra* controlled the *émigré* circles, the majority of committees in Russia were either in the hands of the Bund and the Economists (being composed mainly of workers) or were, in Lenin's eyes at least, of doubtful loyalty, such as the south Russians. And of the minority of committees controlled by *Iskra*, most were not only dominated by intellectuals but even, in some cases, comprised largely of them. With time running out, drastic methods were called for, and employed. Fortunately for posterity, they were carefully documented by one of the three 'token' Economist delegates admitted to the Congress, Vladimir Akimov. He identified no fewer than seventeen non- or anti-'Iskraist' organisations that applied to the Organising Committee to be represented at the Second Congress, only to have their applications rejected on what he regarded as flimsy or spurious grounds. Knowing as we do the actual pattern of voting at the Congress, it is clear that had these excluded groups been permitted to attend, and even allowing for their having (unlike many of *Iskra*'s) only one vote each, the balance of forces at the Congress would have been radically altered. Akimov, surely not without reason, claims that that is exactly what *Iskra* had in mind when determining, through the mechanism of its Organising Committee, whom the Congress delegates should or should not be.[16]

One device employed by *Iskra* (and that meant Lenin) to secure the adoption of its own delegates anticipated the so-called 'Red Trade Unionism' of the Comintern's 'Third Period' (1928-1934), whereby usually small factions of communist-led workers broke away from trade unions with social democratic (the Stalinists preferred the term 'social fascist') affiliations, with invariably disastrous results for the workers involved. Similarly, if the proposed *Iskra* candidate failed to secure a majority in a local committee, the 'Iskraists' would provoke a split, walk out and form a smaller parallel organisation, which would then nominate its own delegate to the Congress, leaving the larger (and usually more proletarian) parent organisation unrepresented. Something like this certainly took place in Yekaterinoslav, where at a general meeting of the organisation, *Iskra* secured four votes to the anti-'Iskraist's' thirty-six. Akimov also gives an account of a similar operation in St Petersburg. Yet, in the case of the Donets Miners' Union, this pro-*Iskra* organisation experienced no difficulty in securing the acceptance of its delegate, despite the Union's apparent lack of any influence or activity in the region's coal fields. (The Union's headquarters were in fact located at a newspaper office in Rostov.) These tactics understandably fed suspicions that *Iskra* was subverting and excluding genuine organisations whilst creating and accrediting phantom ones of its own, purely in order to swell its representation at the Congress.[17]

Certainly, there is ample evidence to suggest that Lenin was prepared to exclude delegates from non-'Iskraist' organisations which had a strong working class base, whilst admitting bogus ones which did not, if the alternative was to risk losing his 'compact majority' at the Congress. An early intimation of the lengths to which Lenin was prepared to go to secure a Congress majority is to be found in his already-quoted letter to F.V. Lengnik. The *Iskra* agent was enjoined to 'push' his 'own people through into the largest number of committees possible' and to be 'bolder, more pushy and more inventive' in the means to be employed. Deception was essential to the success of the undertaking, hence the need to be 'wise as serpents – and (with the committees: the Bund's and St Petersburg [an 'Economist' stronghold]) – harmless as doves'.[18] So with the Congress still more than a year away, Lenin had already begun to pack the assembly with his own supporters. Lenin laid down clear and 'official' guidelines for this policy in a letter, dated December 20, 1902, to the Bureau of the *Iskra* Organisation in Russia:

> The main task now is to strengthen the O. C., to give battle, on the basis of the recognition of this O. C., to all who are opposed, and then prepare for convening the congress as soon as possible. Please do everything you can to ensure that everybody understands this task correctly and that it is carried out.[19]

If the activities of the *Iskra* agents operating in the south, and in Yekaterinoslav and St Petersburg are anything to go by, Lenin need have had no worries on that score. The upshot of Lenin's pre-Congress manoeuvrings was that *Iskra* went to Brussels with the entirely reasonable expectation that its thirty-three votes would prove more than sufficient to impose its will on the proceedings, only provided that the 'Iskraist' delegation remained united. But this, as we know, did not happen. *Iskra's* grip could be loosened, perhaps even broken, if an issue arose which persuaded ten or so of its votes to be cast together with the eighteen either 'soft' or anti-'Iskraist' votes held by the south Russians, the Bund and the Economists, against the 'hard' 'Iskraist' core represented in the first place by Lenin. And thus it was that an apparently incidental quarrel between Lenin and Martov over wording in the Party's conditions of membership presented Lenin's opponents with their great opportunity: to join with Martov's *Iskra* 'softs' to force through his proposed rule by twenty-eight votes to twenty-three. With this act were created, in part fortuitously, the factions soon to be known as Bolshevik and Menshevik.

So it is easy to understand why, with relations on the board of *Iskra* becoming (as we shall see) daily more acrimonious, Lenin did all he could to insure himself against possible defections from or waverings in his own ranks by the device of holding the number of non-*Iskra* delegates to an absolute minimum (hence the importance of his grip on the Organising Committee). Otherwise, it could have been Martov, and not Lenin, who emerged from the Congress as the leader of the party majority, with all that that advantage entailed.

In preparing and carrying through his *coup d'etat* at the Second Congress – for that in effect is what it was – Lenin proved himself the peerless exponent of a style and method of organisational warfare that subsequent generations of revolutionaries would come (and, more often than not, prefer) to recognise and describe as Stalinism.

LENIN'S LESSON

Ironically, it was his future Menshevik antagonist Plekhanov who provided Lenin with his first practical lesson in what would later be known as Bolshevik 'hardness'. In the summer of 1900, in the course of the protracted and often stormy negotiations that led to the formation of *Iskra*, Plekhanov had revealed a side to himself which Lenin at first found very hard to come to terms with. He afterwards confided in a report to Martov how Plekhanov had, for example, denounced opponents within the party as 'traitors' deserving only of execution, and described the Bund (which, as we have seen, Lenin wished to see disbanded no less than Plekhanov) as an 'organisation of exploiters'. The Jews were 'all chauvinists and nationalists' and the RSDLP, being a Russian party, should on no account 'render itself into "captivity" to the "brood of vipers"' (C.W., Vol.4, pp.334,336).

Lenin found the hitherto revered Plekhanov's organizational stance no less distasteful. Already the 'dictator' of the Emancipation of Labour Group, he now sought a similar role in *Iskra*, demanding a guaranteed majority on its editorial board (ibid, pp.336,338). But, in the event, Plekhanov's 'repelling traits' proved no obstacle to the proposed merger of forces. In fact, as we shall see, as new divergences developed within the *Iskra* leadership, Plekhanov's Jacobin intransigence would draw Lenin closer to him.

And same proved to be true of Lenin's relationship with Stalin. Far more afflicted even than Plekhanov with racial bigotry, Stalin on one occasion made no attempt to conceal his chauvinistic attitude towards the Jews, retailing a 'jest' by a fellow Bolshevik delegate to the 5th (London) RSDLP Congress of 1907 that in view of the predominance of Jews amongst the more numerous Menshevik delegation, 'it wouldn't be a bad idea for us Bolsheviks to start a pogrom in the Party' (C.W., Vol.2, p.250). These lines appeared in an official Bolshevik publication, and never occasioned any rebuke from Lenin. Indeed, five years later, he would commission their author to produce a pamphlet on, of all topics, the 'national question'. Then, even more incredibly, another five years on, Lenin approved the appointment of this proven anti-semite and future ethnic cleanser to the post of...Commissar for Nationalities. Evidently, here too, defects in such matters were more than outweighed by the value Lenin placed on Stalin's organisational hardness.

CHAPTER THREE
PARTY AND CLASS

Having looked at the background and preparations for the Second Congress, it would, at this point, be appropriate to examine some of the formative influences of Bolshevism, and in so doing, to question the validity of a number of (Leninist) propositions that were the subject of debate during its proceedings then, and which have remained a subject of debate to this day. They are:

1) that the working class, by its own independent efforts, is unable to develop the degree of political awareness considered to be necessary for its emancipation from capitalist exploitation and rule;

2) that, consequently, a highly centralised party, staffed by 'professional revolutionaries' and with its 'ideology' provided by intellectuals, is necessary for the achievement of a socialist revolution;

3) that such an organisational system is perfectly consistent with 'traditional' or 'classical' Marxism (and by this is meant the writings of Marx and Engels on the related question of class and party);

4) that the Leninist 'vanguard party' or 'party of a new type' was (and remains) the only possible instrument of proletarian revolution and emancipation not just in Russia, but throughout the world;

5) that any other system of organisation, for example, that advocated by the so-called 'Economists' before and at the Second Congress, and then by the Mensheviks and Rosa Luxemburg after it, necessarily predisposes its practitioners to adopt 'opportunist policies'; that, in Lenin's own words, 'opportunism in programme is naturally connected with opportunism in tactics and opportunism in organisation.'[1]

Though seemingly united against what Lenin derisively called Economist 'democratism', even before the Second Congress, several leading 'Iskraists' found themselves at odds with Lenin over the 'party-class' question. The dawning of this awareness came with the drafting, and then publication in early 1902, of Lenin's 'What Is To Be Done?' According to its author, the book examined (together with other subjects) what the preface called 'the fundamental question of the role of the Social-Democrats in relation to the spontaneous mass movement'.[2] These differences first arose when, during the book's drafting stage, Lenin showed the manuscript to fellow *Iskra* board member Paul Axelrod, who found certain of its arguments at odds with traditional Marxist positions on party and class.[3] We know, especially in the light of the later open controversy over the book, that Axelrod was referring to those of its sections which denied the ability of the working class to find its way onto the revolutionary path except under the ideological hegemony of the socialist intelligentsia. Among the most contentious passages which (despite Axelrod's objections) appeared in the published version of the book, are the following:

> We have said that *there could not have been* Social-Democratic consciousness among the workers. The history of all [!] countries shows that the working class, exclusively by its own effort, is able to achieve only trade union consciousness [emphasis in the original].[4]

> All those who talk about 'overrating the importance of ideology', about exaggerating the role of the conscious element, etc, imagine that the labour movement pure and simple can elaborate, and will elaborate, an independent ideology for itself, if only the

workers 'wrest their fate from the hands of the leaders'... [However] the spontaneous development of the working class movement leads to its subordination to bourgeois ideology... the spontaneous working class movement is trade unionism... and trade unionism means the ideological enslavement of the workers by the bourgeoisie. Hence, our task, the task of Social-Democracy, is to *combat spontaneity, to divert* the working class movement from this spontaneous, trade unionist striving to come under the wing of the bourgeoisie, and to bring it under the wing of revolutionary Social-Democracy [emphasis in the original].[5]

It hardly surprises us that Axelrod should have questioned these and other similar formulations, since they run counter to nearly everything Marx and Engels wrote on the 'party-class' question. And it was indicative of the drift of Lenin's thinking at this time that, fond as he was of invoking their authority to support his own arguments, on this occasion neither Marx nor Engels are cited so much as once in the sections devoted to working class spontaneity. Was this, perhaps, because they had nothing of note to say on the question? Quite the contrary, as we shall shortly see. In 'What Is To Be Done?' the word spontaneous (or its derivatives) occurs more than fifty times, almost always, as in the above instances, in a pejorative sense. In view of the obsessive significance Lenin attached to the word in this work, it is an instructive exercise to investigate the use to which Marx and Engels put the same term when employed in a similar context, that is the mode of development of the working class movement.

Lenin, as we have seen, insisted that, invariably (in 'all countries') the spontaneous tendency of the working class was its 'striving to come under the wing of the bourgeoisie' – an absolutely extraordinary formulation for someone usually so concerned to be seen defending Marxist 'orthodoxy', and certainly equalling in its audacity any of the revisions of Marxism then being undertaken by the German Social-Democrat Eduard Bernstein. Marx and Engels were, to be sure, prepared to engage in all manner of intrigues, ruses, combinations and manoeuvres in order to defeat their political opponents. Their war against the no more scrupulous Bakuninist faction in the First International, culminating in the expulsion of its leader at the partially rigged (on both sides) Hague Congress of 1872, undeniably 'anticipated' in certain respects not only Lenin's method of factional warfare, but even, in the conduct of the Marxist and Bakuninist groupings before and at the Hague Congress, several of the tactical devices Lenin was to employ against the Bund and the Economists before and during the Second Congress.[6] However, unlike Lenin, what Marx and Engels never did was to expound in their writings a worked-out doctrine of political *élitism* and organisational manipulation. On the contrary. Whenever they *wrote* about the 'party-class' question, it was to advance principles entirely contrary to those of the founder of Bolshevism. In Lenin's defence, it can, of course, be argued that he was the more honest in the sense of preaching what he practised. Perhaps. But was he honest in continuing to describe himself (as he invariably did) as a faithful, fully 'orthodox' follower of the Marxist pioneers, when what he wrote and practised was so blatantly at odds with the classic texts upon which he and his co-thinkers claimed to base all their political activity?

The debate can, in a sense, be reduced to one simple question: in what sense, if any, was Lenin a Marxist at all? To attempt an answer we must examine, and in some detail, how Marx and Engels attempted to resolve what is generally understood as the 'organisational question' or the 'party-class problem'.

The literary collaboration of Marx and Engels began in 1844 with 'The Holy Family', being a long and, for the most part, tediously over-written polemic against a rival faction of Hegelian radicalism. Our only interest here is in what Marx and Engels had to say in this work about the relationship claimed by their opponents (who included Max Stirner, destined to serve as an intellectual catalyst in Mussolini's transition to fascism) to exist between what they termed the 'mass', that is to say the proletariat, and 'criticism', the conscious, thinking few. 'Critical Criticism,' observed Marx and Engels sarcastically, 'however superior it deems itself, nevertheless has boundless pity for the mass.' Such 'criticism', therefore, saw its mission as one of messianic leadership, in which it would 'redeem the mass from its mass-like [i.e. unthinking] nature.'[7] The problem to be overcome was the workers' alleged passivity, their inability to create, an activity that required 'a stronger consciousness... than that of the worker.'[8] Marx and Engels contested this *élitist* solution, arguing from an appreciation of the workers' active and creative role in the process of production to the conclusion 'that the proletariat can and must emancipate itself', a view which they contrasted with 'criticism's' belief that it alone constituted 'the exclusive creative element in history'.[9] Evidently, what Marx and Engels were already rejecting, as early as 1844, was an (albeit philosophically couched) *élitist* 'party-class' schema in which, as they put it, 'a few chosen individuals as the active Spirit are counterposed to the rest of mankind as the spiritless Mass.'[10] Four years on, in their 'Communist Manifesto', Marx and Engels returned to the same problem, but now in terms, and in a context, which we recognise as those of what we might call a maturing 'classical Marxism'. In the first (German) edition of 1848, in the section devoted to a critique of the early pioneers of socialism, whom they term utopians, we read that 'the proletariat offers to them [i.e. the utopians] the spectacle of a class without any historical initiative or any independent political movement.'[11] This passage remained unaltered until the English edition of 1888 when, with Marx now dead five years, Engels inserted, after 'proletariat', the words 'as yet in its infancy', obviously with the intention of making it clearer exactly why the early utopians came to regard the working class as incapable of acting on its own behalf. No great political significance can be reasonably attached to this alteration. The same, however, cannot be said of the next. In the 1848 edition, the passage in question ran as follows:

> Social action is to yield to their [the utopians'] personal inventive actions, historically created conditions of emancipation to fantastic ones, and the gradual organisation of the proletariat to an organisation of society specially contrived by these inventors. [12]

There are already sufficient indications here to convince us that had Marx and Engels lived to read 'What Is To Be Done?', they would have concurred with Axelrod's criticisms of the book. Sufficient for some maybe – but not for Engels. In the 1888 edition, the passage was altered in such a way as to render even more explicit its rejection of all *élitist* 'party-class' systems:

> ... the gradual, *spontaneous* class organisation of the proletariat [is to yield] to an organisation of society specially contrived by these inventors [emphasis added].[13]

Lenin almost certainly never read this passage in the version just quoted since, in all probability, he would have been familiar only with the Russian edition of 1882, where the text remained in its original form and, consequently, minus the (for Lenin, as we have seen, highly pejorative) word spontaneous. It is an intriguing thought as to how he might have reacted to Engels' insertion of that word had he become aware of it. Of course, Lenin could have argued that a single instance proves very little, even though it would still need to be explained why Engels, forty years after its first drafting, now saw fit to make just this change and insert just this word into a text that on an earlier occasion he, together with its co-author Marx, had insisted they had 'no longer any right to alter'.[14] So to anticipate any such objections – and they are of course legitimate – it will obviously be necessary to cite other instances where not only Engels, but Marx, invested the word spontaneous with a very different meaning and significance to that encountered in its Leninist usage.

Marx's chief concerns, as is well known, tended to be theoretical, but when the opportunity arose, with the formation in 1864 of the International Workingmen's Association (the I.W.A. was later known as the First International), to play a more active role than hitherto in the life of the working class movement, after attending the I.W.A.'s founding meeting he became a secretary of its General Council and, in this capacity, drafted many of the International's more important documents. Some of these necessarily touched on organisational matters and, in particular, the 'party-class' question. It was to this that Marx addressed himself in the fourth (1868) annual report of the I.W.A. General Council:

> [The] Association has not been hatched by a sect or a theory. It is the *spontaneous* growth of the proletarian movement, which itself is the offspring of the natural and irrepressible tendencies of modern society [emphasis added].[15]

A similar (and no less anti-Leninist) conception of organisation is conveyed in another document of the time, where Marx advised that it was 'the business of the I.W.A. to combine and generalise the *spontaneous* movements of the working class, but not to dictate or impose any doctrinaire system whatsoever'[16] [emphasis added]. How different from the 'Marxist' Lenin who, far from proposing to 'combine and generalise' the spontaneous movements of the working class (for the obvious reason that unlike Marx, he believed they led, not towards socialism, but away from it, towards their subordination to capitalism) advocated a 'fierce struggle against spontaneity' so as to 'divert' the working class from its wrongly chosen path.[17] There is little doubt that Marx and Engels would have found that idea both ridiculous and reactionary, because on this point, the 'Manifesto' is unambiguous. The section 'Proletarians and Communists' begins by asking in 'what relation do the Communists stand to the proletarians as a whole?' Here, too, the answer lends no support to any of the organisational proposals advanced by Lenin, first in 'What Is To Be Done?', and then at the Second Party Congress a year later:

> They [i.e. communists] do not set up any sectarian principles of their own, by which to shape and mould the proletarian movement.[18]

Instead, as Marx advised on another occasion, it was necessary to base and advance the struggle of the working class 'solely [on] demands that actually have *spontaneously* arisen out of the labour movement itself.'[19] (emphasis added) Of course, neither Marx nor Engels ever advanced the absurd argument that the spontaneous struggle of the working class was a substitute for scientifically-grounded knowledge of the workings of capitalist society. What they did insist on (rightly or wrongly) was that the natural (and therefore irresistible) tendency and thrust of the spontaneous working class struggle was in the direction of the overthrow of capitalist rule and the eventual establishment of a world-wide classless and stateless society. As Engels once put it so well, 'the general aspirations and tendencies of the working class emanate from the real conditions in which it finds itself placed' and were 'therefore common to the whole class', even though 'the movement reflects itself in their heads in the most diversified forms, more or less phantastical, more or less adequate.'[20] Much the same idea was conveyed by Marx, late in his life, in an interview with a correspondent of the *Chicago Tribune*. The working classes 'moved spontaneously without knowing what the ends of the movement will be.' But for Marx, 'spontaneously' did not imply 'erroneously', as it did for Lenin, but 'naturally'. So the task of socialists was not to 'divert' or 'combat' this movement by imposing upon it a 'vanguard', as proposed by Lenin. 'The socialists have no movement,' explained Marx, 'but merely [n.b.] tell the workmen what its character and its ends will be.'[21] Lenin, while conceding (and it would have been ridiculous for him not to have done so) that the working class struggle displayed anti-capitalist tendencies, nevertheless insisted that 'bourgeois ideology spontaneously imposes itself upon the working class to a still greater degree.'[22] So, it surely follows that the struggle of classes (wherein, according to Marx and Engels, the natural and predominant tendency is for the working class spontaneously and successfully to struggle against capitalist rule) is necessarily replaced by what Leninists call the 'ideological struggle'. This is a contest which, by its very nature, can only be conducted by trained professionals, and which, for the same reason, excludes from any directing role the 'immense majority' of the exploited classes that are to be emancipated by this *élite*. As Marx and Engels once put it in a polemic against Bakunin, the workers are relegated in such schemes to the role of 'cannon fodder'. As we have seen, the founders of Marxism explicitly repudiated this conception, favouring, as against Lenin's model of a tightly centralised, even militarised, party structure (which Lenin once, revealingly, described as 'bureaucracy' rather than 'democracy'[23]) a more flexible and decentralised method of organisation. That is why they rejected the Italian nationalist Giuseppe Mazzini's proposal to organise the I.W.A. after the fashion of an Italian secret society or 'carbonari', which would have the effect of converting a broad international workers' movement into a 'centralised conspiracy giving tyrannical powers to the central body'[24] and why they both, more generally, opposed any *élitist* system which 'treat[ed] the working masses as a flock of sheep, led by a few initiates whom they follow blindly' after the fashion of 'the Jesuits in the Catholic Church'.[25] Again, the reader is invited to compare this style of leadership, not with that of Stalin or Hitler, where the similarities are all too obvious, but of Lenin. Did he not argue for a system of organisation which 'strives to proceed from the top downwards, and upholds an extension [!] of the rights and powers of the centre in relation to the parts',[26] one where it would be perfectly 'natural' to entrust to a small circle or even a single individual what Lenin termed the 'conductor's baton' of party leadership?[27] We should at this point acknowledge that Lenin, always the master tactician, took good care to reserve to himself (and to deny to his opponents) the right to defy his own organisational principles should he find himself in a minority:

> When the revolutionary wing [naturally represented by Lenin] revolts against the opportunist wing, it is a good thing. When the opportunist wing revolts against the revolutionary wing, it is a bad business.[28]

These principles, it should be remembered, were, after the Bolshevik seizure of power in 1917, applied not only to the organisation of Soviet society as a whole, but also to the construction of a world Bolshevik movement, the Third or Communist International (Comintern) whose leading staff were, predictably, drawn from the inner circles of Lenin's Party, and who imposed on the entire international movement a discipline that was fundamentally military in character and structure. 'Building the party from the top downwards'[29] was evidently as valid on a global as on a national level.

And here, too, Lenin's approach was diametrically opposed to that of Marx and Engels. Despite the demise, after the defeat of the Paris Commune in 1871, of the First International, they believed that 'the common struggle for common interests against a common enemy' would bind the workers together 'in a new and greater *spontaneous* international'[30] [emphasis added]. Sure enough, in 1889, one thousand delegates from twenty-two countries met in Paris to found the Socialist (Second) International, a body which, despite its many vicissitudes, and internal divergencies, remains to this day the only organisation which can lay claim to being in any way representative of international labour interests. Meanwhile, Lenin's International, after wreaking twenty-four years of havoc in the working class, was wound up – ostensibly at least – by Stalin in 1943, whilst the Fourth, founded by Trotsky in 1938 to supplant the Stalinised Third, despite its courage and integrity, never became, except locally and episodically (i.e. in Ceylon, Bolivia, the U.S.A. and Greece) anything resembling a genuine workers' movement. Today, for all its claims to the heritage of Bolshevism, it is effectively as dead as its immediate predecessor.

Despite the controversy that Lenin's organisational proposals caused, both at the Second Congress and afterwards, they were, as we have already seen, by no means novel, as his critics were quick to point out. Marx and Engels would have instantly recognised in Lenin's plan for the Party, the organisational principles of the German socialist pioneer Ferdinand Lassalle and his successor, Johann Baptiste von Schweitzer, who inherited from Lassalle the presidency of the General Association of German Workers. In a letter written on behalf of the I.W.A. General Council, Marx observed that the Lassallians had found themselves outside the International because their 'artificial and sectarian organisation' was 'wholly opposed to the historic and *spontaneous* organisation of the working class'[31] [emphasis added]. Lassalle's great failing, Marx wrote to Schweitzer on another occasion, was his insistence on 'prescrib[ing] the course to be followed by this movement according to a certain doctrinaire recipe',[32] whilst Engels derided his (entirely Leninist) obsession with 'extreme centralism and strict organisation'.[33] But whether it was a matter of prescribe, combat or divert the essential idea remains the same: a handful of leaders, or even a single leader, who dictate, 'from the top down', how an entire class should conduct its struggle for emancipation.

'Classical Marxism' evinced no more sympathy for another axiom of Leninism, namely the idea that since the workers by themselves (i.e. spontaneously) were incapable of developing the necessary level of revolutionary awareness, it would have to be 'brought to them from without' by what Lenin described as 'educated representatives of the propertied classes', the 'bourgeois intelligentsia'.[34] Here, too, Lenin was saying nothing new. As far back as the 1830s, the Jacobin pioneer of the socialist *coup d'etat*, Auguste Blanqui, had already pronounced that 'labour is the people', whose allotted task was to 'execute' the practical business of the revolution, whilst those of 'intellect' were 'the dedicated men who lead it'.[35] This schema was, as we shall see, subsequently taken up and further elaborated precisely by those Jacobin tendencies within the pre-Marxist revolutionary movement in Russia which exerted the greatest influence upon Lenin during the formative years of his political thinking. Marx and Engels, however, argued for a very different approach to the problems of revolutionary organisation in general, and the role of the intellectuals in particular. It is, of course, perfectly true that their 'Communist Manifesto' does indeed discuss the relationship between intellectuals and the working class movement. However, it is no less true that it arrives at conclusions altogether different from those advocated by the Jacobin-*élitist* systems of Blanqui, the Russian populists and Lenin. That is why the relevant passages in the 'Manifesto' are not so much as alluded to, let alone cited, in 'What Is To Be Done?', for they lend no support whatever to Lenin's claim (echoing Blanqui) that socialist consciousness must be introduced into the working class 'from without' by bourgeois intellectuals. The authors of the 'Manifesto' believed that 'when the class struggle nears the decisive hour', a 'portion of the bourgeoisie' would 'go over to the proletariat', in particular, 'a portion of the bourgeois ideologists, who have raised themselves to the level of comprehending theoretically the historical movement as a whole.'[36] This is surely proof that neither Marx nor Engels ever envisaged (even less advocated) that renegade bourgeois intellectuals would, could, or should 'guide' or 'lead' the workers to their emancipation, or 'divert' them from a (supposedly false) path of struggle. Rather, as the cited text makes clear, what it describes as 'bourgeois ideologists' were expected to join a movement that was already seen as 'hold[ing] the future in its hands',[37] in other words, one that already appeared capable of victory, and most certainly not one that (according to Lenin) without their guidance, would face a future of continual defeats. On another occasion, Marx and Engels again made it perfectly clear what they understood to be the most fruitful relationship between the working class movement and the intelligentsia. Far from the workers being expected to place themselves under the intellectual tutelage of the educated middle classes, the latter would be expected to themselves 'wholeheartedly adopt the proletarian outlook'.[38]

The scenario envisaged by the 'Manifesto' can be either right or wrong. But, right or wrong, it hardly conveys a picture of a class capable, by itself, of only marching to its doom. In fact, on more than one occasion, the creators of 'classical Marxism' felt obliged to repudiate the idea that the workers required the leadership of intellectuals who supposedly, as they once put it, 'alone possess the "time and opportunity" to acquaint themselves with what is good for the workers'. They even went so far as to make public their refusal to 'co-operate with people who openly state that the workers are too uneducated to emancipate themselves.'[39] This criticism was initially made of an *élitist* trend within German socialism (partly an inheritance from Lassallianism), but was later directed with equal force against the intellectual *élitists* the English Fabian Society, of whom Engels once said they 'would graciously deign to emancipate the proletariat from above if it would only be sensible enough to realise that such a raw, uneducated mass cannot alone emancipate itself.'[40] Again, one is struck by the similarity with Lenin's notion of 'party-class' relations and, in particular, his stress on the leading role of bourgeois intellectuals. (In the 1930s, leading Fabians, including Shaw, Wells and the Webbs, became prominent apologists for the Bolshevik regime, seeing in its claimed successes a vindication of their own version of authoritarian socialism.)

The conflict within the I.W.A. between Marx and Bakunin's International Alliance of Social Democracy still arouses controversy between partisans of each faction. Muddied though the arguments were by clashes of personality and the usual polemical exaggerations of differences, there can be no disputing the fact that in certain crucial respects, and for all his talk of libertarianism, Bakunin conceived of revolutionary organisation in terms that anticipated those of Lenin's 'vanguard party'. One passage in Bakunin's manifesto to which Marx and Engels objected had argued that 'to make the working class the real representative of humanity's new interests', the workers had to be 'guided by the idea that will triumph.' How was this to be achieved? Bakunin's solution clearly anticipates Lenin's introduction of consciousness 'from without':

> To evolve this idea from the needs of our epoch, from mankind's vital aspirations, by a consistent study of the phenomena of social life, then to carry that idea to our worker's organisations, such must be our aim.[41]

Marx's response was to claim that for Bakunin, 'the working class is so much raw material, a chaos into which they must breathe their Holy Spirit before it acquires a shape.'[42] In other words, back to Stirner, with his creative 'criticism' and passive 'mass'.

Irrespective of their 'official' labels, what the authoritarian Lenin and the no less *élitist* 'libertarian' Bakunin shared was a conception of revolutionary consciousness which placed an enormous stress on its formation by a specialist or 'technocratic' group, the intelligentsia. Artificially contrived, this consciousness was then to be 'introduced' (Lenin) or 'carried' (Bakunin) into the class chosen as the medium of revolutionary action. In Russia (as in other industrially underdeveloped societies such as Italy and Spain) the preferred medium was originally the peasantry. And so was born Russian populism. With the arrival of capitalism, and the emergence of an urban proletariat, many younger populists (inspired by the example and writings of Plekhanov) converted to Marxism, without, as was the case with *Iskra*, totally abandoning the old populist belief in the need for a guiding intellectual *élite*. They now began to argue for a similar relationship between themselves and an increasingly self-aware working class, as their populist forbears had sought between themselves and a politically still largely inert peasantry.

Lenin's organisational theories pushed this tendency within Russian Marxism to its extreme. It had no more in common with 'classical' Marxism (with its emphasis on the spontaneous and therefore, in this context, organic development of class consciousness) than had Bakunin's with what might be called 'mainstream' libertarianism. On the contrary, both were products of deeply rooted tendencies within Russian populism. Very much in the spirit of Lenin, though very much to his admirers' embarrassment, Bakunin once described himself as the chief of a small number of 'invisible pilots guiding the revolution',[43] a classical 'carbonari' conspiracy in which 'one hundred revolutionaries, strongly and earnestly allied' would 'suffice for the international organisation of all of Europe.' This select band would operate as a 'revolutionary general staff' (a term later employed by Bolsheviks) selected from the 'dedicated', 'energetic' and 'intelligent'.[44] In the early post-revolutionary years, when Soviet scholars could still discuss such things with a degree of frankness, Bakunin's *élitist* organisational theories were seen as 'a great step forward' from the loose and decentralised structures of the First International.[45] But to argue thus is to side with Bakunin (and therefore with the most *élitist* trends within Russian populism) against Marx and Engels! And it is indeed the case that Bakunin and Lenin both derived their system of revolutionary organisation from the same Jacobin and Blanquist-inspired Russian populism, Bakunin having for years moved in its highest circles. Lenin, too, was also nurtured in a similar, if more provincial, populist milieu, even after leaving it in 1893 for St Petersburg, continuing to insist that the old terrorist conspiracies 'should serve us as a model'.[46] Counterposed to this we have Engels' maxim (being both in spirit and

23

letter precisely what Lenin would later define and decry as Menshevik 'opportunism in organisational questions') 'the looser the organisation,the firmer it is in reality.'[47] In the same spirit, in their struggle against Bakunin, Marx joined Engels in condemning his attempt to foist on the International and the working class a truly Leninist 'despotic and hierarchic secret organisation' that, given its nature and functions, could not but be 'recruited anywhere but from among the privileged classes'.[48] A study of the class origins of the members of Lenin's central committee, the 'immense majority' of whom were from just such backgrounds, will reveal how right they were. But, even if workers (or, rather, former workers) did manage, somehow, to insert themselves into the upper echelons of such a structure, nothing would essentially change except its appearance. It was in the very nature of things for such organisations to subject their members to 'authoritarian, mystical laws which cramp their independence and distort their powers of reason.'[49] Again, anyone who has spent time in a Leninist organisation, and emerged from the experience relatively unscathed, knows how true this judgment is, and how it can, so sadly, be measured in the human lives, qualities and talents that Leninism devours. But hyper-centralism was rejected not only because it threatened to stifle the initiative and energies of the revolutionary movement. Engels saw in such methods no less danger to the development of the post-revolutionary society. In a critique of the tactics of Blanqui, Engels predicted that once the conspiratorial *élite* seized power, 'it necessarily follows that a dictatorship is needed after the success of the revolution,' though 'not of the entire revolutionary class, the proletariat, but of the little handful of those who have made the *coup de main*, and who in their turn are themselves under the dictatorship of one or several individuals.'[50] This is indeed a remarkable 'anticipation', not only of the actual progression of events surrounding the October Revolution but, as we shall see, of the critique of Leninism undertaken after the 1903 split by (amongst others) Plekhanov, Trotsky and Luxemburg; namely, the theory of so-called 'substitutionism'.

This is not to say that Marx and Engels were entirely free from Jacobin-Blanquist conceptions of political action and organisation, especially in their younger years. Engels admitted as much in his 1895 Introduction to a new edition of Marx's 'The Class Struggles in France'. Recalling their participation in the events of the revolutionary year of 1848, Engels confessed that 'all of us, as far as our conceptions of the conditions and the course of revolutionary movements were concerned, were under the spell of previous historical experience, particularly that of France.' It took the disappointments of that year to refute what Engels described as the 'erroneous' strategy of 'turning the revolution of the minority into a revolution of the majority.'[51] Experience had taught that the time of 'surprise attacks, of revolutions carried through by small conscious minorities at the head of masses lacking consciousness', was past.[52] Lenin (who surely must have read these lines) was obviously not convinced, though there is no evidence that the Blanquist strain in Lenin's doctrine was assimilated directly from its French practitioners. All the evidence suggests that it filtered into his political thinking as a result of his saturation in a Russian populist tradition which shared with Blanquism the same Jacobin heritage. Peter Tkachev, a disciple of Blanqui and Bakunin, and the most Jacobin of all Russia's populists has, with some justification, been described as the father of Bolshevism, with his advocacy, thirty years before Lenin, of an *élite* party which was 'able to act according to a single common plan' and was 'subordinated to a single common leadership, and organisation based on the centralisation of power and decentralisation of function.'[53] And it was Tkachev who first expounded, in its most uncompromising form, Lenin's doctrine of the 'introduction from without' of revolutionary consciousness. Only a 'minority' distinguished by its 'higher intellectual and moral development' could organise and lead the forces of revolution, an undertaking which demanded 'centralisation, strict discipline, speed, decisiveness and unity in action'.[54] Like his mentor, Blanqui, Tkachev was also an admirer of Robespierre, and avowedly set out to emulate, in Russia, the Jacobin strategy of terrorist rule by an enlightened *élite* on behalf of an oppressed, but politically immature, majority. The 'revolutionary minority' (and here Tkachev had specifically in mind the intelligentsia) would, after seizing power, 'take upon itself the forcing of consciousness upon the people',[55] a policy which Plekhanov (and here he followed Engels) argued reflected a lack of confidence in the ability of the oppressed classes of Russia to engage in political action on their own behalf. What was being questioned was not, of course, the integrity or courage of Tkachev and his followers, but whether organisational methods and political tactics devised for a peasant-oriented movement (and one, moreover, increasingly inclined after 1879 to resort to terrorism) were suited in any way to the needs of a movement based on the urban working class then emerging in Russia's new industrial centres. The debate over these issues was conducted mainly in public, by means of robust mutual polemics, and it was one that, so far as Tkachev's critics were concerned, helped to lay the theoretical as well as tactical foundations for the development of Russian Marxism and, eventually, in 1898, the founding of the RSDLP. And yet, despite all this, it was to Tkachev rather than any Marxist, Russian or otherwise, that Lenin attributed the origins of Bolshevik revolutionary strategy. One of Lenin's closest colleagues, Vladimir Bonch-Bruevich, revealed in his memoirs that it was an

> irrefutable fact that the Russian Revolution proceeded to a significant degree according to the ideas of Tkachev. The seizure of power was made at a time which was determined in advance by a revolutionary party organised on the principle of strict centralisation and discipline. And this party, having seized power [whatever happened to the Bolshevik pre-revolutionary slogan 'all power to the soviets'?] operates in many respects as Tkachev advised.[56]

But if this was so – and we have no reason to doubt it – what need did Lenin have of Marxism? Nor is this all. The same writer also recalled that Lenin paid 'particular attention to Tkachev', and once even remarked that he was 'closer to our viewpoint than any of the others'.[57] Well! Amongst those 'others' were not only George Plekhanov, the founder of Russian Marxism, but Marx and Engels themselves. After all, Lenin would certainly have known better than most that Tkachev had been attacked, publicly, by Engels as a 'true Bakunist', and his ideas as 'tedious', 'contradictory', mere 'childish nonsense', the work of a 'boring and pompous... green grammar school boy'.[58] So much for Lenin's instructor in revolutionary strategy.

Small wonder, then, that Lenin's organisational proposals in 'What Is To Be Done?' should have perturbed Axelrod when he read its first draft, for he would have found there a revival, in the guise of Marxism, of populist conceptions long since repudiated. Whatever changes Lenin may have made in the final version, when the book appeared it met with mostly only qualified approval from his fellow 'Iskraists'. Plekhanov for one (and his opinion would have carried greater weight than any other) shared Axelrod's reservations concerning the relationship between spontaneity and consciousness, though, like all the other board members, he seems to have kept his reservations largely to himself. Perhaps the *Iskra* board feared that a public debate over the merits of Lenin's book would only have given comfort to their opponents. Be that as it may, no prominent 'Iskraist' was prepared unconditionally to praise the work in the Party press. The only public review, and at that some three years after its publication, came from the pen of a recent recruit to the Party, who waxed enthusiastic and at great length on the merits of Lenin's 'splendid book' and then, albeit very clumsily and tediously, rehearsed its main arguments, dwelling almost obsessively on those passages which expounded the theory of the 'introduction from without' of socialist consciousness. The author was none other than Lenin's future General Secretary, the incomparably hard and self-styled 'man of steel', J.V. Stalin.[59] Lenin's book also featured prominently in two other substantial (at least in length) articles Stalin wrote at this time, suggesting that he may have found in this work compelling ideological and moral incentives to pursue his new career as a professional revolutionary. Ironically, at its very outset, Stalin had run foul of the leading Tiflis Social-Democrats over his insistence that manual workers should not be permitted to sit on the Party's local committee, on the grounds that they had not attained the political maturity of the party's intellectual members.[60] Perhaps it was an 'anticipation' of their later political collaboration that Lenin had already defended the same principle some years previously at a stormy meeting of the St Petersburg League of Struggle shortly before his departure to Siberian exile in March 1897,[61] a confrontation that foreshadowed his later crusade against what he derided as 'democratism'.

Evidently gratified that the seed had not fallen entirely on stony ground, Lenin completed the recycling of his own theory by congratulating Stalin on the 'splendid [!] way in which the problem of the celebrated [sic] "introduction of consciousness from without" had been posed.'[62] But from the board of Iskra – scarely a word. At least, not in public. It was as if there was some kind of understanding whereby Lenin's colleagues would refrain from any open criticism of the book for fear of giving encouragement to Iskra's political adversaries before and during the Second Party Congress. Plekhanov, for one, certainly seems to have exercised an uncharacteristic reticence, because not long after the Congress, and following his defection to the Mensheviks, he expressed regret at not having from the beginning exposed Lenin's 'theoretical mischief to a bright light'. Poor Axelrod rather lamely explained to Plekhanov that he had 'put [his] own construction on [Lenin's] words',[63] little suspecting what use might be made of them when the time came at the Congress to transform Lenin's 'plan' for the Party into a reality or, even less, that when opposed by the Iskra 'softs', this would in turn provoke Lenin to eject the insufficiently resolute Axelrod, together with Zasulich and Potresov, from the editorial board of Iskra. Yet despite his inner reservations, Plekhanov did his best to defend Lenin's book when the Economist delegates cleverly used the debate on the party programme to tease out what they must have suspected were incipient differences of opinion among the 'Iskraists' over the 'party-class' question.

CHAPTER FOUR
HARD AND SOFT

To what extent, if any, was *Iskra* troubled by internal differences in the period prior to the Second Congress? In the first two years of *Iskra*'s activity, conflicts on the board, apart from those of a purely episodic nature, tended to run along generational lines, with the younger trio of Lenin, Martov and Potresov (Starover), ambitious and newly arrived from Russia, pitted against the old guard establishment, the exiles of the Emancipation of Labour Group, Plekhanov (with his two votes), Axelrod and Zasulich, with Lenin and Plekhanov respectively assuming the role of principal antagonists. When, in preparing for the Congress, these two again locked horns – this time over the merits of their rival drafts for the Party programme – the result was to obscure, if only temporarily, a new tension arising not between but within the two groupings, a development which only became properly visible at the Congress itself. Of these two rifts, that between Martov and Lenin in the younger trio proved to be more significant and enduring than the temporary rupture in the old guard between Plekhanov and Axelrod. In fact the previously intimate relations between Lenin and Martov had, by all accounts, already cooled somewhat following their move from Munich to London in the summer of 1902, with Martov now tending to spend more of his time in the company of Zasulich, and then, following his arrival in October from Siberia, with Trotsky. The fact that they shared the same lodgings (not far from Lenin's flat, at Sidmouth Street, near King's Cross) surely played its part in drawing together these three co-founders of Menshevism. Already pre-occupied with his campaigns against the Bund and the Economists, and still at odds with Plekhanov, Lenin must have found his worsening relations with Martov an added source of worry. Krupskaya recalled that in the weeks before the Congress, Lenin's 'nerves were in such a bad state that he developed a nervous disease caused by inflammation of the nerve endings of the back and chest.' On the board, 'the situation was intolerable', while among some of the delegates ariving for the Congress, there were already 'signs of discontent about *Iskra* wanting to boss the show.'[1] The very idea!

Little wonder, then, that in this period of flux and uncertainty, Lenin had begun to cast around for new allies, proposing that Trotsky be co-opted onto the board of *Iskra* as its seventh member. This move was immediately vetoed by the ever-suspicious Plekhanov, who construed the move, probably rightly, as an attempt by the ambitious Lenin to break the old deadlock of the two trios by giving a guaranteed majority to his own supporters. But it might also have occurred to Lenin that Trotsky's vote (and Lenin was always calculating votes) would lessen the damage of any future defections from his own camp. For, no later than the spring of 1903, Martov and Lenin, once the very best of comrades and friends, had begun to feel at odds with one another in all manner of ways; first, as can be so often the case, morally, psychologically and socially, and only later, politically. Increasingly irked by what he described as the 'omnipotence' and 'despotism' of Lenin's regime within the *Iskra* organisation, and the special role within that regime allotted to his wife, Martov had begun to press the case for ending the 'state of siege' which *Iskra* (acting as a Jacobin 'Committee of Public Safety', chiefly at the instigation of Plekhanov and Lenin) had declared in its war against the Economists and the Bund. Martov now increasingly favoured a party leadership based on a coalition of different political tendencies (thereby opposing Lenin's plan for a monopoly exercised by *Iskra* 'hards'), and criteria for membership which would open up the Party to rank and file workers. To this end, Martov, at the request of like-minded

27

fellow 'Iskraists', set about drafting, for adoption at the Second Congress, a Party constitution which would allow for the broadening of Party membership beyond the existing core of professional revolutionaries and *Iskra* 'agents'. Martov's endeavour proved to be the very issue which provoked the initial rupture with Lenin at the Congress,[2] chiefly because the latter (now with the encouragement of an avowedly Jacobin Plekhanov[3]) was planning to propose a constitution in keeping with the ideas advanced in his 'What Is To Be Done?'

Some idea of the drift of Lenin's thinking at this time can be gleaned from his pamphlet 'A Letter to a Comrade on our Organisational Tasks', which complained of the 'immoderate application of the elective principle'[4] by Party activists, and advised that instead the leadership of the movement should be entrusted to the 'smallest possible number of the most homogeneous possible groups of professional revolutionaries.'[5] (Time would show that not only in theory, but in practice, this number could be reduced to one.) And then, as if to emphasise the 'technocratic' thrust of his proposals, Lenin used the phrase 'cogs and wheels of the party machine'[6] to illustrate his ideal of the relationship between the different parts and levels of a revolutionary organisation, an image to which he would return in the 1921 debate with Trotsky on the post-revolutionary role of trade unions.

Partly as a consequence of Lenin's hardening resolve, despite Martov's objections, to press ahead with an ever more stringent centralisation of the Party's structures, the old fault lines of the board began to be surreptitiously supplanted by a new, cross-generational antagonism between incipient 'hards' and 'softs'. At its root, the differences were obviously political. Yet the incident that announced and crystallized this regroupment within *Iskra* seemed to have nothing to do with the conventional stuff of party politics. The issue that first divided the board between 'hards' and 'softs', or, as they would become known after the Congress, Bolsheviks and Mensheviks, was Lenin's adamant refusal to support a demand by three of the board's members – Martov, Potresov and Zasulich (Axelrod was not present at the meeting in question) – to call to account a fellow-'Iskraist' for his vile abuse of a female Party comrade. The woman, who was married to another Party member, had had an affair with N.E. Bauman while they were both in exile in Siberia. After making her pregnant, Bauman deserted her, and then drove her to suicide by a campaign of insults and mockery which included, incredibly for someone supposedly committed to the cause of women's emancipation, circulating amongst the exile community pornographic cartoons and verses. Before taking her life, she wrote a letter to the Party denouncing what she called its 'prevailing indifference' to the 'personal morality' of its members, and expressing the hope that her tragic fate would 'draw the attention of comrades to the question of the private morals of public figures.'[7]

Well she might! For when this letter was eventually presented by her husband, in the spring of 1903, to the *Iskra* board for action, Lenin, supported by the no less Jacobin Plekhanov, threatened to resign if the matter was not immediately dropped. Lenin had already earmarked the up-and-coming *Iskra* agent for a key role at the Congress, and when compelled to make a choice, placed a higher value on the impeccably 'hard' Bauman's services than on the need to uphold the Party's ethical standards. Lenin contemptuously brushed aside the whole business, chiding the protestors for their confusion of 'the personal and the political' in 'an incident of a purely personal character'.[8] The ever-dutiful Krupskaya cut an even more wretched figure, if that were possible. She dismissed the tragedy as 'some gossip about an incident supposed [*sic*] to have taken place in Siberian exile.'[9] So far as the present writer is aware, no Leninist, male or female, either then or since, has seen fit to condemn Lenin's (or, for that matter, Krupskaya's) role in what would, in any other circumstances, be denounced as a cover-up of a scandal. And so, having faced down their over-sensitive opponents over what they obviously regarded as nothing more than a storm in a tea cup, Lenin and Plekhanov moved on to next business. Yet for Potresov, it was to prove the parting of the ways. As far as he was concerned, Bolshevism and Menshevism were born, not at the Congress, in the row over rules, but in the course of a struggle for the honour and dignity of a cruelly wronged comrade:

> Six months before the party Congress of 1903, relations between Lenin on the one hand and Martov, Vera Zasulich and myself on the other, which were already tense, went completely to pieces. The incident which drew our attention to Lenin's amorality and brought matters to a head was his utterly cynical resistance to the investigation of a charge levelled by the damaged party against one of his outstanding agents.[10]

Yet how different from Lenin's reaction, exactly twenty years later, when a mere 'rude summons' (over the telephone at that) to his own wife by Stalin was sufficient to provoke Lenin into severing all personal relations with the offender.[11] What the two episodes had in common was most certainly not any consistent attitude by Lenin towards the abuse of women Party comrades, but the exigencies of political alignments. In the spring of 1903, with the outcome of the Congress still far from certain, and his own position on the board insecure, Lenin found Bauman far too valuable an ally to be sacrificed to the conscience of the Party. By March 1923, with his grip on the Party reins almost lost, Lenin had finally resolved upon a break with his too indiscriminately 'hard' (and therefore potentially disloyal) General Secretary, and had, ironically, turned for support to his 'soft' antagonist at the Second Congress, Trotsky.

But then certain questions naturally arise: why was Lenin so attracted to the Baumans and Stalins of the Party machine? What was it about their undoubted 'hardness' that he preferred to the integrity, enlightenment and selfless dedication of a Martov or an Axelrod? And, bearing in mind his astuteness in so many other matters, why did it take Lenin so long (in fact too long) to discern in Stalin traits which, from the very outset of his political career, were acutely pronounced, and notorious amongst numerous Party activists?

Many times must Trotsky have asked himself these questions. After all, without Lenin's patronage, someone of Stalin's limited political sophistication would have occupied at best only an intermediate position in the Bolshevik hierarchy. For whatever reasons, and despite encountering considerable and repeated opposition to his preference, rung by rung Lenin guided Stalin up the Party ladder from the obscurity of a provincial 'committeeman' in the Caucasus to the summits and nerve centres of Bolshevik power in the Kremlin. In the entire history of Russia, there had never been an ascent quite like it (nor, after his death, such a fall).[12] More than once, Trotsky tried to grapple with this problem. He could hardly very well avoid it, in view of the incalculable impact Lenin's choice had on his own political and personal fortunes. And yet there was an obvious difficulty. For tactical reasons, after his fall from power Trotsky found it expedient to justify as well as to explain why his mortal enemy, whom Lenin once described, in a rare moment of enthusiasm, as a 'marvellous Georgian',[13] was entrusted with so many sensitive positions and important tasks within the Party apparatus, while Trotsky himself was given none. Hard though it must have been to restrain himself, on no account was Trotsky prepared to invite the charge that he was in any way impugning Lenin's political sagacity or objectivity. We are asked to believe that it was all perfectly straightforward, a simple matter of Lenin's liking for 'people who showed resoluteness', of his valuing 'men of action'.[14] Trotsky recalled how, after the revolution, Stalin was deliberately 'advanced' by Lenin, who perceived his 'firmness, grit, stubbornness, and to a certain extent his slyness, as necessary attributes in the struggle.'[15] Slyness? Exactly where that struggle might lead, and the uses to which Stalin could put his slyness, only became evident when it was too late to undo Lenin's choice. One by one (and beginning with Lenin) the Party's leaders fell victim to the machinations of the 'irreplaceable assistant' selected, before all others, by Lenin to administer the apparatus of Bolshevik rule. It was Stalin's 'ability to "exert pressure"' that 'Lenin prized so highly',[16] admitted Trotsky with remarkable candour, even his 'ruthlessness and conniving'.[17] Conniving. But again we must ask: against whom? Surely all Bolsheviks were comrades? What could Lenin have been thinking of? What Stalin had in mind came as something of a shock to those who, like Lenin, had fondly believed for far too long that Stalin's gifts were at the disposal of the Party or, at the very least, of its ruling circles.

The chain of events that culminated in the split at the Second Congress strongly suggests that Lenin's preference for 'hard' Party cadres, so revealingly discussed by Trotsky, was already well established no later than 1903. What is more, as the case of Bauman indicates, he was, even then, not prepared to let any personal deficiency or misdemeanour influence his choice of political allies. The issues raised by the 'Bauman affair', and the new alignments which it precipitated, confirm that even before the Congress began, the ground had begun to move beneath the feet of the old *Iskra*. Perhaps it was this very episode, arising from events that had, on the surface at least, absolutely no bearing on the Party's programme, strategy, tactics or theory, which finally persuaded Lenin, after several months of increasing doubts, that his new opponents on the board were not made of the 'right stuff'. Maybe it was time to change tack, to seek new allies, to promote new cadres, and to placate old rivals. And there was always the hope that his old, but now increasingly estranged friend, Martov, could be separated from his weaker allies on the board, Zasulich, Axelrod and Potresov. They were probably lost. But not Martov. Not yet.

Such thoughts as these must have raced through Lenin's mind as the Congress drew nearer. And as he lay awake at night, he must have toyed with this and that plan to inoculate *Iskra*, and with it, the entire Party, against the virus of 'softness' that was infecting all but himself and Plekhanov. What was needed was an injection of Jacobin intransigence, or maybe even a bloodletting, a purge of waverers and doubters. Certainly, it was in the weeks preceding the Congress that Lenin became convinced that it was time to reduce the size of the *Iskra* board from six to three, a measure that once proposed, would announce to the Party Lenin's intention to make his bid for the 'conductor's baton'.

It was now midsummer in Brussels. The delegates were gathering. But so were the storm clouds. The greatest drama of our century was about to begin.

CHAPTER FIVE
ISKRA DIVIDED

And here I prophesy – this brawl today grown to this faction shall send a thousand souls to death and deadly night.

Henry VI, Part One

Iskra's opponents – principally the Bund and the Economists – were still unaware of these new tensions. Threatened as they were with virtual extinction by the Second Congress, both groups understandably pinned their hopes of survival on divisions within the ranks of the 'Iskraists'. With this obviously in mind, the Economist delegates in particular set about attempting a kindling of the old and well-known rivalries between Lenin and Plekhanov. With this in mind, they tried to insert between them the wedge of Lenin's 'What Is To Be Done?', little suspecting that it would be Martov and not Plekhanov, who would be the first 'Iskraist' to break ranks. Akimov (and Martynov) began their attack by drawing attention to what they saw as similarities between Lenin's approach to the 'party-class' issue in his book and the draft programme's treatment of the same question. After referring to the growing 'discontent' of the workers (and not their increasing political consciousness), the programme had described in some detail how the Party 'guide[d] all the manifestations of the class struggle', 'reveal[ing]' and 'explain[ing]' to the workers the causes of their exploitation and the means by which it could be brought to an end. As far as the Economist delegates were concerned, the overall impression created by this section of the programme was one of a proletariat capable of playing only a subordinate part in its own emancipation:[1]

> We see here [declared Martynov] the influence of the recent fight against so-called Economism, and in particular the influence of a basic theoretical argument that was advanced during that fight by Comrade Lenin.[2]

Martynov then convincingly demonstrated, by deftly counterposing Lenin's formulations to a series of quotations from the writings of Marx and Engels (as well as extracts from other Social-Democratic party programmes), how Lenin's and the programme's treatment of the 'party-class' question was anything but classically Marxist. Martynov detected in both a 'conspiratorial plan of organisation which is essentially suitable not for the class party of the proletariat but for a radical party basing itself upon a variety of revolutionary elements.'[3] In other words, its inspiration was not Marxist, but Jacobin-populist, in the tradition of those who argued, before the emergence of Marxism in Russia, that the 'revolutionary minority that understands the tasks of working class socialism' needed to unite in a 'powerful organisation' that would be joined by 'suffering masses' at 'the moment of the explosion', an arrangement necessary because 'complete awareness of ends and means' was to be found only 'in small groups and in individual units.'[4]

Martynov's was a serious and substantial critique of Lenin's book, being by far the longest speech delivered to the Congress. As such, it could hardly be totally ignored. That would simply invite the suspicion that the 'Iskraists' did indeed have something to hide. So Martov gamely sprang to Lenin's defence, though in a manner suggesting that he would have preferred to have remained silent. Feigning bewilderment at Martynov's strictures on spontaneity and consciousness, Martov protested, rather unconvincingly, that he could not see 'any connection between a passage in Lenin's book and the absence of the word consciousness' from the Party programme. But even so (and this may well have been an indication of his subterranean and soon to erupt quarrel with Lenin on this very question) Martov went some way towards meeting Martynov's objections by adding that he had 'nothing against inserting this word'.[5] But why was it missing in the first place? The explanation could be that although Lenin had shared with Plekhanov the drafting of the Party programme, this particular section was more the result of his handiwork than Plekhanov's. Obviously with the purpose of drawing attention to Martov's equivocations, and perhaps also with the intention of encouraging him to take them further, Martynov observed that Martov had 'tried to defend Comrade Lenin's thesis', but that in order to do so, he had 'first touched it up' by softening the harshness of Lenin's formulations. But even in its modified form, said Martynov, 'Comrade Lenin's theory is wrong'.[6] Possibly sensing a hint of 'softness' on the part of Martov, and with no other members of the *Iskra* board prepared to take the floor, Plekhanov stepped into the breach. But even he was less intransigent than usual. Adopting the same evasive tactics as Martov, he advanced the opaque objection that Martynov had 'transferred the argument to a terrain on which it is inexpedient to argue.' Hardly a whole-hearted defence, one might well say. But then worse followed. Although obliged to refute Martynov's criticisms of the Party programme, he also sensed the need to distance himself just a little from their target. The criticised passage (by now obviously not his, but Lenin's) was perhaps 'unfortunate', but even so, it had been misunderstood. As for Lenin's book, it was not intended as a 'treatise on the philosophy of history, but a polemical article against the Economists.'[7] But, objected Akimov, however one described Lenin's book, it was still wrong. Moreover, the contentious section of the programme differed radically from what Plekhanov had himself written elsewhere on the same topic. For this reason, Akimov was 'sure that Plekhanov [did] not agree with Lenin.' (In this he was soon proved to be correct.) The danger was, Akimov continued, that as the programme stood, it could be interpreted to mean that 'the role of the leading organisation is to relegate to the background the class it is leading and to separate the former from the latter' and that 'consequently, the formulation of our political tasks is exactly the same as that of [the Jacobin terrorist] Narodnaya Volya.'[8] Indeed! With the 'Iskraists' now palpably embarrassed in their role as reluctant defenders of Lenin's book, the Bund, until this point on the defensive, saw an opportunity to hit back. Its view on the subject had already been made quite clear before the Congress by Vladimir Medem, when he insisted that 'a workers' movement cannot be created from the top down [but] must arise from below.'[9] So it should hardly have been a surprise when the Bundist Mark Liber agreed with the Economist delegates that Lenin's book 'underestimate[d] the influence of pro-letarian psychology' in the formation of working class consciousness, though he failed to detect a similar tendency in the programme.[10]

As the debate rolled on, and finding his own comrades making heavy weather of the Economist offensive against his book, it must have become increasingly evident to Lenin that he was obliged, even if only for tactical reasons, to enter the lists in his own defence. He did so by explaining, ingenuously, that the controversies it addressed were no more than an 'episode in the struggle against economism' and had been 'confused with a principled presentation of a major theoretical question, namely, the formation of socialist ideology.'[11] But this was simply not true, and all the delegates, 'Iskraists' included, must have known it. In the Preface to his book, Lenin refers to its treatment of the 'fundamental question of the role of social democrats in relation to the spontaneous mass movement.'[12] Now it was a different story. All he had done, Lenin explained, was to bend the stick of 'Economist' opportunism in the other direction so as to straighten it out.[13] And with that, he sat down.

The debate was rounded off by two 'Iskraist' contributions, one from Trotsky and another by Plekhanov. Trotsky's was intriguing in that he did not even attempt a defence of Lenin's book (which he was soon to subject to a vigorous criticism) but chose instead to expound views on the 'party-class' question that clearly distanced himself, even if only implicitly, not only from Lenin, but also from his own later theory of 'permanent revolution', a conception which, amongst other things, argued that the workers could come to power whilst still constituting but a small minority of the total population. Rejecting Akimov's accusations of *Iskra* Jacobinism, Trotsky predicted that the proletarian dictatorship 'will become possible only when the Social-Democratic Party and the working class – the counterposing of which worries him so much – have come closer than now to identification one with the other. The dictatorship of the proletariat will not be a conspiratorial "seizure of power" [which is just what it proved to be – ironically, largely under the practical direction of none other than Trotsky himself] but the political rule of the organised working class, constituting the majority of the nation.'[14] It should be recorded here that at the moment of the Bolshevik seizure of power, the Russian working class (defined, that is, in classical Marxist and not populist terms) comprised, at the most, ten per cent of the total working population of the Russian Empire, whilst a few weeks later the Bolsheviks won no more than twenty-five per cent of all votes cast in the elections to the Constituent Assembly, which the Bolsheviks then promptly dispersed by force after one sitting. (See Appendices Two and Three.) So, whether one uses social or political criteria, these proportions hardly comprised the 'immense majority' the author of the 'Communist Manifesto' (and, in 1903, Trotsky) considered essential for a successful proletarian revolution. But it was enough for Lenin who, two years after October, explicitly reversed the 'Manifesto's' priority of first winning what it called 'the battle of democracy'[15] (i.e. a majority), with a formulation that could just as easily have come from the pen of Blanqui, Tkachev or Bakunin:

[T]he proletariat must first overthrow the bourgeoisie and win for itself state power and then use that state power for the purpose of winning the sympathy of the majority of the working people.[16]

Machiavelli put it more honestly, if also more cynically:

[T]he nature of the people is variable, and whilst it is easy to persuade them, it is difficult to fix them in that persuasion. And thus it is necessary to take such measures that, when they believe no longer, it may be possible to make them believe by force.[17]

(In fairness to the founder of the world's first totalitarian state, it must be conceded that when it came to this plan's actual execution Lenin, following the example of Richard of Gloucester, 'set the mur'drous Machiavel to school'.[18])

These fascinating, and truly anticipatory, exchanges took place in Brussels during the ninth session of the Congress, on August 4, 1903, with the division over the rules still some way off (it occurred, after the enforced move to London, at the twenty-third session on August 15). Up to that point it was therefore still possible and expedient for all 'Iskraists' to close ranks when Lenin's book came under sustained attack from the Economists. But it is obvious from the proceedings that, one way or another, Akimov and Martynov had divined that all was not well in the

Iskra camp, and that its troubles were connected in some way with incipient unease over Lenin's *élitist* organisational principles. As we have seen, their first sally against Lenin's book failed to draw any more blood than a few blushes of embarrassment from its author's comrades. But then, seemingly over a mere form of words, there exploded the rift between Martov and Lenin in the commission charged by the Congress with drawing up the Party rules. In retrospect, however, it was, as we have seen, closely related to the differences that had already been concealed as much as revealed in the debate over Lenin's book. This fissure, once open, now provided the anti-'Iskraists' with a second opportunity to insert their wedge, this time to devastating effect. Lenin's 'compact majority', already fraying at the edges, disintegrated. In the division over the rival drafts of the first rule, Martov's broader condition of membership secured twenty-eight votes, Lenin's more narrow version, twenty-three. At that moment, in (of all places) a church hall in a London suburb, on August 15, 1903, fifty or so atheists (most of them Jews), acted as unwitting midwives to Bolshevism and Menshevism, non-identical twins of the same populist-Marxist parentage.

An important question needs to be answered at this stage: why did Plekhanov find himself (albeit only briefly) on the same side as his most serious and consistent opponent on the board of *Iskra*? For more than a year, he and Lenin had waged war over the Party programme, only at the last moment to close ranks over what might have seemed to be the far less crucial issue of a matter of wording in the Party rules. Could it have been that, like Lenin, Plekhanov saw the 'party-class' question in Jacobin-populist, rather than classically Marxist terms? Here the record is ambiguous, perhaps helping to explain how, even after deserting the Bolsheviks, Plekhanov could be enticed by Lenin into combinations directed against his own Menshevik comrades. For example, in an early (1883) polemic against Russian Jacobinism (principally Tkachev and his school) Plekhanov could insist in one passage that 'there is no more difference between heaven and earth than between the dictatorship of a class and that of a group of revolutionary intelligentsia' (thereby distancing himself from what Trotsky would, after the split of 1903, describe as Lenin's theory of 'substitutionism' in which the select organisation of professional revolutionaries thinks, acts and eventually rules in the place of the working class); and, in another, no less fervently argue that this very same intelligentsia 'must become the leader of the working class in the coming emancipation movement'.[19] Undoubtedly, Plekhanov shared Lenin's tendency (though never to the same excess) to resort to rough-handed, highly centralised solutions to what were often intensely complex political problems. This tendency usually co-existed quite happily, at least up until 1903, with Plekhanov's public opposition to the *élitist* assumptions and tactics of his former populist colleagues. Following his separation in 1879 from the peasant-oriented, and, increasingly, terrorist inclined 'Land and Liberty', Plekhanov had indeed loosed off a fusilade of vituperative polemics against his former comrades, aimed, in part, at their advocacy of Jacobin methods of revolutionary action and organisation. On the other hand, privately (as was also the case with Lenin until his publication of 'What Is To Be Done?') Plekhanov continued to nurse a respect and even longing for the old ways. In 1888, he admitted to Axelrod that the mood was again upon him, and asked his friend to restrain his 'centralist and Jacobin tendencies', confessing (as he would have done to no-one else) that he had 'sinned on that score'.[20] Twelve years on, when locked in battle with what he regarded as the twin heresies of Bernstein's German revisionism and Russian Economism, and totally convinced of his theoretical correctness, Plekhanov wrote once more to Axelrod, only this time to reassure him that 'as a member of the Emancipation of Labour [Group] you are infallible and must not and cannot err,' adding (revealingly, in the light of his choice of allies at the Second Congress), 'you know I am beginning to lean toward Jacobinism.'[21] So, as the Congress approached, and with the smell of gunfire and blood already in his nostrils, it is not difficult to see why, when hostilities actually began, Plekhanov found himself, albeit only briefly, in the company of Lenin's 'hards', even if this involved, as it did for Lenin, a painful rupture with his oldest comrades and most cherished friends. After all, was it not Robespierre, the most intransigent Jacobin of them all, who, when faced with the same choice between friendship and the good of the cause, without hesitation took the path of revolutionary virtue? Ironically, at the Congress, it fell to Plekhanov, and not Lenin, to make the most Jacobin pronouncement of all, during the debate on the Party programme. A proposed amendment stipulating the Party's support for biennial elections had been met with the objection that its strict application might prove 'awkward for the party', whilst another delegate went even further by opposing inclusion in the programme of any democratic demands 'capable of restricting our freedom of action in the future.'[22] With the Congress now in uproar, Plekhanov threw his prestige behind the exponents of *Iskra Realpolitik*. In accordance with the thoroughly Jacobin maxim, 'the success of the revolution is the highest law', he declared himself ready to sacrifice any democratic principle – even universal suffrage – or to contemplate the most repressive measures – including the dispersal of a freely elected parliament – if the interests of the cause could be advanced thereby.[23] And that, of course, is exactly what the Bolsheviks later did.

To his credit, Plekhanov would soon come to bitterly and publicly regret his role at the Second Congress. In fact his alliance with Lenin did not last out the year. But there was much in his past, and in his character, that helps to explain why he came to share with Lenin (though not to the same degree) the responsibility for the creation of what later became known as Bolshevism.

CHAPTER SIX
LENIN AS *ÉLITIST*

Now to consider what is perhaps the most important question of all: of what, precisely, was Lenin's 'hard' caucus an anticipation? The party of proletarian emancipation? Or of totalitarian manipulation? Lenin's faction initially defined itself not in relation to any questions of policy, programme or tactics, but in the struggle over the Party constitution, supporting his proposed rule confining Party membership to those who 'participated personally in one of the party's organisations',[1] while Martov's extended it to those who worked under their direction. The distinction, though initially believed by everyone involved to be small (and certainly not worth splitting the Party over) was nevertheless important in that Lenin's rule would have tended to restrict Party membership to professional revolutionaries. Lenin had already explained in 'What Is To Be Done?' that 'the organisation of the revolutionaries must consist first and foremost of people who make revolutionary activity their profession',[2] thereby creating a 'powerful and secret organisation which concentrates in its hands all the threads of [the Party's] secret activities.'[3] *Élitist* (and conspiratorial) though this conception undoubtedly was, it was something else again to propose, as Lenin now did, that this revolutionary *élite* should not only comprise the Party's inner core, but make up a considerable, even the greater part, of its total membership. Under Lenin's rule, workers who supported the Party but remained at their jobs would almost inevitably find themselves outside its ranks. Hence Martov's objections, which were then endorsed by Trotsky and Axelrod. In 'What Is To Be Done?', Lenin had been quite specific on this point:

> A worker-agitator who is at all gifted and 'promising' [sic] *must not be left* to work eleven hours a day in a factory. We must arrange that he be maintained by the Party; that he may go underground [emphasis in the original].[4]

Here is the germ-cell – and, at the same time, the justification – of what after the revolution became the Leninist *nomenklatura*, a ruling formation which, at its lowest echelons, was indeed comprised, for the most part, of assimilated (and therefore declassed) former workers, these then being dominated and directed from its summits by cadres selected predominately from the radical (and no less declassed) intelligentsia. The social composition of the leading bodies of Lenin's post- as well as pre-revolutionary Party conformed very closely to this schema, with (former) plebians holding positions of real influence being as rare then as they are today in the British Labour Party, and rarer than has been the case with the (Thatcherite) Conservative Party.

In this respect, too, Lenin's intentions diverged from the views of the founders of Marxism. Marx saw the Blanquist practice of the segregation and elevation of former workers into an *élite* of 'professional conspirators' as an impediment to the development of the broader working class movement. He observed amongst such types a strong tendency to live a life outside of and above the class they claimed to represent, and an inclination to use the proletariat as a vehicle for their own political ambitions.[5] Marx also, on another occasion, warned of the harm that would be done to the movement by workers leaving their jobs (as Lenin proposed) to 'join muddleheads from the allegedly "learned" caste.'[6] So, whatever their actions, the public stance of Marx and Engels towards *élitism* was clear, and would consequently have been known by all the leading participants in the life of the RSDLP. Furthermore, as we have seen, not long before his death Engels had inserted into the text of a new edition of the 'Manifesto' the word 'spontaneous' with what could only have been the intention of making yet more explicit its rejection of the idea that the working class was in need of guidance by an *élite*. Nor was this his only textual change. In the same (English) edition of 1888, Engels interpolated into the following passage the words that are emphasised:

> The proletarian movement is the *self-conscious*, independent movement of the immense majority in the interests of the immense majority.[7]

What could be clearer? The forces and motives impelling Lenin to challenge this tradition and conception must, therefore, have been strong indeed, especially in view of his understandable concern always to appear as the custodian of Marxist orthodoxy. Yet there is evidence that even before the Congress, Lenin had countenanced such innovations. It is to be found in an article written by him for the journal *Rabochaya Gazeta* whilst in Siberian exile, and dating from the second half of 1899:

> We do not regard Marx's theory as something completed and inviolable; on the contrary, we are convinced that it has only laid the foundation stone of the science which socialists *must* develop in all directions if they wish to keep pace with life. We think that an *independent* elaboration of Marx's theory is especially essential for Russian socialists, for this theory only provides general *guiding* principles, which, *in particular*, are in England applied differently than in France, and in France differently than in Germany, and in Germany, differently than in Russia [emphasis in the original].[8]

The founder of 'revisionism', Eduard Bernstein, was, of course, saying something rather like this (at exactly the same time) in Germany, arguing that his party, still 'officially' orthodox, had to take account, in its programme, of new developments in German social, economic and political life.[9] What Bernstein also shared with Lenin was the conviction that the class struggle and, specifically, the direction given to it by what were seen as the spontaneously reformist tendencies of the working class, put in question long-established orthodoxies concerning the inevitability of socialism. Where the two differed was in their response. While Bernstein recommended that his party align its programme and theory with these processes and tendencies, Lenin proposed an all-out war against them. Hence his call for a struggle against working class spontaneity. But Lenin did not arrive at that conclusion overnight. Still feeling his way, he did not at first clearly indicate in what areas he was proposing to revise or 'violate' (his own term) Marxism in its application to Russian problems. But there were clues. Nearly all the articles he wrote at this time – 'Our Immediate Task', 'An Urgent Question', 'A Retrograde Trend in Russian Social-Democracy' and 'Apropos of the "Profession De Foi"'[10] (these last two being directed against 'Economism') – were Lenin's first serious attempts to explore and resolve the problem that was only finally answered to his own satisfaction in 'What Is To Be Done?' We should, however, place Lenin's quest for the resolution of the 'party-class' question in a broader setting. The idea of a directing (almost invariably intellectual) *élite* is at least as old as Plato's 'Republic', where it is argued at great length and with much eloquence that a system where 'philosophers are to rule the state'[11] was the only salvation of a society plagued by the 'evil' of 'discord and plurality'.[12] In fact Stalin's argument (which he derived directly from Lenin) that manual workers had 'neither the time nor the opportunity to work out socialist consciousness' and that therefore, this had to be done for them by 'a few social-democratic intellectuals who possess the time and opportunity to do so'[13] is 'anticipated' not only by Plato, who derided the very idea (which lay at the foundation of Athenian democracy) of a 'cobbler or any other man designed by nature to be a trader' presuming to 'meddle' in the affairs of state,[14] but in the Old Testament, where Ecclesiasticus, although evincing a certain sympathy for the lot of the labourer, nevertheless concluded that the 'wisdom of a learned man cometh by opportunity of leisure' and asked, rhetorically:

> How can he get wisdom that holdeth the plough, and that glorieth in the goad, that driveth oxen; and is occupied in their labours; and whose talk is of bullocks?[15]

Given that the idea was so old, and had served so often as a justification for the rejection of democratic principles, we can understand why Lenin's brand of *élitism*, even though it eventually secured for itself a significant following, aroused such a controversy in Russian (and later, international) social-democracy that the dispute left in its wake a trail of envenomed political feuds, blighted friendships and organisational rifts. Moreover, at the time of the birth of Leninism, the idea of an endemic incapacity or inertness of the mass, and the call for an 'organising' or 'dynamic' minority, came (as one would expect) chiefly from beyond the confines of the socialist movement and, when within it (until, that is, Lenin wrote 'What Is To Be Done?'), from tendencies that could hardly be regarded as typically Marxist. Often originating at the cultural margins of the political world of late nineteenth and early twentieth century Europe, we find this contempt for the 'herd' and cry for a ruthless ('hard') new caste of masters in the works of writers as diverse in other respects as Henrik Ibsen ('fools are in a terrible, overwhelming majority, all the world over'[16]); Friedrich Nietzsche ('morality in Europe today is herd-morality'[17]); Bernard Shaw (the main hindrance to socialism is 'the stupidity of the working class'[18]); Gaetano Mosca ('even in democracies the need for an organised minority persists'[19]); Georges Sorel ('Lenin, like Peter the Great, wants to force history'[20]); Roberto Michels ('the majority is permanently incapable of self-government'[21]); and Vilfredo Pareto, with his theory of a never-ending 'circulation of *élites*'. There were no compelling reasons to assume that Russia's younger would-be Marxists, with their country's long tradition of *élitist* conspiratorial theories and organisations, would prove totally immune to the seductive idea of an organising *élite* that could drive forward the often frustratingly slow pace of Russia's social and political development. After all, if even an economically matured and liberal England could have the Fabian Bernard Shaw addressing the question of how to politicise what he described as the 'raw material of Socialism – otherwise the Proletarian man'[22] only to arrive at conclusions which would later enable him to endorse, simultaneously, the policies of Bolshevism and Italian fascism, why not Russia its Lenin, a land which, from the time of the Tartars, on through Ivan IV and Peter the Great, had been organised 'from the top down'? Also at this time, but in Austria, an ambitious, though as yet unheeded, failed artist and political agitator was already blaming his lack of public recognition on the 'inertia of the mass', and learning to despise the judgment of a 'fluctuating majority... thrown together by more or less savoury accidents',[23] while in Italy his future mentor was embarking on an extraordinary political career that, inspired more by the writings of Blanqui, Sorel, Nietzsche and Pareto than Marx and Engels, would transport him from positions of total intransigence on the extreme left of the Socialist Party, through war-time 'interventionism' to the founding of Fascism and the destruction of the Italian workers' movement. Yet throughout all these phases, he would remain what he had been at the beginning – 'hard' to the point of callousness, convinced of the necessity of a guiding *élite* and answering, always, to the title of 'Duce', 'the Boss'. Whilst still editor of the Socialist Party daily *Avanti*, Mussolini painted in lurid colours an approaching revolution that would be 'mad, violent and bestial' which would 'kill, destroy and sack'.[24] All these it would be, but its victims would not be the bourgeoisie, but the organisations of the Italian proletariat. Surely it is instructive that, so far as Mussolini was concerned, the same means that were initially intended to hasten the victory of socialism could later equally well be employed to bring about its defeat?

In all, the last years that preceded the war were a time of the breaching of traditional barriers, of strange intellectual mutations and exotic syntheses ('national syndicalism' in Italy, 'national socialism' in Germany, 'Jacobin Marxism' in Russia); a flux out of which, in the crucible of war and failed, defeated or cheated revolutions, would crystallize the doctrines and methods of modern totalitarianisms, being, in each of its varieties, very much an affair of impatient and intolerant 'young men in a hurry'. Neither should too much be made, in this respect at least, of conventional distinctions between 'left' and 'right'. Whilst still a socialist, Mussolini could already be heard echoing Lenin's strictures on the limitations of trade unionism, complaining that 'the worker who is merely [economically] organised becomes a petit bourgeois who only obeys the voice of his own interests. Any ideal finds him deaf.' To counteract this deplorable tendency of the workers (to quote Lenin) to 'come under the wing of the bourgeoisie', the Party had to become an 'organisation of warriors', a 'small, determined bold nucleus', a 'proletarian *élite*',[25] since it was impossible to 'incorporate the majority of the proletariat' into the movement for socialism.[26] (In his day, Plato also found that the 'corruption of the majority' was 'unavoidable'.[27]) An old comrade of Mussolini's echoed this idea when he wrote:

> We are not worried about recruiting the mass; let us pick the *élite* of the proletariat, and with this minority we will govern the majority.

The author was not an Italian Leninist – but he easily might have been. For was it not Lenin himself who developed the so-called 'conveyor-belt' theory of organisation? Did he not argue that a partly 'divided', 'degraded' and 'corrupted' proletariat could not 'directly exercise' its own rule, and had therefore delegated this task to a 'vanguard that has absorbed the revolutionary energy of the class', and this would in turn require 'an arrangement of cog-wheels', a 'number of "transmission belts" running from the vanguard to the mass of the working people'?[28] *Élitist* and technocratic to be sure, but hardly Marxist. With its Futurist overtones, it smacks much more of Mussolini.

And what of the previous quotation, with its equally Leninist (and Stirnerite) contempt for the 'mass', and advocacy of domination through a 'proletarian *élite*'? Like Mussolini, Roberto Farinacci had, before the war, stood on the 'intransigent' wing of the Italian Socialist Party. This declaration, however, belongs to his period of office as secretary of the Italian Fascist Party.[29] Though by this time supposedly a man of the extreme right, Farinacci's ideal of leadership shared an obvious kinship with Comintern chief Grigori Zinoviev's conception of revolutionary organisation. One of Lenin's closest associates (they shared years of exile together), Zinoviev faithfully echoed his mentor in demanding, for the fledgling parties of the newly-founded International, the formation of 'a really determined minority of the working class' whose task would be to 'organise the struggle of the masses' by means of a 'disciplined organisation of the working class *élite*.'[30]

Two questions. Firstly, who defined socialism as a system where an 'all-embracing' party, by creating organisations in which the 'whole of individual life will be reflected' would, as the 'representative of the common good', regulate 'each activity and each need of the individual'?

Secondly, which of these statements was made by Mussolini the *élitist* socialist, and which by Mussolini the no less *élitist* fascist? 'Majorities are inevitably static, minorities dynamic. We wish to be an active minority,' and, 'The struggle in human society has always been and will always be a struggle of minorities. To aspire qualitatively to an absolute majority is absurd [because] the majority always follows and obeys.'

Revealing though the answers are (and it has been left to the reader to puzzle them out), in one respect they hardly matter. All the quotations are equally remote from 'classic' Marxism's insistence that 'the proletarian movement is the self-conscious, independent movement of the immense majority in the interests of the immense majority'[31] and infinitely closer in spirit to Lenin's battle cry: 'Give us an organisation of revolutionaries and we shall overturn Russia,'[32] or his totalitarian blueprint of 'building the party from the top downwards.'[33] So why should we be surprised that Lenin could confide to an Italian Socialist Party delegation that Mussolini's defection to fascism was a 'great pity', being the loss of a 'strong man who would have led our party to victory'? Or that Trotsky should have scolded the same delegation for having lost their 'trump card', the 'only man who carried through a revolution'? Or, that Trotsky again – and this was after Mussolini's 'March on Rome' – could have described the gravedigger of the Italian labour movement as 'our best pupil'?[34] Or that, as early as 1923, a Soviet publication could recognise in Italian fascism 'a politically conscious imitation' of Bolshevism;[35] or, finally, that Mussolini's *Critica Fascista* of July 15, 1937, could publish an article entitled 'The Fascism of Stalin'?[36]

Late in his life, and without (of course) admitting any significant continuity between early Bolshevism and Stalinism, Trotsky went yet further, averring that 'Stalin's political apparatus' differed from that of fascism only in its 'more unbridled savagery,'[37] 'Stalinism and fascism' being 'symmetrical phenomena' sharing a 'deadly similarity.'[38] Despite the claims of its rulers that it was the land of socialism, the USSR had, concluded Trotsky in 1936, 'become "totalitarian" in character several years before this word arrived from Germany.'[39] As for the Bolshevik Party, under Stalin 'the fascist, counter-revolutionary elements' were 'growing uninterruptedly'.[40] In truth, they were present, in embryo, from the very outset, in Lenin's *élitist* doctrine of the political incapacity of the masses and consequent need for a 'vanguard' party led by 'professional revolutionaries', a system of thought and action which, as it evolved, provided the natural and necessary ideological, organisational and moral culture for the emergence and triumph of what Trotsky and his followers have invariably described as Stalinism.

Another question: who might have said this?

> Revolution is a task for a determined minority immune to discouragement. It is the task of the minority whose first steps will not be understood by the majority.

Immediately, one recognises the same Jacobin intransigence which is the animating spirit of Leninism. But the words are, as it happens, those of the *Jefe* of the Spanish fascist Falange, José Antonio Primo De Rivera.[41] And here, too, there was a certain symmetry. Just as the founder of fascist 'national syndicalism', Ramiro Ledsma Ramos, proclaimed the need for 'revolutionary efficiency' exercised by 'audacious and valiant minorities' (and coupled to the predictable slogans 'Long Live Fascist Italy' and 'Long Live Hitler Germany', a defiant 'Long Live Soviet Russia'[42]), so the pioneers of Spanish Bolshevism (many having been reared in the school of Bakunist *élitism*) scolded the workers for their 'superlative incapacity and ignorance', while the Andalusian Anarchist, Paulino Diez, temporarily mesmerised by the myth of a 'Bolshevik libertarianism', insisted on the need for a 'conscious minority who carry along the masses by means of their convictions and their decisions'.[43] Irrespective of formal doctrinal labels, what is revealed in each instance is a similar, if not identical, conception of an inert, recalcitrant, corrupt or misguided proletariat that must be manipulated, press-ganged and frog-marched towards its salvation. And it was a view which, in turn, they each shared with Lenin's 'conveyor-belt', 'cog-wheel' specifically Bolshevik 'national syndicalism'.

However unpalatable Leninists and their fellow-travellers might find these affinities, they surely need to be acknowledged and their significance debated. To help them take their first tentative steps in such an exchange, let them begin with their own Trotsky's admission (in his last work, the uncompleted biography of Stalin) of the existence, from the very birth of Leninism, of what he described as the 'negative aspect of Bolshevism's centripetal tendencies', which were first manifested, according to Trotsky, at the Third (in fact all-Bolshevik) Party Congress of April 1905. Trotsky shows how Stalin, 'the "Committeeman" par excellence', was subsequently irresistibly attracted to the Leninist 'political machine', the same apparatus which, in later years, served as the vehicle of his ascent from Tiflis 'practico' to Party General-Secretary, becoming by stages 'the very personification of the bureaucracy and its peerless leader.'[44] And whilst conceding that there was 'not a little that [was] immature and erroneous' in his criticism of Lenin (Trotsky is referring here to his pamphlet of 1904, 'Our Political Tasks', a polemic against Lenin's views on the 'party-class' question), Trotsky claimed that it nevertheless contained 'pages which present a fairly accurate characterisation of the cast of thought of the "committeemen" of those days,' 'professional revolutionaries' who, like Stalin, had 'forgone the need to rely upon the workers after they had found support in the principles of centralism.'[45] Anxious, as always, to avoid the charge of anti-Bolshevism, Trotsky took immense care to avoid implying that there was any necessary causal link between Lenin's organisational principles and the bad habits (to put it at its mildest) of his apparatchiks – a difficult task, since the connection was all too evident. Nevertheless, he refers (daringly) to the 'erroneousness' of Lenin's theory (expounded in 'What Is To Be Done?') that the 'labour movement, when left to its own devices, was inclined irrevocably toward opportunism' and that therefore, necessarily, 'revolutionary class consciousness was brought to the proletariat from the outside, by Marxist intellectuals.' Of course, Trotsky at once hastens to point out that Lenin 'subsequently acknowledged' the fallaciousness of that theory,[46] though without specifying when and where. Even if Trotsky had in mind Lenin's defence of his book at the Second Congress (and the context suggests that he does), far from acknowledging what Trotsky calls its 'biassed nature', Lenin, as we have already observed, justified the sharpness of its formulations on the ground that it was necessary to 'bend the stick [made crooked by the 'Economists'] the other way' in order to straighten it out.[47] The same is true of his 1908 Preface to 'Twelve Years' (a collection of Lenin's writings that included an edited version of 'What Is To Be Done?') which, far from admitting any error, boasted that the book's critics had been made to 'look ridiculous' by the triumph of the organisational principles expounded therein.[48] In neither instance, then (and there are no others), is there a case to be made out that Lenin accepted the need to qualify (let alone admitted the erroneousness of) the principles he expounded in 'What Is To Be Done?'

Precisely what Trotsky found 'immature' in his polemic against Lenin he does not say, but the reader will find in 'Our Political Tasks' the beginnings of a serious discussion of what some political analysts (including Trotskyist adherents of the theory of 'bureaucratic collectivism'[49]) have subsequently described as the phenomenon and process of the rise of the 'new class'. As such, Trotsky's essay represents an attempt to understand the social and ideological origins of revolutionary *élitism*, with its obsessive centralism, fear of heresy, dishonest methods of debate, mistrust of spontaneity, militarised methods of organisation and subordination, and the primacy of the 'plan' and the will of the leaders (or even single leader) over the objective tendencies of the class struggle. Trotsky's critique of early Leninism is, like several others of its time (for example, those of Akimov, Plekhanov and Luxemburg), an 'anticipation' of later theories of totalitarianism, with its dawning awareness of what he understood as the process of 'substitution-ism'. According to this conception the party, having first substituted itself for the mistrusted spontaneous movement of the working class, then succumbs, from the bottom upwards, to the same process of usurpation, until all the conscious functions of organisation become concentrated in the hands of a single infallible leader.[50] (Trotsky's rejection of Lenin's ideal of the 'barracks' or 'factory' regime[51] is ironic in that after the revolution he would, as Commissar for War, be cast in the role of chief executant of Lenin's 'War Communism' and, in that capacity, advocate the militarisation of labour and the statification of the already largely Bolshevised trade unions.)

Although undertaken independently of Trotsky's work, several other Marxist studies of proto-Leninism arrived at very similar conclusions. Rosa Luxemburg, no less than Trotsky, defended the traditional Marxist attitude towards working class spontaneity, scorning a 'pitiless centralism' that demanded 'the blind subordination in the smallest detail, of all party organs,' to an *élite* 'which alone thinks, guides and decides for us all', and a style of command in which leaders acted towards the led 'as troops are instructed in their training camps.'[52] But, unlike Trotsky who, in 1917, without any theoretical accounting (though with political motives that were all too transparent) renounced his earlier opposition to, and implicitly, his analysis of, Lenin's Jacobin methods, Luxemburg continued to subject them to a searching critique. After the Bolshevik seizure of power, she denounced a system of rule in which

> a dozen outstanding heads do the leading and an *élite* of the working class is invited from time to time to meetings, where they are to applaud the speeches of the leaders, and to approve proposed resolutions unanimously.

For all its claims to represent the masses, the Bolshevik regime was, she concluded, 'a clique affair, a dictatorship, to be sure, not of the proletariat, but only the dictatorship of a handful of politicians.'[53]

Axelrod, who at the Congress found the inner strength to break from Plekhanov's Jacobinism, afterwards rounded on Lenin himself, who was, after all, the prime mover in the entire enterprise. For all its insistence on Marxist orthodoxy, the tendency represented by Lenin was in reality a 'Jacobin club' composed of the 'revolutionary-democratic elements of the bourgeoisie' (that is to say, the socialist intelligentsia) which saw its task as leading 'the most active sections of the proletariat'.[54] This and other similar jibes from Axelrod goaded Lenin into a passionate defence of Jacobinism. For him, it exemplified and symbolised above all else 'a struggle to achieve the end in view', one 'without kid gloves, without tenderness, without fear of resorting to the guillotine.' Anticipating his own 'Red Terror', Lenin warned that like the Jacobins in the French Revolution, Marxists in the socialist revolution had to understand that it could not be carried through 'without a proper Jacobin purge', because the 'dictatorship of the proletariat' was 'absolutely meaningless without Jacobin coercion.'[55] Lenin was particularly incensed when his old ally Martov declared, shortly after the Second Congress, that there could be nothing in common between Jacobinism and Marxism. All such views were simply proof for Lenin of the 'bourgeois spinelessness'[56] of his critics, and the correctness of his divisive tactics at the Second Party Congress. Meanwhile, the Mensheviks were in the process of recruiting to their ranks (which already included Martov, Axelrod, Zasulich, Potresov and Trotsky) Lenin's only prominent ally, the formidable figure of George Plekhanov. Hoping for a reconciliation with his old comrades, and discovering that Lenin's intransigence was making it impossible to achieve, Plekhanov quickly tired of his role as peace-maker between the two factions, and by the end of 1903 had made his way over to the Mensheviks. Now hopelessly isolated, Lenin resigned from the board of *Iskra*, which then reverted to its old management (minus Lenin and with the inclusion of Trotsky) and resumed publication until the onset of the revolution of 1905. Lenin, starting early in 1904, then set about collecting and organising, under his personal direction, reliably 'hard' cadres for his own, Bolshevik, faction. From this period begins the rise to prominence of not only Stalin, but two other of Lenin's principal lieutenants, Grigori Zinoviev and Lev Kamenev. It was, of course, precisely these three who combined in 1923 to form the so-called 'old Bolshevik' 'Troika' to exclude their old enemy Trotsky from the leadership contest then unfolding.

Having helped Lenin engineer the split at the Second Congress, and then failed to heal it afterwards, Plekhanov doubtless felt obliged to make what amends he could. He did so in the best Plekhanov tradition, with a furious tirade against the same Jacobinist tendencies he had found so hard to resist in himself. Inviting his readers to suppose that Lenin's plan of an all-powerful central committee had indeed been realised, he then suggested to them what might ensue:

> Since a congress is in the offing, the Central Committee everywhere "liquidates" the elements with which it is dissatisfied, everywhere seats its own creatures, and, filling all the committees with these creatures, without difficulty guarantees itself a fully submissive majority at the congress. The Congress constituted of the creatures of the Central Committee amiably cries "Hurrah!", approves all its successful and unsuccessful actions, and applauds all its plans and initiatives. Then, in reality, there would be in the party neither a majority nor a minority, because we then would have realised the ideal of the Persian Shah.[57]

True, such a state of affairs was only finally realised at the Byzantine court of Joseph the Terrible. But the tendencies in Bolshevism which helped make it possible were already discernible to Plekhanov's perceptive mind as early as 1904, as they were also to Akimov, Martov, Luxemburg, Trotsky and Axelrod. Then, after 1917, what had hitherto been implicit rapidly became explicit. It was a time when not only the actions, but also the statements of the most prominent Bolshevik leaders confirmed that the previous criticisms of Leninism had not been so wide of the mark after all.

As early as November 27, 1918, Lenin could (publicly) declare that 'we reserve state power for ourselves, *and for ourselves alone*'[58] [emphasis in the original] and, seven months later, that so-called Soviet power was in fact 'a dictatorship of one party' and that 'that is what we stand for.'[59] And by now, Trotsky had overcome – albeit rather self-consciously – his earlier qualms concerning the dangers of Leninist substitutionism:

> We have more than once been accused of having substituted for the dictatorship of the Soviets the dictatorship of the party.
> Yet it can be said with complete justice that the dictatorship of the Soviets became possible only by means of the dictatorship of the party.[60]

Very much in the manner of 'our best pupil' Mussolini, Trotsky poured scorn on the 'fetishism of the parliamentary majority' and the 'mystery of majority and minority':[61]

> If there is one question which basically not only does not require revision but does not even admit the thought of revision, it is the question of the dictatorship of the party.[62]

Nor was it now just a question of one-party rule but, increasingly, of the one-party state:

> We are the only party in the country, and in the period of the dictatorship it could not be otherwise... the Communist Party is obliged [*sic!*] to monopolize political life.[63]

Or, as Nikolai Bukharin, Lenin's 'favourite', once quipped, Russia might have two parties, but only on the condition that 'one must be the ruling party and the other must be in prison'[64] – a political outlook identical to Robespierre's conviction that he recognised 'only two parties, the party of the good citizens and the party of the bad.'[65] Need it be said that both Bukharin and Robespierre spent their last hours in one of their own prisons?

But it was not only a question of the one-party state but, following the 10th Party Congress's endorsement (in March 1921) of Lenin's proposal to outlaw all internal party groupings within the sole Party, the one faction party. Ignoring the universally-known fact that his entire political career had been one long and frequently brutal struggle for the triumph of his own faction, Lenin warned that 'all class-conscious workers must clearly realise that factionalism of any kind is harmful and impermissible.'[66] This sentiment was no less Jacobin. Hell-bent on creating, by terror, a government of a 'single will' – his own – the Jacobin leader Maximillien Robespierre, in his last speech to the National Convention before his own downfall, demanded new emergency powers to 'punish the traitors' (who included his own comrades) and, like Lenin and later, Stalin, to 'crush all the factions' – all, that is, save his own.[67]

There has grown up, largely at his own instigation, something of a myth concerning Trotsky's supposed commitment to what is usually called 'Soviet' and 'inner party' democracy. (See Appendix One.) In reality, the record shows that he was their vehement opponent so long as he felt his position in the Party leadership to be secure, and that he began to modify his position, and in so doing re-write the history of Bolshevism, only after the definitive victory of Stalin.[68] (Trotsky's summersaults on this question, like Lenin's, suggest that for certain politicians at least, how they view a police state varies acording to whether they are the jailer or the jailed.) Precisely because of his Menshevik past (to which he partially returned in his last exile) Trotsky, after 1917, sought to pre-empt or deflect allusions to his earlier 'softness' by such 'super-Bolshevik' (not to say rash) assertions as 'the party does not want factions and will not tolerate them'.[69] Least of all, as it turned out, Trotsky's.

Crowning this edifice of what the founders of Marxism would surely have failed to recognise as the rule of the 'immense majority' was the Party central committee (comprised, at first, of a score or so members in a country of 150 millions), a body which, Zinoviev insisted, must needs be 'single, strong, powerful', a 'leader of everything'.[70] The Bolshevik slogan 'all power to the Soviets' – invaluable as a means of outbidding their more cautious and constitutional rivals – had by now become an encumbrance. 'The last word,' declared Trotsky, 'belongs to the central committee of the party.'[71] 'Soviet power' thus defined was Robespierre's 'single will' by another name, and accorded with Machiavelli's dictum that 'in all states, whatever their form of government, the real rulers do not amount to more than forty or fifty citizens.'[72]

And so we have all the phases of Trotsky's 'substitutionism' bar the last – the domination of the entire pyramid by a single leader, the Bolshevik Tsar, Shah or Pharaoh, his emergence marking that point at which 'the dictator substitut[es] himself for the central committee'.[73] This stage, it is true, was only fully attained under the Byzantine tyranny of Stalin. But it was Lenin (again with the endorsement of Trotsky) who, characteristically, furnished his successor with not only the necessary practical precedents, but their theoretical justifications. Consolidation of Bolshevik rule required that 'thousands subordinat[ed] their will to the will of one' (Robespierre again) and that since there was 'absolutely no contradiction in principle between Soviet democracy (*that is*, socialist democracy) and the exercise of dictatorial power by individuals', it was essential that workers submitted 'with unquestioning obedience to the will of a single person, the Soviet leader'[74] [emphasis in the original]. Any workers resisting what Trotsky called, with his usual bluntness, 'the methods of militarisation of labour'[75] would, he warned, be 'put into concentration camps'.[76] And this was called the 'dictatorship of the proletariat'.

The question has to be asked: where, in all these citations – and there are many more – is there to be found the smallest hint of the 'classical' definition of working class rule provided by Marx and Engels in the 'Communist Manifesto', 'the proletariat organised as the ruling class'?[77] The Leninist conception, as these quotations demonstrate, is, in fact, much closer in word and spirit to how the 'Manifesto' saw the state institutions of the capitalist class; namely, as 'a committee for managing the common affairs of the whole bourgeoisie.'[78] Out of its own collective mouth, the Bolshevik leadership confirmed that it did indeed regard its Central Committee (and very soon its even smaller Politburo and, finally, Stalin's Secretariat) as the natural and only possible body, after the manner of Robespierre's twelve-man Committee of Public Safety, to 'manage the common affairs of the whole proletariat' – and not only of Russia but, with the founding in 1919 of the Comintern and its subsequent domination by these same Bolshevik institutions, of the entire world. Again, the Jacobin inspiration, with its line of descent through Russian populism, of 'What Is To Be Done?' and the principles advocated by Lenin at the Second Congress, is not so hard to detect and trace. And yet, despite his early insights into Lenin's political mind, Trotsky seems to have recognised little or nothing in proto-Bolshevism that was of universal or enduring significance. Essentially, he saw Leninism, at its birth, as no more than a difficult stage in the development of the Party, one which owed its origins to an over-reaction by *Iskra* to the earlier and opposite, allegedly anti-political excesses, of Economism. It was a Jacobin phase which, like its Economist predecessor, would be overtaken by the force and logic of objective events. Luxemburg and, it must be said, Plekhanov saw further. She directed her attentions towards the danger inherent in the ambitions of 'an intellectual *élite* hungry for power,' one seeking to 'enslave a young labour movement' by imposing on it a 'bureaucratic straitjacket' that would 'turn it into an automaton manipulated by a Central Committee.'[79] What is, however, common to both approaches is their rejection of Lenin's unshakeable conviction that hyper-centralism (so-called 'democratic centralism') invariably served the best interests of the working class and that opposition to his version of centralism necessarily constituted 'opportunism in questions of organisation'. Subsequent history has furnished more than sufficient proofs that 'opportunist' socialist parties (and others that are almost exclusively devoted to the struggle against socialism) can be directed by leaders no less 'hard' and 'centralist' than Lenin's Bolshevik cadre. It was, after all, the same Social-Democratic Party apparatus hitherto so revered by Lenin that marched the German proletariat off to war in August 1914, and subsequently, by invoking the imperatives of centralism 'from the top down', hounded from its ranks all those who (like Rosa Luxemburg) resisted its chauvinist policies. Neither was the suppression, in January 1919, of the so-called 'Spartacist Uprising' and the murder of, amongst other of its leaders, Rosa Luxemburg and Karl Liebknecht, by forces under the direction of the SPD Defence Minister Gustav Noske, any less merciless than the Bolshevik response to the revolt of the Kronstadt sailors two years later. Lenin's views on the virtues of 'hardness' are also put into question by the case of Plekhanov whom, despite his desertion to Menshevism shortly after the Second Congress, Lenin continued to regard as essentially sound on the organisational question, heading what Lenin described as a group of 'pro-party Mensheviks'. Sadly for Lenin (and like a number of Bolsheviks including, almost certainly, Stalin) Plekhanov's enduring 'hardness' did not prevent his adopting a defencist stance on the outbreak of the First World War, nor, for that matter, his defection to the right from the mainstream of Menshevism after the February revolution of 1917. By contrast, the prototypical 'softs' Martov, Trotsky, Axelrod and Luxemburg (and the 'revisionist' Bernstein) adhered throughout the war to internationalist positions, albeit of a different hue and motivation to Lenin's potentially pro-German defeatism. The same objections apply with even more force in the case of fascist and Nazi totalitarianism which, in their crusade against democracy and organised labour, elevated the 'leadership principle', centralism and 'hardness' (what might now be termed 'machismo') to the level of a fanatical religious cult. While no serious political commentator or historian has ever detected a tendency on the part of either Hitler or Mussolini to imitate the organisational principles of Menshevism, Trotsky certainly was prepared to concede that 'Mussolini stole from the Bolsheviks', and that Hitler, in his turn, stole from both.[80] Precisely what they stole from Bolshevism we are not told, but amongst its features they found attractive must surely have been what Luxemburg saw as its 'pitiless centralism', hunger for power and ability to manipulate the masses with radical slogans. Trotsky was also commendably honest in admitting that even in its pre-revolutionary years, when it stood closest to the workers, 'the political machine of the Bolshevik Party was predominantly made up of the intelligentsia, which was petty bourgeois in its origins and conditions of life,' a state of affairs which meant that the professional revolutionary 'lacked independent daily contact with the labouring masses.'[81] What he could not admit (which does not mean he never entertained the idea) was that Leninism, from 1903 onwards, provided the doctrinal justification and organisational means whereby the professionals of the apparatus (the germ-cell of the future *nomenklatura* 'new class' of 'Soviet' rulers) could raise themselves above the proletariat while, at the same time, sustaining their claim to lead and, after 1917, to govern it.

With their tragic (and predicted) outcomes plain for all to see, the pretensions of Leninism are today openly defended in the West (frequently with all manner of cowardly reservations) largely by a dwindling fraternity of third-rate intellectuals, Trotskyist zealots and Stalinist neanderthals. In the land of Bolshevism's birth and greatest crimes, genuine support for its claims approaches zero. There, as the failed *coup* of August 1991 demonstrated, insofar as Leninism is seen to have any utility at all, it chiefly serves as a means and pretext for restoring the power and privileges of the as yet only partially-ousted *nomenklatura*.

If these accusations have any substance to them, they point to only one conclusion, namely, that Leninism's claim to being the one and only true Marxism is bogus, a fraud perpetrated, with catastrophic consequences for the cause of working class emancipation, on generations of revolutionaries. For, despite Bolshevism's superficial similarities, in certain respects, to Marxism (for example, lip-service to its theory of the class struggle and the progression of society through distinct economic modes of production), in their everyday activity Leninist regimes and organisations have for decades routinely and shamelessly violated these same principles. 'Marxism-Leninism' is as absurd a concoction as Christian Satanism.

He who can still believe me a dishonourable man, is a man who deserves to be stifled.

J.-J. Rousseau

So, if Bolshevism is not Marxism, how, then, shall we describe it? As has already been argued, its lineage is not hard to establish, and it is one that begins with Jacobinism. And here, just as in so many other areas, Lenin's appreciation of its political character diverged radically from that of Marx and Engels. In fact, when evaluating what Marxists would describe as the 'class role' of Jacobinism, Lenin at different times came up with highly contradictory answers. In 1905, he followed the traditional Marxist (though questionable) approach of depicting the Jacobins as essentially upholding the 'interests of the advanced class of the eighteenth century' (i.e. the 'rising bourgeoisie' of the Third Estate) and likened them, in this respect, to the 'revolutionary social democrats' (i.e. Marxists) who upheld 'the interests of the advanced class of the twentieth century' (i.e. the proletariat).[1] But by June 1917, and actively engaged in the preparations for seizing power, Lenin was praising the Jacobins for something altogether different, for their 'great example of a truly revolutionary struggle against *the class of the exploiters by the class of the working and the oppressed who had taken all state power into their hands*'[2] [emphasis in the original]. So, according to this (totally inverted) representation, the Jacobin reign of terror (two thirds of the victims of which, incidentally, were from the very classes whose interests the Jacobins were supposedly advancing[3]) was nothing less than an 'anticipation' of a Leninist-style 'dictatorship of the proletariat.' And, in support of this claim, one must indeed agree that in their struggle to gain and hold onto power, the Jacobins anticipated many of the tactics deployed by the Bolsheviks during and after 1917. Following their *coup* of June 1793, the Jacobins (naturally in the name of preserving democracy and liberty) saw to it that effective power moved by degrees away from the repeatedly purged and cowed National Convention (the revolutionary parliament) and the popular revolutionary societies of Paris (the soviets of their day) into the hands of an ever-smaller circle of professional revolutionary leaders, who, in their turn, were dominated and intimidated by Robespierre's own faction. Only the overthrow of this group by an alliance of the ousted and threatened factions (some to his left, others to his right) frustrated Robespierre's final bid for total power. So, in a way, despite his obvious confusion concerning its social tendencies, Lenin was right to see in Jacobinism the precursor of Bolshevism. And not only in matters of political tactics. As, with each passing day, economic centralisation required that the Bolshevik 'Red Terror' fell ever more harshly on the masses it claimed to be emancipating so, following their *coup* in May-June 1793, the clumsy Jacobin attempts at interventionism involved the severest measures against the very classes on whose backs they had ridden to power. One such was the so-called 'maximum', a statutory limit to wages, imposed at a time of rampant inflation and the acutest shortages. Another was their ruthless utilisation of a law, dating from 1791 (known after its proposer as the 'Loi Chapelier') outlawing trades unions and strikes. But while Lenin had nothing but praise for the 'great example' of Jacobinism, Marx found it 'so characteristic of Robespierre that, at a time when it was a crime punishable by the guillotine to be "constitutional", as defined by the [National] Assembly of 1789, all of its laws directed against the workers remained in force.'[4] As for the Jacobin terror, which Lenin explicitly took as a model for his

48

own, Engels confided to Marx that, far from being the 'rule of people who inspire terror' it was 'on the contrary', 'the rule of people who are themselves terror stricken', involving 'mostly useless cruelties perpetrated by frightened people in order to reassure themselves', the work of 'small philistines crapping their trousers, and the underworld who know how to coin profit from the terror.'[5] So much for Lenin's 'great example'! But to understand why it exerted such a great influence upon Lenin's political thought and actions, it is necessary to discuss, even if only briefly, the ideas of the most influential ideological precursor of Jacobinism, Jean-Jacques Rousseau.

'Anticipating' Lenin's view of the proletariat as a class (to quote again the 'Manifesto') 'lacking historical initiative', it was Rousseau who first confronted (even if only theoretically) the conundrum of how a 'blind multitude which often does not know what it wants' could ever be trusted to manage its own political affairs.[6] Rousseau's solution, a government embodying the so-called 'General Will', anticipated in this respect Lenin's 'vanguard party', one which, although it might never enjoy majority support, would nevertheless claim to represent, at all times, the true historic interests of the proletariat. But Rousseau's 'General Will' was more than an anticipation. Through the mediations of first, French Jacobinism (Robespierre and its socialist extension by Blanqui) and then its Russian variant (Tkachev), the theory undoubtedly contributed to the maturing of Lenin's desire and design for an *élite* (or as Trotsky initially described it, 'substitutionist') revolutionary party which knew better than the proletariat what the proletariat needed. Like Lenin's attempts to 'divert' a spontaneously bourgeois (even, at times, counter-revolutionary) proletariat, Rousseau urged that the erring people 'must be made to see things as they are, sometimes as they ought to be [!]', to 'learn what it is they want.'[7] For 'it does not follow that the deliberations of the People are always equally beyond question... they do not at all times see where [the] good lies.' They are 'often deceived' and 'appear to will what is evil', because there is 'often a considerable difference between the will of all [i.e. the actually existing and expressed will of the people] and the general will.'[8] How, then, to ensure that the latter triumphs over the former? Surely by suppressing those 'intriguing groups and partial associations'[9] (i.e. parties or 'factions') who lead the gullible astray. And this totalitarian quest, one of seeing to it that 'there be no subsidiary groups within the state',[10] (or as Plato has it, 'discord and plurality') was pursued by Rousseau's disciples and Lenin's mentors, the Jacobins, through the deployment of an all-enveloping system of spying, informing, false accusations, frame-up trials, mass terror and summary executions. After all, had not Robespierre, at the very outset of his political career, apostrophied Rousseau as the 'divine man' who had, through his writings (most notably the 'Social Contract', which Robespierre kept at his bedside) enlightened him in the 'great principles which govern the social order'?[11] One such axiom was that, whatever the people might think, want or believe, their rulers (provided only that they are guided by reason and virtue) determine what is the 'general will'. And to those who have become convinced (by whatever means) that they have indeed unravelled the hidden processes which govern human actions and, by so doing, devised an infallible method of securing given political objectives, Rousseau's doctrine is a seductive one. It has been invoked by every ruler who, while concerned to be seen governing in the name and with the consent of the people (and what modern dictator is not?) is equally concerned to avoid the hazards of ruling in accordance with the genuine will of a people which, if allowed to express itself freely, would invariably prove to be divided, changeable and perverse. This supposed 'immaturity' of the people has, in recent times, been a pretext for numerous 'Third World' dictatorships, with their exponents here, as in other matters, following the examples set first by Jacobinism (a spurious model for 'nation building' democratic revolutions) and then by Bolshevism (with its no less fraudulent claims to have overtaken, by the methods of coercive collectivism, the performance of the market economies of the capitalist/imperialist West). When he on one occasion justified the lack of majority support for Bolshevik rule, Trotsky at the same time, even if unwittingly, made a more general case for all such minority regimes. They 'achieve meaning' not by 'statically reflecting a majority' (which, as we have seen, his undoubtedly lacked) 'but in dynamically creating it.'[12] As we all know, examples abound. Like that of the genocidist Saddam Hussein who, while admittedly not renowned for his subtlety, has certainly learned and, thus far, with the West's no less than the Kremlin's assistance, successfully applied the 'creative' totalitarian mathematics of Leninism, whereby two plus two does indeed become five, and a 'politically correct' minority, without having to increase its magnitude, becomes a majority:

> [Our] party constitutes a minority in proportion to the population... But when it represents, by its will and daily conduct, the people's will, when its acts correspond to the people's objectives, in present and future calculations, then it constitutes a majority.[13]

Who, one might well ask, is best qualified to divine and interpret the people's will, if not the people themselves? 'Anticipating' Lenin's advocacy of the workers' ideological subordination to the socialist intelligentsia, Rousseau (again like Plato) believed the 'most natural arrangement that can be made is that the wise should govern the masses.'[14] Exactly! It is then but a small step to the Jacobin 'Angel of Death' Saint-Just's cynical aphorism on the hazards of popular rule – 'where the feet think, the arm deliberates, the head marches' – and his conclusion that permitting 'liberty to a bad people' was 'total treason'.[15] From such precepts necessarily flow the use of, and justification for rule by terror, whether it is that of a Robespierre, Lenin, Trotsky, Stalin, Hitler – or Saddam Hussein (to whose side the Leninists shamefully rallied at the time of the Gulf War of 1990-91, under the slogan 'Victory to Iraq').

There should be no misunderstandings. Lenin was fully aware of the link between his own political doctrine and the *élitist* and manipulative precepts of Jacobinism, declaring on one occasion that his ideal of a revolutionary socialist was a 'Jacobin who identifies himself with the *organisation* of the proletariat'[16] [emphasis in the original]. Organisation, be it noted, not emancipation. But Bolshevism's historical, ideological – and moral – debt to Jacobinism was perhaps never more frankly acknowledged than by the Spanish 'communist syndicalist' turned Leninist, Andreas Nin. In an attempt to justify the Bolshevik repression of the Kronstadt sailors in March 1921, he argued:

> The Russian Communist Party is the only guarantor of the Revolution and, just as the Jacobins saw themselves obliged [!] to guillotine the Herbertists, even though they represented a tendency to the Left... so our Russian comrades see themselves inevitably obliged to smother implacably every attempt to break their power. It is not only their right but their duty. The health of the Revolution is the supreme law.[17]

In other words, sometimes it is necessary to save the workers from themselves, from their own ignorance – or, as Rousseau chose to phrase it, 'compel a man to be free'.[18] But what kind of freedom is it that is forced upon a people against its will? And what kind of 'general will' is it that contradicts and annihilates the wills of those who make up the body politic? Evidently, that of the rulers, and not of the ruled. This principle did not die with either Rousseau or the Jacobins. The repression of popular resistance under Lenin, and then by his successors – in East Germany in 1953, Hungary in 1956, Czechoslovakia in 1968, Poland in 1956, 1970, 1976 and 1981 – invariably called forth the same Jacobin (and Jesuitical) rationalisations. When the workers allow themselves to be misled (invariably, so we are told, by the intelligence agencies of imperialism) they must, by all means necessary, be led back onto the path of virtue. A noble goal permits, in fact demands, the use of any means. How could Nin have known that, fifteen years later, when it was his turn to find himself no less to the left of the by then thoroughly Stalinised Spanish Communist Party than were the ill-fated Herbertists to the left of the Jacobins, precisely this argument would serve equally well to justify the crushing of the Barcelona proletariat by the Spanish Stalinists, and Nin's murder by agents of Stalin's secret police? Just as Robespierre's terror machine, once set in motion, finally lopped off the heads that created it. In the light of such outcomes, one has to conclude that what all the advocates of Rousseau's precepts seem to have overlooked – and this despite the repeated lessons of history – is that they can just as easily, no, more easily, become the victims of this process as its executants. Why so? Because, in the final analysis, as Lenin's opponents understood from the very birth of Bolshevism, the logic of a system built on a disbelief in the capacity for self-government by 'ordinary people' demands (as Trotsky demonstrated in his early polemic against Lenin) that, at the most, only one leader can be trusted. To dramatise his argument, Trotsky predicted that under Lenin's party regime, 'Marx's lion-like head would have been the first to fall under the guillotine.'[19] And so it would, since Lenin operated according to Rousseau's dictum that it was 'against the natural order that a large number should rule and a smaller number be ruled.' Democracy might be suited to a 'nation of Gods', but not 'mere men'.[20] History would soon prove just how right Trotsky was when he observed that the 'practice of organised distrust' advocated by Lenin at the Second Congress demanded 'an iron hand', a 'system of terror crowned by a Robespierre', and that of all the party's leaders, Lenin was best suited to direct it.[21] And how fitting that, after their seizure of power, the Bolsheviks should erect, close to the Kremlin, a monument to Maximillien Robespierre, the father of revolutionary terrorism.

Perhaps part of the difficulty in understanding the nature of Leninism resides in the fact that, like all modern political doctrines, it cannot be analysed purely in terms of the conventional and one-dimensional spectrum of 'left' and 'right', a system of political measurement derived, almost accidentally, from a seating arrangement in the French Estates-General of 1789 and, therefore, hardly applicable to political, social and economic issues that have arisen in subsequent historical periods. Yet, locked as it has been in permanent combat with the bourgeois world, and at war with precisely those of its features and tendencies Marx and Engels regarded as progressive, Leninism has succeeded in convincing friend and foe alike that it is indeed the authentic heir to the revolutionary traditions of 1789, and the one true exponent of the theory created by Marx and Engels. But appearances can deceive. Bolshevism's claim to being the only true left, in the traditional senses of the term, is no less fraudulent than its pretensions to Marxism. Hence the uncontrollable urge, from its very inception, to slander and, if possible, destroy, in true Jacobin fashion, all its leftist competitors and critics. After 1917, and now armed with all the resources of state power, the achievement of this monopoly of revolutionary virtue became not only a necessity, but a very real possibility, and Lenin, following his Jacobin exemplars, set about the task with equal verve and determination, and with the same weapons of judicial terror:

> For the public manifestations of Menshevism our revolutionary courts must [!] pass the death sentence, otherwise they are not our courts, but God knows what.[22]

It was measures such as this which Lenin must surely have had in mind when he described his regime as being 'unrestricted by any laws';[23] or Trotsky, when, to justify the taking of hostages,[24] he invoked the 'iron dictatorship of the Jacobins';[25] and Stalin, when he likened the party to an 'Order of Knights of the Sword'.[26] Whatever their differences (and they were real enough), they each advocated and practised rule by what Lenin candidly described as 'terrorist purge, summary trial and the firing squad'.[27] To those who, like Martov, protested that a revolution was compromised by employing the methods of its enemies, Lenin retorted that 'a revolutionary who does not want to be a hypocrite cannot renounce capital punishment.'[28] Not to be outdone, Trotsky derided opposition to summary execution as 'vegetarian-Quaker prattle about the "sacredness of human life".' Bolshevik rule could only be maintained by 'blood and iron'.[29] So much for Engels' condemnation of capital punishment as the 'civilised form' of 'blood revenge'[30] and Marx's description of hostage taking as a 'brutal custom'.[31] So what then, in the light of Bolshevik attitudes towards the use of terror, are we to make of the traditional socialist opposition to the death penalty, and campaign for its abolition, at least in capitalist countries? Lenin explained that it was simply a matter of 'against which class a particular government would use it',[32] though this precept never seems to have unduly troubled Bolshevik executioners when, as was usually the case, they found themselves following the Jacobin example of exterminating not only members of the old ruling classes (some of whom had had the good sense to join the Bolsheviks), but those whom Lenin categorised as 'wavering and unstable elements among the working masses' against whom 'revolutionary coercion' was 'bound to be employed'.[33] That the brunt of the Bolshevik terror was indeed borne by the classes supposedly now ruling Soviet Russia was admitted by Felix Dzerzhinsky, the head of Lenin's political police, the Cheka, when he reported that with the civil war won and Bolshevik power secure, Russia's prisons were 'packed, chiefly with workers and peasants instead of the bourgeoisie'[34] – an odd outcome, to say the least, to a workers' revolution, especially when we learn that of the twenty leading Chekists responsible for their arrest and detention, at least twelve were of either gentry or bourgeois pedigree.[35] This they shared, no less than their *modus operandi*, with their Nazi counterparts, the commanders of the SS extermination units, or *Einsatzgruppen*.[36]

Though usually delegating the day-to-day routine of repression to others, Lenin, with his lawyer's training (and this, too, he shared with Robespierre and his fellow terrorists), took good care to ensure that no legal loopholes were left open for his opponents to exploit. A typical example of Lenin's thoroughness in such matters was his recommendations for tightening up the proposed new Soviet penal code. Lenin was anxious not only to introduce a clause which would extend the use of the death penalty to cover 'all forms of activity by the Mensheviks' but also, in the many cases where sufficient evidence to convict was lacking, to formulate the proposed law in such a way 'as to identify these acts [whatever they might in fact be] *with those* of the international bourgeoisie'[37] [emphasis in the original]. In other words, Lenin's intention was to have the Mensheviks 'fitted up', accused and then convicted of treason. It was inquisitional methods such as these that prompted Plekhanov to observe, even before the split of 1903 (and approvingly, it should be said) that Lenin was of the stuff that Robespierres were made. And, sure enough, once in power, Bolshevism followed, in small things as in great, the path pioneered by its Jacobin precursors. Lacking either legitimacy or majority support, both regimes, naturally enough, were ever ready to use and justify rule by terror. Having argued, under the monarchy, that the death penalty was 'fundamentally unjust', being 'nothing but cowardly murder',[38] Robespierre would soon convince himself – and others who included those he was shortly to execute – that with his incorruptible hand at the helm of state, this 'atrocious penalty'[39] could be harnessed to the cause of virtue. And in those many cases where any proof of guilt was lacking, the Jacobin Revolutionary Tribunal would, in the manner of Lenin (and later, Stalin), shamelessly fabricate it, Robespierre and his co-factionists perhaps not realising that, once legitimised, this practice could just as easily be turned against its inventors. And indeed it was, with their overthrow, on the by now routine (and as on all previous occasions, absurd) accusation of involvement in a royalist conspiracy, in July 1794. And even here, Bolshevism re-enacted the history of Jacobinism. Nearly all of Lenin's closest comrades died in the same fashion, after being convicted, at the court of Stalin, of a no less fictitious complicity with the enemies of the revolution and the USSR. Yet all of Stalin's victims – Trotsky, Bukharin, Zinoviev and Kamenev being the most prominent – had been, together with Lenin (and, of course, Stalin), only too willing to resort to such methods when they found them a convenient alternative to tolerating opinions and organisations other than their own. Like the Jacobins, they seemed to have been hell-bent on proving the truth of Machiavelli's contention that politicians, 'having first striven against ill-treatment, inflict it next upon others.'[40] So our outrage at the crimes of Stalinism, and sympathy for its Bolshevik victims, should not blind us to the fact, unpalatable though it still is for many on the left, that the mechanism and ideological underpinning of the Stalinist terror were the legitimate offspring of Jacobinist Leninism.

CHAPTER EIGHT
LENINISM AND THE LEFT

An end which requires unjustified means is no justifiable end.
                                                    Karl Marx

Not only in Britain but throughout the world, the left stands at a crossroads, for reasons that are surely in no need of elaboration here. What route it now chooses to take depends to a large degree on its ability to learn from past mistakes, especially the generally far too indulgent attitude towards the crimes of Bolshevism. Quite apart from matters of policy or tactics, what now needs to be challenged, without inhibitions or preconceptions, are above all else the Jesuitical amoralism and *élitist* political methods of Leninism, both of which are accepted, sometimes unthinkingly, far beyond the narrow confines of Leninist organisations. Only by doing so does it become possible to appreciate the stultifying, corroding, corrupting and above all dehumanising effect Bolshevism has had on the Marxist and, more broadly, the entire socialist tradition. One of its corrosive effects has undoubtedly been to generate and justify the most cynical of political double standards. The left universally (and justly) abhors and denounces the use of the death penalty on those tragic, even if rare, occasions when it is deployed in democratic capitalist countries – for example, in certain states of the USA – but has had little or nothing to say about the scandal that for decades what passes for Soviet justice has routinely been executing upwards of eight hundred offenders per year, and in China many times more. No less hypocritically, British and other western pro-Soviet trade union officials, though always ready (and again quite rightly) to condemn any curtailment of trade union liberties in capitalist countries – in, say, Chile or South Africa – often have found it expedient to look the other way when campaigners for workers' rights in the Soviet bloc and China have been victimised not only by the customary term in a labour camp, but by detention in 'psychiatric hospitals' or even execution. And, hardly surprisingly, the same individuals (together with many other prominent personalities on the left) have proved to be no less selective in choosing whose nuclear weapons, or acts of military aggression to oppose. Can it be doubted that such attitudes invariably repel people from, rather than attract them towards, the ideals and goals of socialism?

Then there is the double standard many on the left adopt towards freedom of the press. While demanding it for themselves, they are perfectly capable of denying, under various pretexts and guises, the same freedom to those whose opinions they find unacceptable, or of ignoring its blatant suppression in countries deemed to be more 'progressive'.It needs to be said again: as in the case of capital punishment, the precedents for such conduct cannot be found in 'classical' Marxism. Marx, it should be remembered, made his debut as a journalist with a passionate defence of press freedom, 'the ubiquitous vigilant eye of a people's soul',[1] denouncing its suppression as 'the most frightful terrorism',[2] a device to 'spy on people's hearts',[3] and recommending that the 'real, radical cure for the censorship would be its abolition.'[4] Engels was no less forthright. 'Freedom of the press, free competition between opinions' meant 'giving freedom to the class struggle in the sphere of the press.' For that very reason, what Engels described as the 'party of law and order' would be tempted to resort to the 'gagging of oppressed classes' by means of 'press laws, bans etc',[5] a policy he denounced as 'disgraceful perfidy.'[6] In its battle for press freedom, the workers' movement was 'fighting to establish the environment necessary for its existence, for the air it needs to breathe.'[7] And on yet another occasion, Engels specified the liberties the proletariat required for its victory as: 'the right of assembly and association and the freedom of the press.'[8] So once again, the record is clear.

What of the Bolsheviks? In their second day of power, Lenin made haste to introduce 'press laws and bans',[9] though not without meeting (and with Trotsky's support, overcoming) opposition from within his own party. But before becoming Russia's new 'party of law and order', the Bolsheviks (like all other parties of the Second International) had, as members of the RSDLP, publicly defended the traditional Marxist position on press freedom. It was inscribed in the RSDLP programme adopted unanimously at the Second Congress of 1903, the specific clause (number five) having been drafted by Lenin personally. Following Marx and Engels, it demanded 'unrestricted [n.b.] freedom of conscience, speech, publication and assembly, freedom to strike and freedom of association.'[10] All of these freedoms were, as we know, destined to be trampled underfoot by Lenin after 1917. But in 1903, he had pledged to fight for them to 'the last drop of blood'.[11]

How, then, did Lenin explain away his *volte face*? Predictably, with the same Jacobin argument that he used to justify the death penalty. Merely to suggest, let alone permit, the breaching of the Bolshevik press monopoly was to 'cease to be socialist',[12] simply 'helping the class enemy'. It therefore followed that his own party's demand for press freedom (for which he was once prepared to give his own blood) had, in the meantime, become an 'anti-proletarian slogan'.[13] Lenin's post-revolutionary diatribes against press freedom call to mind another self-styled socialist's contention that 'this fetish of the liberty of the press' constituted a 'mortal danger "par excellence"' to 'the interest of the state'.[14]

Whilst still in opposition Robespierre, too, had drafted a declaration which, like Lenin's, protected 'the right to manifest one's opinions by means of the press or in any other manner.'[15] And yet it would appear that Robespierre (again, like Lenin) had chiefly the opinions of his own party in mind, because at the very moment of the Jacobin seizure of power, he recorded, in a private memorandum, his intention to permit only 'republican [that is, Jacobin] papers'.[16] And, sure enough, within a matter of months, Robespierre had unleashed a campaign of intimidation intended, in his own words, to 'repress the journalist imposters'.[17] Its climax arrived when, taken to task for his betrayal of press freedom by his old friend Camilles Desmoulins (whom he was soon to accuse of treason, and dispatch together with his protesting wife to the guillotine), Robespierre demanded that the offending article (which prophetically concluded 'the Gods are athirst'[18]) be ceremonially burned at the Paris headquarters of the Jacobin club.[19]

It is, for obvious reasons, impossible to be sure whether Lenin any more than Robespierre ever sincerely believed in genuine press freedom, though they both most certainly always wanted it for themselves. What one can do is point out the many discrepancies between what Lenin, at different times, said and did about it. There is, for example, Lenin's varying attitude towards public libraries. Here we have a classic instance of his apparently limitless ability to adopt and then discard, without the least hint of embarrassment, a principle which is at one moment the acme of revolutionary rectitude and the next a total betrayal of the proletarian cause. In early 1914 Lenin interpolated into an article on education written by his wife a passage condemning the autocracy's 'ignominious police measures to hamper the cause of education', including not only the 'foul [*sic!*] institution' of censorship, but, more to the point, 'special rules against libraries' which 'no civilised country' would tolerate. Police censorship of libraries was 'an outrageous policy of benighting the people.'[20] And who could disagree? Three years then pass by. The Bolsheviks seize power, thereby assuming responsiblity for, amongst many other things, the libraries. Now holding a high post in the People's Commissariat for Education, Lenin's wife has the opportunity to rectify the policies denounced by Lenin, presumably with her approval, in her article. At last, one would surely be entitled to expect, the libraries will truly belong to and serve the people. But what happens? Acting on the highest authority of the Soviet government (the Council of Peoples' Commissars, headed by none other than her husband) Krupskaya, beginning in 1920, launches a purge of Soviet libraries on a scale, and with a zeal and thoroughness, that would have left the Tsarist police simultaneously gaping in admiration and smarting with jealousy.

Over the next few years, under Krupskaya's supervision, there were removed from public libraries (and then often destroyed) all works deemed to be 'obsolescent', 'counter-revolutionary' and 'harmful'.[21] Books falling under this rubric were listed in a Bolshevik index entitled 'A guide to the removal of Anti-Artistic and Counter-Revolutionary Literature from Libraries Serving the Mass Reader'. They included, amongst the works of hundreds of other writers, books by Plato, Kant, Descartes, Schopenhauer, Ruskin, Nietzsche, Tolstoy, Kropotkin, Pushkin, Gogol, Verne, Cervantes, Kipling, Gorky (a close friend of Lenin's) and... Shakespeare, who, long before Lord Acton, had discovered a thing or two about the corrupting effects of absolute power.[22] In all, lists of removed works ran to some 2,000 pages (pages, not items).[23] One is left wondering – did Krupskaya pursue her crusade for 'literary correctness' to the extent of removing from the shelves of her husband's private library the many offending volumes she would undoubtedly have found there? Or was the Bolshevik 'purging of the books' confined, as seems to have been the intention, to libraries frequented only by the 'mass reader'? Almost certainly yes, since this term denoted precisely those classes which, according to the Leninist canon, could not be trusted with anything other than party-approved texts. And is it not ironic that under the justly despised, but nevertheless, by comparison with the Bolsheviks', still considerably milder Tsarist censorship, some of Lenin's most important writings were legally published and distributed, and, being legal, could presumably be borrowed from public libraries?

Of course, this shameful episode was not the first occasion on which, out of concern for the security of the rulers and the sanctity of the faith, institutions of learning had been reduced to instruments of state policy and the enforcement of doctrinal conformity. Nor would it be the last. Just as, two thousand four hundred years ago, Plato demanded a censorship to 'fashion the mind',[24] the Nazis set about the same task with no less gusto and urgency than Lenin's Thought Police, likewise removing from the shelves of their far more numerous and better stocked public libraries all publications deemed offensive to, or subversive of, the new Germany.[25] The advantages of such measures were obvious. But they could also, at times, create new difficulties. Being obliged, no less than their Soviet counterparts, to faithfully follow each twist and turn of their rulers' policy, the librarians of the Third Reich found themselves, on the conclusion of the Stalin-Hitler pact in August 1939, confronted with a directive entitled (very much after the style of Krupskaya's index) 'Adjustment of Public Libraries to the Political Situation' and instructing them to remove from their shelves publications 'disagreeable to the Soviet regime' of which, up to that point, there had been a more than adequate supply.[26] Needless to say, Stalin returned the compliment.[27] But when we recall that Lenin unleashed his purge of the libraries thirteen years before the Nazi burning of the books in Berlin, we see the delusion (at best) that Mussolini invented totalitarianism, and Stalin 'Stalinism' for what it is. And whose model were our own local authorities following when they decided in recent times to purge their libraries, not only of political texts, but also, like Krupskaya, of literary works deemed to violate the canons of 'Political Correctness'?

And yet some will doubtless object (and they will not by any means all be Leninists), even if all this were to be proved true, Bolshevism surely still deserves to be recognised as a genuine, if flawed, revolutionary current, as somehow part of 'the left'. After all, unlike any other socialist parties, when Leninist organisations, even Stalinist ones, come to power, they introduce – though with what methods, and at what costs! – the principles of state ownership and central planning. Yes, and so they do. But is state ownership necessarily emancipatory? 'Interventionism', invariably 'from the top down' and on the grandest of scales, has been practised by despotisms from the very dawn of civilization, and not least, in the Russia of the Tsars. Does that oblige us to depict as being in any way progressive the economic policies of a Romanov, an Egyptian Pharaoh or a Chinese emperor? To be on the left, at least in the pre-1917 sense of the term, should surely have nothing to do with slavery, even if the slave owner is the state and the slavery centrally planned, and everything to do with the traditional socialist (including Marxist) objectives of the self-emancipation of oppressed classes and the ever-broader extension of individual liberty.

Then what remains of the claims of Leninism? Let us consider its attitude to war. Did not Bolshevism, we might be asked, oppose imperialist aggression, even when to do so involved denouncing, as did Lenin in the First World War and Trotskyists in the Second, the actions of one's own government? Yes, it did. But Bolsheviks have not been alone in doing so:

> [W]here do you find the Labour Party? Sitting in parliament and agreeing with the Government in its plans for capitalist war... You find the Labour Party asking for world war to fight in the service of capitalism, the capitalism they used to fight... War is a crime against the peoples of all lands.

Unlike Lenin, who conducted his campaign against Tsarist aggression from the safety of neutral democratic Switzerland, the speaker was made to pay for his opposition to his 'own' imperialism, being detained for four years without proper charges or trial. His name was Sir Oswald Mosley, the would-be Fuehrer of British national socialism.[28]

But, our Leninists might persist, surely it has to be agreed that even though Bolshevism did not fulfil all that was expected of it, the revolution of 1917 nevertheless did, by challenging world capitalism, set a socialist example to the world's oppressed. But others have made similar claims:

> Great Britain... the regime of money grabbers, the bastion of capitalism, seeks to strangle [we] who have given the world the example of Socialist order. They fear the effects on their position in England itself, even more they fear for their huge colonial empire. Their subjects inside and out are no longer to have [our] state before their eyes which, by its mere existence, might turn them into rebels against their exploiters. This means that [we are] waging war not only for [our] own existence, but at the same time for *all* oppressed nations of the world.

The voice of socialist internationalism? Hardly. It is the Nazi Party daily, the *Volkische Beobachter*, of November 20, 1939 [emphasis in the original].[29]

Then again, it is possible to respond to the British empire in a more conciliatory fashion and, far from seeking to undermine Britain's grip on its colonies, to undertake, as one statesman in fact did, that his government would 'not carry on any official propaganda' directed against Britain's imperial possessions, and even to aver that there was 'no intention of infringing on any of Britain's interests in the East.' Hard to credit though it is, these were undertakings given, not by Hitler (who, until the outbreak of the war, repeatedly sought an accommodation with Britain) but by Lenin.[30] The truth of the matter is that, even before the 1917 revolution, Bolshevik foreign policy was susceptible to the temptations, and therefore the imperatives, of *Realpolitik*, an orientation first embarked upon by Lenin as the price for his return to Russia from Switzerland in the Kaiser's 'sealed train', and subsequent German financial support for the Bolshevik bid for power and withdrawal from the war.[31] And, for all their revolutionary and internationalist rhetoric, once in power the Bolsheviks conducted themselves in practice as the rulers of an imperial state, albeit one in acute crisis. In the East, as we have seen, Lenin sought a *modus vivendi* with the colonial concerns of Britain, whilst taking care to reserve what he described as Russia's 'certain interests'[32] in territories that were, by ethnic and not imperialist criteria, anything but Russian. So much for the Bolshevik policy of the 'right of nations to self-determination.'[33] And as Lenin courted and appeased Britain in the Orient, in the West the Bolshevik regime sought a counter-weight to a hostile France by conniving with and even inciting in Germany the most rabid and reactionary groupings of the chauvinist, anti-semitic right, even as its terror units, the so-called 'Free Corps' (the prototypes for Hitler's Brown Shirts and death squads) waged, under their Swastika flag, a relentless terror campaign against Jews, Poles and the German workers' movement.[34] What did it matter that the 'German Black Hundreds' (Lenin's apt analogy with the pogrom gangs unleashed by the autocracy against the revolution of 1905) were prepared to 'shoot down their own communists'?[35] Far more to the point was their willingness to seek the support of the Soviet Union in a war of revenge against the West. It was, explained Lenin, 'natural for Germany to be prompted towards an alliance with Russia',[36] a tendency which had encouraged the emergence of what he called a 'bloc between the Black Hundreds and the Bolsheviks'.[37] Following Lenin's cue, the Soviet Comintern official Karl Radek avowed that 'even with the people who murdered Liebknecht and Luxemburg [i.e. the Free Corps] we shall make common cause.'[38] Radek's cynical invitation did not go unheeded. Prepared to go to any lengths in their quest for revenge against the West, the German 'radical right' saw in Russian Bolshevism not only an ally against the despised 'Jewish' liberalism of the Entente, but a model of revolutionary organisation and national renewal. And, as Moscow's principal specialist on and contact with German 'national Bolshevism', Radek saw to it that the Soviet authorities (and this would have been in the first place Lenin and after him Trotsky) were kept fully informed as to the attitude of this group towards the Soviet Union as a potential ally against the West. He would, for example, have been heartened by Hitler's public declaration, in the summer of 1920 – at the climax of the Soviet invasion of Poland supported, with fanatical enthusiasm, as Lenin readily acknowledged, by the entire German extreme right – that in order to liberate Germany from the burden of the Versailles Treaty, he would be prepared to ally himself 'not only with Bolshevism, but even with the devil'.[39] Such sentiments, although not always voiced so publicly (after all, the rightist movement presented itself as Germany's last defence against Marxism) nevertheless contributed to the ideological as well as strategic thinking of leftist tendencies within German national socialism. Josef Goebbels, before his capitulation to Hitler in 1926,[40] argued that it was necessary to 'look to [Bolshevik] Russia because it is the country most likely to take with us the road to socialism,'[41] that it was 'better to go down with Bolshevism than live in eternal capitalist servitude.'[42]

Despite Goebbel's subsequent deference to Hitler in doctrinal matters, Nazi 'National Bolshevism' lived on. One of its most consistent devotees was Herbert Backe, who in 1942 succeeded his former patron, the eclipsed Walter Darré (advocate of the lunatic doctrine of 'blood and soil') as Hitler's Minister of Food and Agriculture. Originating from the German community at Baku, Backe was well-informed on the trends in Russian revolutionary socialism, to the extent that after becoming a Nazi, he cited, of all books, Lenin's 'What Is To Be Done?' to support his case for a centralised and professionalised leadership structure for the party.[43] Nor was this all. Backe articulated a belief widely shared by the Nazi *élite* (for example, von Ribbentrop) that once Russian Bolshevism had purged itself of its 'Jewish' (and therefore internationalist) elements and tendencies, it would prove itself a more reliable ally of 'national' Germany. As Backe put it, 'Lenin, Rykov, Chicherin, Krylenko, Dzherzhinsky are worthy of admiration', while the Jews Trotsky, Kamenev and Zinoviev were deemed 'unworthy'.[44]

The goal of a 'united front' of Bolshevik Russia and a revanchist Germany against what both were pleased to call the 'decadence' of western democracy[45] was eventually realised (after Stalin's elimination of the 'unworthy' Jews) with the conclusion in August 1939 of the Stalin-Hitler pact, a treaty hailed, in one Nazi publication of the time, as the 'first act of liberation of the peoples from the straight-jacket of Western European plutocracy.'[46] The pact, as we know, stunned the world. How was it possible that Nazis and Bolsheviks could find so much common ground? Yet all Stalin had done (and would continue to do) was to follow, to the letter, the example and policy guidelines laid down by his predecessor, namely, to 'set America against Japan, the entire Entente against America, and all Germany against the Entente.'[47]

Neither was this mere talk. Lenin came closer than is generally appreciated to pulling off the very same *coup* by which Stalin, together with Hitler, finally erased Poland from the map in the autumn of 1939. Under the terms of a secret agreement between War Commissar Trotsky and Reichswehr chief Hans von Seeckt, Soviet and German forces were to combine to crush the newly independent state of Poland, with the objective of achieving a fourth partition along the frontiers of the pre-war Russian and German empires.[48] So much for the Bolshevik rejection of 'secret diplomacy'. The opportunity to activate this strategy presented itself in the latter stages of the war between Russia and Poland which, by August 1920, had brought the Red Army close to the outskirts of Warsaw. Lenin then issued to the Cheka (the Bolshevik political police) a secret directive (so secret, in fact, that it has been censored out of all editions of his 'Collected Works') which instructed that 'under the guise of Greens [irregular units outside the control of the Red Army] we shall go forward for 10-20 versts and hang the [Polish] kulaks, priests and landowners.' As an incentive to commit such atrocities, Lenin proposed the award of a 'bounty [of] 100,000 roubles for each man hanged'.[49]

Need we go on?

This book has advocated a return to the values of the 'traditional', that is, pre-Leninist left, and, as part of that left, to what has been defined as 'classical' Marxism, best epitomised by its founder's assertion that 'the emancipation of the working class must be conquered by the working classes themselves'.[50] But on no account should there be an uncritical acceptance of this tradition. It surely goes without saying that any movement or system of ideas which chooses to name itself after its founders or founder, and what is worse, refuses to question any of their teachings must, sooner or later, degenerate into a cult. Everything – principles, tactics, projections, programmes and theories – should be subjected to the closest scrutiny, so that if and when they are found wanting, they can be either amended or rejected outright. This undertaking is unavoidable if the cause which first brought the left into being is to have any prospects of success. And it will involve, amongst other things, having the courage to think what is, for far too many, still the unthinkable; to be prepared to consider the possibility that, contrary to the claims of Trotskyism, Stalinism was the necessary outcome of Leninism; to be prepared to discuss, open-mindedly, whether Menshevism and not Bolshevism more truly represented the most enlightened tendencies within the Russian working class; to be ready to admit that what goes by the name of the October Revolution could perhaps be better described as Lenin's Petrograd *putsch*, one which, moreover, has proved to be an unmitigated disaster for the cause of world socialism. The purpose of this book is to encourage such an exchange. For, unless it begins and prospers, all future attempts to advance beyond the injustices of our present world will simply re-enact the failures of the past and consign the movements responsible to the 'dustbin of history'. And that is a fate they would deserve.

REFERENCES

Foreword
1. K. Marx and F. Engels: *Collected Works* [*C.W.*], Vol.5, p.52
2. K. Marx and F. Engels: *C.W.*, Vol.4, p.37
3. V. Lenin: *Collected Works* [*C.W.*], Vol.5, p.422
4. *Ibid*, p.461
5. *Ibid*, p.452
6. *Ibid*, p.465
7. I. Getzler: *Martov*, p.86
8. *Ibid*, p.162
9. *Ibid*, p.163
10. K. Kautsky: *Selected Political Writings*, p.148
11. K. Kautsky: *Communism Versus Social Democracy*, p.89
12. Cited in: R. Abramovitch: *The Soviet Revolution*, p.360
13. G. Orwell: *The Collected Essays*, Vol.4, pp.200-201
14. D. Laurence (ed.): *Bernard Shaw: Collected Letters*, Vol.4, 1926-1950, p.103
15. G.B. Shaw (ed.): 1930 Preface to *Fabian Essays in Socialism [1889]*, p.x
16. G.B. Shaw: *Everybody's Political What's What?*, p.90
17. D. Laurence, *op. cit.*, p.70
18. *Ibid*, p.72
19. *Ibid*, p.336

Introduction
1. *Soviet News*, Nov. 4, 1987
2. *Ibid*, Nov. 11, 1987
3. *Ibid*, Feb. 24, 1988
4. *Ibid*, April 13, 1988
5. *Ibid*, May 11, 1988
6. *Morning Star*, Nov. 7, 1989
7. *Ibid*, Aug. 26, 1991
8. *Ibid*, Aug. 26, 1991
9. *Ibid*, Sept. 26, 1991
10. *Ibid*, Sept. 25, 1991
11. *Marxist Monthly*, Vol.3, No.2, p.70
12. L. Trotsky: *The Revolution Betrayed*, p.248
13. V. Lenin: *C.W.*, Vol.25, p.358
14. V. Lenin: *C.W.*, Vol.27, p.216
15. P. Fryer: 'In Defence of October', *Workers Press*, Nov. 14, 1992
16. *Ibid*
17. V. Lenin: *C.W.*, Vol.33, p.27
18. P. Fryer: *op. cit.*
19. E. Heffer: Preface to: V. Haynes and O. Semyonova: *Workers Against the Gulag*, p.4
20. J. Stalin: *Collected Works* [*C.W.*], Vol.5, p.200
21. V. Lenin: *C.W.*, Vol.32, p.23
22. V. Lenin: *C.W.*, Vol.7, p.281
23. V. Lenin: *Ibid*, p.19

Chapter One: Bolshevism and Menshevism
1. V. Lenin: *C.W.*, Vol.7, pp.379-409
2. V. Lenin: *C.W.*, Vol.31, p.28
3. *History of the CPSU ('Short Course')*, pp.52-53
4. *Ibid*, p.63
5. *Ibid*, p.95
6. *History of the CPSU*, p.122
7. L. Trotsky: *My Life*, pp.178-182
8. V. Lenin: *C.W.*, Vol.9, p.28
9. V. Lenin: *C.W.*, Vol.10, p.369
10. *Ibid*, p.252
11. L. Engelstein: *Moscow in the 1905 Revolution*, pp.371-372
12. *Lenin: A Biography*, pp.105-106
13. L. Trotsky: *Lenin*, p.28
14. L. Trotsky: *My Life*, p.183

Chapter Two: Lenin Prepares
1. V. Lenin: *C.W.*, Vol.7, p.211
2. G. Zinoviev: *Lenin*, p.21
3. *Ibid*, p.21
4. *Ibid*, p.21
5. V. Lenin: *C.W.*, Vol.7, pp.336-343
6. V. Lenin: *C.W.*, Vol.34, p.101
7. *Ibid*, p.147
8. V. Lenin: *C.W.*, Vol.36, p.112
9. *Ibid*, p.120
10. V. Lenin: *C.W.*, Vol.34, p.118
11. *Ibid*, p.152
12. *Ibid*, p.163
13. See: J. Brennan: *The Origins, Development and Failure of Russian Social Democratic Economism*
14. *Ibid*, p.227
15. V. Lenin: *C.W.*, Vol.36, p.104
16. V. Akimov: 'The Second Congress of the Russian Social Democratic Labour Party' in: J. Frankel: *Vladimir Akimov on the Dilemmas of Russian Marxism*, pp.101-109
17. J. Keep: *The Rise of Social Democracy in Russia*, p.109; Brennan, *op. cit.*, p.341; Akimov, *op. cit.*, p.102
18. V. Lenin: *C.W.*, Vol.36, p.112
19. V. Lenin: *C.W.*, Vol.43, pp.100-101

Chapter Three: Party and Class
1. V. Lenin: *C.W.*, Vol.7, p.398
2. V. Lenin: *C.W.*, Vol.5, pp.350-351
3. L. Schapiro: *The Communist Party of the Soviet Union*, p.39
4. V. Lenin: *C.W.*, Vol.5, p.375
5. *Ibid*, pp.383-385
6. See: *The [1872] Hague Congress of the First International*
7. K. Marx and F. Engels: *C.W.*, Vol.4, pp.9-11
8. Cited in: *Ibid*, p.19
9. *Ibid*, p.37

10. *Ibid*, p.85
11. K. Marx and F. Engels: *C.W.*, Vol.5, p.513
12. *Ibid*, p.515
13. *Ibid*, p.515
14: K. Marx and F. Engels: *C.W.*, Vol.23, p.175
15. *Documents of the First International*, Vol.II, p.176
16. *Ibid*, Vol.I, p.346
17. V. Lenin: *C.W.*, Vol.5, pp.384-385
18. K. Marx and F. Engels: *C.W.*, Vol.6, p.497
19. K. Marx and F. Engels: *Selected Correspondence* [*S.C.*], pp.40-41
20. K. Marx and F. Engels: *C.W.*, Vol.43, p.485
21. K. Marx and F. Engels: *C.W.*, Vol.24, p.573
22. V. Lenin: *C.W.*, Vol.5, p.386
23. *Ibid*, p.397
24. K. Marx and F. Engels: *C.W.*, Vol.44, p.185
25. *Ibid*, p.397
26. V. Lenin: *C.W.*, Vol.7, p.397
27. *Ibid*, p.300
28. *Ibid*, p.407
29. V. Lenin: *C.W.*, Vol.7, p.206
30. K. Marx and F. Engels: *S.C.*, p.414
31. K. Marx and F. Engels: *C.W.*, Vol.44, p.309
32. *Documents*, Vol.III, p.407
33. K. Marx and F. Engels: *S.C.*, pp.257-258
34. V. Lenin: *C.W.*, Vol.5, p.375
35. Cited in: S. Bernstein: *August Blanqui and the Art of Insurrection*, p.62
36. K. Marx and F. Engels: *C.W.*, Vol.6, p.494
37. *Ibid*, p.494
38. K. Marx and F. Engels: *S.C.*, p.394
39. *Ibid*, p.389-395
40. F. Engels: *On Britain*, p.580
41. Cited in: *Documents*, Vol.III, p.398
42. *Ibid*, p.398
43. M. Bakunin: *On Anarchism*, p.180
44. *Ibid*, p.155
45. Cited in: A. Kelly: *Mikhail Bakunin*, p.245
46. V. Lenin: *C.W.*, Vol.5, p.474
47. Cited in: B. Wolfe: *Marxism: 100 Years in the Life of a Doctrine*, p.195
48. K. Marx and F. Engels: *C.W.*, Vol.23, pp.465, 470
49. K. Marx and F. Engels: *C.W.*, Vol.22, p.470
50. K. Marx and F. Engels: *C.W.*, Vol.24, p.13
51. K. Marx and F. Engels: *C.W.*, Vol.27, pp.510-512
52. *Ibid*, p.520
53. Cited in: A. Weeks: 'The First Bolshevik' in: *Problems of Communism*, Nov./ Dec. 1967, p.100
54. D. Hardy: *The Critic as Jacobin*, pp.140-141
55. Cited in: A. Weeks: *The First Bolshevik: A Political Biography of Peter Tkachev*, p.77
56. Cited in: A. Weeks, *Problems...*, p.101
57. Cited in: *Ibid*, p.102
58. K. Marx and F. Engels: *C.W.*, Vol.24, pp.24-31

59. J. Stalin: *C.W.*, Vol.1, pp.90-132
60. A. De Jonge: *Stalin*, p.46
61. See: R. Pipes: *Social Democracy and the St. Petersburg Labour Movement 1886-1897*, p.114-115
62. V. Lenin: *C.W.*, Vol.9, p.388
63. J. Keep, *op. cit.*, p.111

Chapter Four: Hard and Soft

1. N. Krupskaya: *Reminiscences of Lenin*, pp.86-88
2. I. Getzler: *Martov*, pp.68-74
3. S. Baron: *Plekhanov: The Father of Russian Marxism*, p.129 and pp.213-214
4. V. Lenin: *C.W.*, Vol.6, p.235
5. *Ibid*, p.248
6. *Ibid*, p.249
7. Cited in: Getzler, *op. cit.*, pp.68-74
8. V. Lenin: *C.W.*, Vol.34, p.169
9. N. Krupskaya, *op. cit.*, p.96
10. Cited in: Getzler, *op. cit.*, p.67
11. V. Lenin: *C.W.*, Vol.45, pp.607-608
12. See: A. De Jonge, *op. cit.*, and L. Trotsky, *Stalin*
13. V. Lenin: *C.W.*, Vol.35, p.84
14. L. Trotsky: *Stalin*, p.109
15. *Ibid*, p.243
16. *Ibid*, p.258
17. *Ibid*, p.373

Chapter Five: Iskra Divided

1. *Second Congress [1903] of the RSDLP*, pp.4-5
2. *Ibid*, p.142
3. *Ibid*, p.151
4. Cited in: T. Dan: *The Origins of Bolshevism*, p.68
5. *Second Congress*, p.152
6. *Ibid*, pp.157-158
7. *Ibid*, p.158
8. *Ibid*, pp.159-161
9. Cited in: R. Brym: *The Jewish Intelligentsia and Russian Marxism*, p.85
10. *Second Congress*, p.167
11. *Ibid*, p.168
12. V. Lenin: *C.W.*, Vol.5, pp.350-351
13. *Second Congress*, p.70
14. *Ibid*, pp.169-170
15. K. Marx and F. Engels: *C.W.*, Vol.6, p.504
16. V. Lenin: *C.W.*, Vol.30, p.263
17. N. Machiavelli: *The Prince*, p.30
18. W. Shakespeare: *Henry VI, Part III*, Act III, Scene II
19. G. Plekhanov: *Selected Philosophical Works*, Vol.1, pp.110, 117
20. S. Baron, *op. cit.*, p.129
21. Cited in *ibid*, p.213
22. *Second Congress*, pp.220-221
23. *Ibid*, p.220

Chapter Six: Lenin as Élitist

1. *Second Congress*, p.511
2. V. Lenin: *C.W.*, Vol.5, p.452
3. *Ibid*, p.476
4. *Ibid*, p.472
5. K. Marx and F. Engels: *C.W.*, Vol.10, pp.31-32
6. K. Marx and F. Engels: *S.C.*, p.376
7. K. Marx and F. Engels: *C.W.*, Vol.6, p.495
8. V. Lenin: *C.W.*, Vol.4, p.211-212
9. See: E. Bernstein: *Evolutionary Socialism*
10. V. Lenin, *op. cit.*
11. Plato: *The Republic*, p.493
12. *Ibid*, p.474
13. J. Stalin: *C.W.*, Vol.1, p.164
14. Plato: *op. cit.*, p.435
15. Ecc., Ch.xxxviii, Verse 25
16. H. Ibsen: *The Enemy of the People*, Act IV
17. F. Nietzsche: Cited in: *Dictionary of Quotations*, London, 1990, p.250
18. Cited in: A. McBriar: *Fabian Socialism and English Politics 1884-1918*, p.86
19. G. Mosca: *The Ruling Class*, p.331
20. G. Sorel: *Reflections on Violence*, p.280
21. R. Michels: *Political Parties*, p.390
22. G.B. Shaw: *Fabian Essays in Socialism*, pp.x-xi and p.75
23. A. Hitler: *Mein Kampf*, pp.79-80
24. Cited in: G. Urban: *European Communism*, p.155
25. Cited in: E. Nolte: *Three Faces of Fascism*, pp.205-209
26. Cited in: G. Urban, *op. cit.*, p.157
27. Plato, *op. cit.*, p.512
28. V. Lenin: *C.W.*, Vol.32, p.21
29. Cited in: A. Lyttleton: *The Seizure of Power*, p.315
30. Cited in: J. Degras (ed.): *The Communist International, Documents*, Vol.I, pp.131-133
31. K. Marx and F. Engels: *C.W.*, Vol.6, p.495
32. V. Lenin: *C.W.*, Vol.5, p.467
33. V. Lenin: *C.W.*, Vol.7, p.206.
34. Cited in: G. Urban, *op. cit.*, pp.61, 64
35. Cited in: A. Antonov-Ovseyenko: *The Time of Stalin*, 257
36. Cited in: B. Souvarine: *Stalin*, p.634
37. *Documents of the Fourth International*, p.213
38. L. Trotsky: *The Revolutional Betrayed*, p.278
39. *Ibid*, p.100
40. *Documents of the Fourth International*, p.211
41. J. Primo De Rivera: *Selected Writings*, p.204
42. Cited in: S. Payne: *Falange: A History of Spanish Fascism*, pp.13-14
43. Cited in: G. Meaker: *The Revolutionary Left in Spain 1914-1923*, pp.373, 237
44. L. Trotsky: *Stalin*, p.61
45. *Ibid*, p.62
46. *Ibid*, p.58
47. *Second Congress*, p.179
48. V. Lenin: *C.W.*, Vol.13, p.107
49. See: M. Shachtman: *The Bureaucratic Revolution*

50. L. Trotsky: *Our Political Tasks*, p.77
51. *Ibid*, p.103
52. R. Luxemburg: *Rosa Luxemburg Speaks*, pp.116, 118
53. *Ibid*, p.390
54. Cited in: A. Valentinov: *Encounters with Lenin*, p.117
55. *Ibid*, p.128
56. *Ibid*, p.128
57. Cited in: S. Baron, op.cit., p.248
58. V. Lenin: *C.W.*, Vol.28, p.213
59. V. Lenin: *C.W.*, Vol.29, p.535
60. L. Trotsky: *Communism and Terrorism*, p.108
61. *Ibid*, p.21
62. L. Trotsky: *Leon Trotsky Speaks*, p.158
63. L. Trotsky: *The Challenge of the Left Opposition*, pp.78-79
64. Cited in: S. Cohen: *Bukharin and the Bolshevik Revolution*, p.201
65. G. Rudé (ed.): *Robespierre*, p.75
66. V. Lenin: *C.W.*, Vol.32, p.241
67. G. Rudé, *op. cit.*, p.78
68. See: L. Trotsky: *The Revolution Betrayed*, pp.94-105
69. L. Trotsky: *The Challenge*, p.97
70. Cited in: E. Carr: *The Bolshevik Revolution*, Vol.I, p.231
71. L. Trotsky: *Communism and Terrorism*, p.107
72. N. Machiavell: *The Discourses*, Vol.1, p.255
73. L. Trotsky: *Our Political Tasks*, p.77
74. V. Lenin: *C.W.*, Vol.27, pp.268-271
75. L. Trotsky: *Communism and Terrorism*, p.137
76. Cited in: M. Brinton: *The Bolsheviks and Workers' Control*, p.61
77. K. Marx and F. Engels: *C.W.*, Vol.6, p.504
78. *Ibid*, p.486
79. R. Luxemburg, *op. cit.*, pp.126-127
80. L. Trotsky: *Stalin*, p.412
81. *Ibid*, p.203

Chapter Seven: 'The Stuff of Robespierres'

1. V. Lenin: *C.W.*, Vol.8, p.222
2. V. Lenin: *C.W.*, Vol.25, p.178
3. C. Jones: *The Longman Companion to the French Revolution*, p.120
4. K. Marx and F. Engels: *C.W.*, Vol.42, p.71
5. K. Marx and F. Engels: *C.W.*, Vol.44, p.180
6. J.-J. Rousseau: *The Social Contract*, p.289
7. *Ibid*, p.290
8. *Ibid*, p.274
9. *Ibid*, p.275
10. *Ibid*
11. Cited in: J. Loomis: *Paris in the Terror*, pp.266-267
12. L. Trotsky: *Communism and Terrorism*, p.45
13. Cited in: Samir Al Khail: *Republic of Fear*, p.138
14. J.-J. Rousseau, *op. cit.*, p.335
15. Cited in: J. Talmon: *The Origins of Totalitarian Democracy*, pp.84, 86
16. V. Lenin: *C.W.*, Vol.7, p.383
17. Cited in: G. Meaker, *op. cit.*, p.423

18. J.-J. Rousseau, *op. cit.*, p.261
19. L. Trotsky: *Our Political Tasks*, p.124
20. J.-J. Rousseau, *op. cit.*, pp.331-333
21. L. Trotsky: *Report of the Siberian Delegation*, p.28
22. V. Lenin: *C.W.*, Vol.33, p.282
23. V. Lenin: *C.W.*, Vol.28, p.236
24. L. Trotsky: *Communism and Terrorism*, p.53
25. *Ibid*, p.50
26. J. Stalin: *C.W.*, Vol.5, p.73
27. V. Lenin: *C.W.*, Vol.32, p.355
28. V. Lenin: *C.W.*, Vol.42, p.170
29. L. Trotsky, *op. cit.*, p.63
30. K. Marx and F. Engels: *C.W.*, Vol.26, p.202
31. K. Marx and F. Engels: *C.W.*, Vol.22, p.352
32. V. Lenin: *C.W.*, Vol.30, p.28
33. V. Lenin: *C.W.*, Vol.42, p.170
34. Cited in: G. Legett: *The Cheka*, p.329
35. *Ibid*, pp.258-259
36. See: R. Breitman: *The Architect of Genocide*, p.67; and: H. Hoehne: *The Order of the Death's Head*, pp.328-330
37. V. Lenin: *C.W.*, Vol.42, p.419
38. G. Rudé, *op. cit.*, p.24
39. *Ibid*, p.25
40. N. Machiavelli, *op. cit.*, p.315

Chapter Eight: Leninism and the Left

1. K. Marx and F. Engels: *C.W.*, Vol.1, p.164
2. *Ibid*, p.119
3. *Ibid*, p.122
4. *Ibid*, p.131
5. K. Marx and F. Engels: *C.W.*, Vol.9, p.327
6. *Ibid*, p.386
7. K. Marx and F. Engels: *C.W.*, Vol.20, p.78
8. K. Marx and F. Engels: *C.W.*, Vol.22, p.417
9. Cf: *First Decrees of Soviet Power*, pp.29-30
10. *Second Congress*, p.6
11. V. Lenin: *C.W.*, Vol.6, p.350
12. V. Lenin: *C.W.*, Vol.26, p.285
13. V. Lenin: *C.W.*, Vol.32, pp.505-508
14. H. Trevor-Roper (ed.): *Hitler's Table Talk*, p.480
15. Cited in: G. Rude, *op. cit.*, p.55
16. J. Fishman: *The Insurrectionists*, p.13
17. Cited in: J. Loomis, *op. cit.*, p.335
18. Cited in: R. Postgate (ed.): *Revolution from 1789 to 1906*, p.53
19. Cited in: J. Loomis, *op. cit.*, p.294
20. V. Lenin: *C.W.*, Vol.41, pp.323-324
21. Cited in: B. Wolfe: 'Krupskaya Purges The People's Libraries' in: *Survey*, Summer, 1969, No.72, pp.141-149
22. *Ibid*, pp.141-152
23. *Ibid*, p.152
24. Plato, *op. cit.*, p.353

25. M. Stieg: 'The Second World War and the Public Libraries of Nazi Germany' in: *Journal of Contemporary History*, Vol.27, No.1, Jan. 1992, pp.23-40
26. *Ibid*, p.27
27. G. Higler and A. Meyer: *The Incompatible Allies*, p.311
28. Cited in: R. Skidelsky: *Oswald Mosley*, p.439
29. Cited in: J. Noakes and G. Pridham (eds.): *Documents on Nazism 1919-1945*, p.640
30. V. Lenin: *C.W.*, Vol.31, p.474
31. See: M. Pearson: *The Sealed Train*; R. Pipes: *The Russian Revolution*, pp.378-391; R. Clark: *Lenin*, pp.162-170 and pp.195-200; M. Futrell: *Northern Underground*; Z. Zeman: *Germany and the Revolution in Russia*
32. V. Lenin: *C.W.*, Vol.31, p.473
33. V. Lenin: *C.W.*, Vol.22, pp.143-156
34. See: A. Westoby and R. Blick: 'Early Soviet Designs on Poland' in: *Survey*, Vol.26, No.4 (117), Autumn 1982
35. V. Lenin: *C.W.*, Vol.31, p.475
36. *Ibid*, p.475
37. *Ibid*, p.276
38. Cited in: A. Spencer: 'National Bolshevism' in: *Survey*, 44-45, Oct. 1963, pp.141-142
39. See: A. Westoby and R. Blick, *op. cit.*
40. See: R. Black: *Fascism in Germany*, Vol.1, pp.461-491
41. Cited in *ibid*, p.474
42. Cited in *ibid*, p.479
43. A. Bramwell: *Blood and Soil*, p.96
44. *Ibid*, p.96
45. *Neues Wiener Tagblatt*, Oct. 1, 1939, cited in: S. Duff: *A German Protectorate*, p.27
46. V. Lenin: *C.W.*, Vol.31, p.450
47. See: A. Westoby and R. Blick, *op. cit.*
48. Cited in: C. Floud: *Hitler: The Path to Power*, p.156
49. J. Meijer (ed.): *The Trotsky Papers*, Vol.II, p.235
50. K. Marx: 'Provisional Rules of the International Workingmen's Association' in: *Documents*, Vol.I, p.288

APPENDIX I

The following letter, dated April 2 1990, was sent by the author to the American Trotskyist journal *Workers' Vanguard*. The editors of *Workers' Vanguard* undertook to publish this letter, together with an extensive reply, in a future issue of an associated journal *Sparticist*. Notice of the forthcoming publication of these two items then appeared in *Sparticist* number 45-6, Winter 1990-91, p.2. Despite a subsequent written reminder of this undertaking, at the time of writing as far as the author is aware, neither the letter nor the reply has been published. (The text of the letter has been edited for style, but remains the same in substance.)

Dear Editor,

I was surprised to read in your publication (*Workers' Vanguard*, February 23, 1990, page 6) that Lenin and Trotsky did not consider the one-party Soviet state 'either normal or desirable'. Their writings in the period between the Bolshevik Revolution until, in the case of Lenin, his last illness, and in that of Trotsky, until his expulsion from the Bolshevik Party in October 1927, do not provide any evidence to sustain your claim. Perhaps that is why, on this occasion, no quotations from the hallowed texts are forthcoming. However, Trotsky especially furnishes us with ample evidence that the early Bolshevik leadership held a contrary view to the one you suggest. Let me bring a small sample of it to the attention of your readers.

On April 5, 1923, to a conference of the Ukrainian Communist Party, Trotsky said:

'If there is one question which basically not only does not require revision but does not even admit the thought of revision, it is the question of the dictatorship of the party... Our party is the ruling party... To allow any changes whatsoever in this field, to allow the idea of a partial, whether open or camouflaged, curtailment of the leading role of our party would mean to bring into question all the achievements of the revolution and its future.' ('Leon Trotsky Speaks', New York, 1972, pp.158-160)

This quotation, it is true, says nothing about the necessity of banning all other parties, only of all power remaining in the hands of the Bolsheviks (a 'dictatorship of the party', not of the Soviets or of the proletariat). But the next quotation has a force and phrasing which should resolve all doubts. On December 22, 1923, Trotsky wrote:

'We are the only party in the country, and in the period of the dictatorship it could not be otherwise.' ('The Challenge of the Left Opposition', New York, 1975, p.78)

Let me repeat: '... could not be otherwise...'

You speak, in the same article (page 6) of the 'democratic contention of factions and tendencies within the Bolshevik party' as 'serving in a sense as a substitute for a multi-party soviet democracy.' Two questions arise from this. Trotsky, not once, but many times, insisted that all power was necessarily concentrated in the hands of a single party. Thus he defended, in 1927, the 'Leninist principle, inviolable for every Bolshevik, that the dictatorship of the proletariat is and can only be realised through the dictatorship of the party' ('Platform of the Left Opposition', London, 1963, p.62); and again, in the same work, the principle that the 'dictatorship of the proletariat demands at its very core a single proletarian party.' (*ibid*, p.112)

If this is indeed so, just how, under the rule of that single party, would what you describe as a 'multi-party soviet democracy' operate? Your readers will, no doubt, share my interest as to the textual sources of your belief that such an arrangement was indeed the intention of the Bolshevik party in the first years of its rule.

This leads to the next question. You speak of the 'democratic contention of factions'. Yet at their March 1921 (10th) Party Congress, the Bolsheviks outlawed this last residue of political pluralism, in a resolution drafted and moved (with the support of both Stalin and Trotsky) by Lenin himself. It declared 'factionalism of any kind' to be 'harmful and impermissible' as it 'inevitably' led to 'the weakening of team work and to intensified and repeated attempts by the enemies of the governing party, who have wormed their way in to it, to widen the cleavage and to use it for counter-revolutionary purposes.' (V. Lenin: 'Collected Works', Vol.32, p.241) How depressingly familiar!

The resolution did not stop there. It also banned the submission 'to groups formed on the basis of "platforms" ' etc' any 'analysis of the Party's general line, estimates of practical experience, check ups in the fulfilment of its decisions, studies of methods of rectifying errors etc.' (*ibid*, p.244) The penalty for any infraction of these draconian rules was 'unconditional and instant expulsion from the party'. (*ibid*, p.244)

The specific target of the new party regime was, of course, the Workers' Opposition. Indeed, another resolution (also drafted by Lenin) declared the propagation of its ideas as being 'incompatible with membership of the Russian Communist Party'. (*ibid*, p.248) And, sure enough, just a few months later, Lenin attempted, only to fail by just one vote, to secure the expulsion from the party, under its new rules, of the Workers' Opposition's most authoritative spokesman, that Central Committee rarity, a genuine (former) proletarian, Alexander Shlyapnikov.

Please tell me and your readers how the Soviet proletariat could have gone about organising a substitute for a 'multi-party soviet democracy' in a one-party state ruled by (after March 1921) a no-faction party dominated by a clique of a score or so intellectuals? While it is hardly surprising that this problem never seems to have greatly troubled Trotsky so long as he continued to enjoy the privileges of the Bolsheviks' political monopoly, what is remarkable is his reluctance to re-consider his position on 'Soviet pluralism' during and even after the decline in his political fortunes that set in towards the end of 1923. Factions, he still insisted, were dangerous, and the party was 'obliged [*sic!*] to monopolize the direction of political life'. ('Leon Trotsky Speaks', p.79) And again: 'The party does not want factions and will not tolerate them.' (*ibid*, p.86) No... this is not Stalin – or Zinoviev. It is Trotsky, digging his own political grave. Five months later, he was again arguing that 'freedom for factional groupings' was 'extremely dangerous for the ruling party, since they always threaten to split or divide the government and the state apparatus as a whole.' (*ibid*, p.153) (If that was so, then why did Lenin wait until March 1921 to ban them?) To make the point yet stronger, Trotsky insisted it was 'impermissible to draw distinctions between factions and groupings', adding, for the benefit of doubters, that he had 'never [please note, 'never'] recognised freedom for groupings inside the party, nor do I now recognise it.' (*ibid*, p.154) That is surely pretty clear.

And, even as the noose tightened around his neck, Trotsky continued to soap Stalin's rope: 'Various assertions to the effect that the [Left] Opposition is in favour of factions and groupings are lies spread for factional purposes.' ('The Challenge', p.102)

And once again:

'We categorically reject the theory and practice of "freedom of factions and groupings" and recognize that such theory and practice are contrary to Leninism and the decisions of the party [i.e. the ban at the 10th Party Congress]'. (*ibid*, p.127)

It would take Trotsky several more years yet before he even began to revise that position, together with his no less totalitarian views on the virtues of the one-party state. And when he did so, the revision was accomplished in classic Orwellian fashion, with the claim (from which you presumably derive yours) that party and factional pluralism had always been a principle of Bolshevism. Unfortunately, there is not a shred of documentary evidence to suggest that this is true. If it existed, Trotsky and his followers such as yourselves, would have been only too eager to produce it.

In his 'The Revolution Betrayed', written in 1936, Trotsky relates how the 'opposition parties were forbidden one after the other.' It was a measure 'obviously [*sic!*] in conflict with the spirit of Soviet democracy', and, moreover, one 'the leaders of Bolshevism regarded not as a principle [see above!], but as an episodic act of self-defence.' (*ibid*, London, 1957, p.96) The contradiction between this claim and the preceding quotations which, in different ways, say the exact opposite, must be as apparent to you and your readers as it is to me. Which of the two Trotskys one prefers is obviously a matter of political inclination, but we can all surely agree with Trotsky when he goes on to argue, even if only with the advantage of hindsight, that the 'prohibition of oppositional parties brought after it the prohibition of factions', and that the latter 'ended in a prohibition to think otherwise than the infallible leaders.' (*ibid*, pp.104-105)

I trust your paper does not intend to institute a new school of historical falsification to replace that of disintegrating Stalinism, and that you will be able to confront honestly the issues evaded by your rather fanciful excursion into early Soviet history.

Robin Blick

APPENDIX II
'OVERTAKE AND OUTSTRIP'

How ripe was Russia in 1917 for a socialist revolution? According to Marx and Engels, the 'premise of Communism', capitalism, should not only have 'rendered the great mass of the people 'propertyless' but realised 'a great increase in productive power' (K. Marx and F. Engels, 'The German Ideology', 'Collected Works', Vol.5, pp.48-49). Unless this condition was fulfilled, all attempts to advance beyond capitalism would simply render want 'general' and in turn revive the 'old filthy business' (*ibid*, p.49). Communism was not, at least for Marx and Engels, an 'ideal to which reality will have to adjust itself' (that is, be imposed by an act of will from the 'top down' in the manner of Bolshevik 'Petro-Jacobinism') but was rather the outcome of a 'real movement which abolishes the present state of things' (*ibid*, p.49); one which arises on the foundation of a certain level of development of the 'productive forces' and, even more fundamentally, matures within 'civil society', the 'true focus and theatre of all history' (*ibid*, p.50). Given their (necessary) conclusion that communism could, in the first place, only be the work of the '[economically] dominant peoples' (*ibid*, p.49), it is hardly surprising that Marx and Engels should have been sceptical, at the very least (and Engels, it should be said, more so than Marx) of the prospects of a successful socialist revolution in Russia while it continued to lag culturally, politically and economically so far behind the industrialised and liberalised countries of the West.

Whilst respecting their courage, Engels especially berated the populists for their advocacy of a unique Russian path to communism rooted in the traditional system of communal land tenure, the commune or 'mir'. To Plekhanov he once complained, at the very end of his life, that it had become 'impossible to discuss things' with those Russians who still believed in the 'communist mission' that distinguished 'truly Holy Russia' from the 'profane peoples'. ('Selected Correspondence', p.561) Marx was no more sympathetic to the claims of Slavophilism, however socialist its coloration, warning all too presciently, in the light of the history of the Muscovite-dominated Comintern) of the consequences of allowing the workers' movement of the West to be 'commanded in Russian' and afflicted with all the 'private intrigues and brawls' that would ensue from this subordination ('C.W.', Vol.43, p.500). Yet, as early as 1902, in his 'What Is To Be Done?' (where else?) Lenin argued differently. Even in the 1870s, when it was still explicitly anti-Marxist, oriented chiefly towards the peasantry, and increasingly influenced by terrorism, he advanced the claim that above all others, the Russian revolutionary movement had earned the 'honourable title' of the 'vanguard of the international revolutionary proletariat' ('C.W.' Vol.5, p.373). The same conviction, now nourished and seemingly vindicated by the victory of 1917, encouraged Lenin to make his bid for the leadership of the world labour movement with the formation, in March 1919, of the Third Communist International which, from very early in its life, increasingly served as the fifth column of Russian state interests within the organisations of the western working classes and colonial peoples. In this, as in so many of its other aspects, Bolshevism evolved more and more in the direction of a radical (and, under Stalin, pan) slavophilism.

From its formation prominent in the affairs of the Comintern Trotsky, no less than Lenin, argued that the pre-eminence of its Russian leadership arose from the fact and example of the Bolshevik victory of 1917, which had enabled the new regime to become the 'living embodiment' of the 'programme and methods' of the new world movement ('Lenin', p.194). Lenin's role had been to 'take[n] from [Russian] nationalism all that he needed for the greatest revolutionary action in the history of humanity' and, by so doing, raised himself to the level of the 'revolutionary leader of the proletariat of the world' (*ibid*, p.195). We do not have to speculate as to what Marx or Engels might have said about this truly Byzantine cult of Lenin as the holy Russian messiah of the world proletariat. Summing up the arguments for and against slavophile 'mir communism', Engels concluded that 'the age of chosen peoples' had 'gone forever', and that the path to communism in Russia, as elsewhere, lay through, and not around, the development of the productive forces by capitalism, and would follow, and not precede, the victory of the socialist revolution in the West ('C.W.', Vol.27, pp.425-433). And, obviously, to argue otherwise would put in question Marx's famous axiom that 'new superior relations of production never replace old ones before the material conditions for their existence have matured within the framework of the old society' (K. Marx, 'A Contribution to the Critique of Political Economy', London, 1971, p.21).

Perhaps the most prescient comments on the dangers and consequences of 'forcing history' are to be found, not in any writings on Russia, but in an early work by Engels, his 'Peasant War in Germany'. There he warns what might ensue when 'an extreme party is compelled to assume power at a time when the movement is not yet ripe' for the class it represents. In such a case, the rule of this party would advance, not the interests of this class, but those of an 'alien' one ('C.W.', Vol.10, p.470). And this 'alien class', once raised to power, on the backs of the masses, by Lenin's *coup*, and then entrenched and enlarged by its imposition upon Russia of Bolshevik state socialism, is what eventually defined itself as the *Nomenklatura*, the Leninist apparatus, the real victor of October.

Yet, ironically, Russian Marxism, largely at the instigation of Plekhanov, separated itself from the populist movement on this very question. And Lenin, no less than any other of his pupils, religiously followed this tradition, at least in words, right up to the very eve of the events of 1917. Then, just as Lenin had revived (some twenty years previously) the populist model of an *élite* party, so he now embarked on another populist regression, once again away from Marx and back to the Slavophile dream of a 'unique' Russian road to socialism. But on this occasion, and perhaps fittingly, in the light of subsequent developments, it was Stalin who not only consummated but also anticipated Lenin's conversion (if such it was) to a Russophile national socialism. At the August 1917 Congress of the Bolshevik Party, during the course of a debate on the current political situation, the future Trotskyist E. Preobrazhensky moved an amendment to the main resolution which made the victory of the socialist revolution in Russia conditional upon the onset of the proletarian revolution in the West. Stalin objected to this amendment, entirely Marxist in pedigree and spirit, on grounds that derived from an altogether different tradition. 'The possibility is not excluded that Russia will lay the road to socialism. ... We must discard the antiquated [sic] idea that only Europe can show us the way' ('C.W.', Vol.3, pp.199-200).

How the rest of the party *élite* might have responded to this dispute is partly a matter of conjecture, since most of them were absent. Lenin, together with Zinoviev, had recently fled from Petrograd after the 'July Days', while Trotsky and Kamenev were briefly under arrest. Even so, Lenin's views on this issue soon became known. What is more, his support for Stalin's 'Russian road' was unequivocal, only with this difference: that whereas Stalin had spoken merely of its possibility, Lenin now urged its necessity. In the September of that year, and therefore even before the Bolshevik seizure of power, Lenin was already insisting that, faced with the choice of 'perish or forge full steam ahead', it was both necessary and possible for Russia to 'overtake and outstrip the advanced countries economically' through the 'most radical transition to a superior mode of production' ('C.W.' Vol.27, p.340).

Once in power, and despite repeated assertions that Russia would advance to socialism only by means of world revolution, Lenin's Petrine inspiration and orientation became increasingly explicit. Emulating Russia's supreme autocrat (and first technocrat) the Bolsheviks would, vowed Lenin, 'not shrink from adopting dictatorial methods' to accelerate the country's economic development, like Peter and 'even more', 'not hesitat[ing] to use barbarous methods in fighting barbarism' ('C.W.', Vol.27, p.340). And in this at least, Lenin was as good as his word, save for the fact that the chief targets of his Red Terror were those very westernising 'bourgeois democratic' tendencies that were Russia's only hope of progress towards a more civilised society and by this route, to socialism.. This ascendency of the 'national' element in Bolshevism was consumated and reflected in Lenin's very last published writings, where he attempted, rather self-consciously, to prove that Russia (this was in 1923) possessed 'all that is necessary and sufficient' to 'build a complete socialist society' ('C.W.', Vol.33, p.468). Lenin rejected categorically the Menshevik argument (derived directly from the previously cited passages from Marx and Engels) that the Bolsheviks had been 'rash in undertaking to implant socialism in an insufficiently cultured country' . Once accomplished, the Bolshevik 'cultural revolution' (Lenin's term) would 'suffice' to make Russia 'a completely socialist country' (*ibid*, pp.474-475). Surely rhetorically, Lenin asked why the Bolshevik regime could not begin by 'first achieving that level of culture in a revolutionary way, and then, with the aid of the workers' and peasants' government and the Soviet system, proceed to overtake the other nations?' (*ibid*, pp.478-479) Ironically, in insisting that Menshevik objections to such an implicitly slavophile perspective were to be expected only from 'pedants' (*ibid*, p.475), Lenin perhaps forgot that Russian Marxism was born out of a dispute over this very question, and that he in the past had parted company with comrades over issues that at the time seemed less substantial.

Not with total consistency, Lenin's anticipation of what would soon become known as 'socialism in one country' was endorsed by the author of the theory of 'permanent revolution'. Amongst their many sins, his former Menshevik comrades were guilty of 'perverting Marx's conditional and limited conception that "the country that is more developed industrially, only shows, to the less developed, the image of its own future" into an absolute' (L. Trotsky, 'Lessons of October [1924]' in 'The Essential Trotsky', p.143). For good measure, Trotsky also rejected the no less traditionally Marxist proposition that 'the road to power [that is to say, to socialism] runs necessarily through bourgeois democracy' (*ibid*, p.143). Yet that is exactly what Marx and Engels did say, explicitly and repeatedly and, until 1917, Lenin also. But if Russia's road to socialism was indeed to follow another and more direct route than that charted by Menshevism, the problem remained – how was it to be done?

Ever the technocrat, Lenin's solution, like Peter the Great's two centuries before him (and Stalin's later when, in defending the inflated targets of his first Five Year Plan, he too invoked the example of Peter – 'C.W.', Vol. 11, p.258) was to deploy the power of the despotic state. Russia would have its 'cultural revolution' not before, but after the socialist revolution (*ibid*, p.475). And so, seemingly carried away by the vision of of what can perhaps best be described as a Bolshevik 'Petro-Jacobinism', Lenin took the final step. He now 'anticipated' by two years Stalin's doctrine of 'socialism in one country', insisting that the Bolsheviks could indeed 'create the fundamental prerequisites of civilization in a different way from that of West-European countries' and, what is more, without the assistance, hitherto regarded as indispensable, of successful socialist revolutions in these same lands. The order of march of the world socialist revolution envisaged by Marx and Engels was now not amended, but totally reversed, and in a manner that prefigured Mao's Sinophile doctrine of the 'East wind' prevailing over the 'West wind'. In his last published article, of March 4, 1923, Lenin insisted that 'in the last analysis, the outcome of the struggle will be determined by the fact that Russia, India, China, etc., account for the overwhelming majority of the population of the globe' (*ibid*, p.500) – a strange argument coming from someone normally so indifferent to the need for the support of a 'formal' majority.

No longer were world politics to be seen in the traditional Marxist terms of the development of the productive forces and the class struggle, with the western proletariat acting as the principal, self-acting agent of revolutionary change. Indeed, Lenin now predicted a conflict between the 'counter-revolutionary imperialist West and the revolutionary and nationalist East, between the most civilised countries and the Orientally backward countries' (*ibid*, p.500). And what was this if not the rebirth, in a new garb, of that debilitating Tartar yoke of Asiatic barbarism which Russian Marxism was, from its inception, dedicated to uprooting and extirpating from the soil of Muscovy, and which had rendered its exponents, in the eyes of European socialism, as the 'gendarme of Europe'? Nor did Lenin's revisionism end here. Why, he asked, 'cannot we begin by first achieving the pre-requisites for that definite level of culture in a revolutionary way' and then 'proceed to overtake the other [that is, advanced capitalist] nations?' (*ibid*, pp.478-479). And Stalin would soon respond, why not indeed? With some justice, he could argue, against Trotsky's internationalist objections, that 'Leninism answers in the affirmative' that 'we can build socialism by our own efforts' ('C.W.', Vol.7, p.111).

And, after the project had been attempted and, according to its executants, accomplished, even the regimes's sternest Bolshevik critic would affirm that Stalin's Five Year Plans had provided the 'experimental proof' of the 'practicability of socialist methods' (L. Trotsky, 'The Revolution Betrayed', p.1). Slave camps, mass terror and famine notwithstanding (and about these Trotsky , although he must of known of them better than most, had little or nothing to say), socialism had 'demonstrated its right to victory, not on the pages of *Das Kapital*, but in an industrial arena comprising a sixth of the earth's surface' (*ibid*, p.8). And it is perfectly true;

nowhere in the pages of that work can there be found the advocacy or theoretical basis for Stalin's 'socialist methods'. Trotsky's readiness to accept them brings to mind Bertrand Russell's admission that he was 'completely at a loss to understand how it came about that some people who are both humane and intelligent could find anything to admire in the vast slave camp produced by Stalin' ('Why I am not a Communist', in 'The Basic Writings of Bertrand Russell, p.480).

To bring the story into our own era. Twenty five years on, Lenin's plan to 'overtake and outstrip' the West underwent yet further embellishment, with Party chief Nikita Krushchov's boast, at the 22nd CPSU congress of 1961, that by the year 1970, the USSR would 'surpass the strongest and richest capitalist country, the USA, in production per head of population' ('The Road to Communism', Moscow, 1961, p.512).

The following tables should assist the reader in deciding firstly, how prepared was Russia for the Bolshevik 'great experiment' and, secondly, the viability of Lenin's dream for 'overtaking' the Soviet Union's capitalist rivals.

Table A: Comparative Per Capita National Income (as % of Russia)

	In 1861	In 1913
Russia	100	100
Spain	?	167
Italy	258	219
France	211	254
Germany	246	314
U.K.	323	487
U.S.A.	450	868

Source: P. Gatrell, *The Tsarist Economy*, London, 1986, p.32

Table B: % of Total Labour Force Engaged:

	Agr.	Industry	Construction	Transport
Russia (1926)	90	6.5	0.5	1.6
Spain (1910)	55	14	3.8	2.6
Italy (1911)	56	27		3
France (1911)	42	27	3	3.5
Austria (1920)	25	45	6.2	2.5
Belgium (1910)	28	44	6.3	6.3
Germany (1907)	36	36	7.6	4
U.K. (1911)	9	52	6	9

Source: B. Mitchell, *European Historical Statistics*, London, 1987, pp.161-171

Table C: % Contribution to National Income, by Sectors:

	Agr.	Industry	Construction	Transport
Russia (1926)	48	?	?	?
Italy (1913)	45	21	2	6
France (1909)	35	36	2	7
Austria (1919)	11	41	4	6
Germany (1913)	23	45	?	6
U.K. (1907)	6	34	4	10

Source: Ibid, pp.842-854

Table D: Comparative Urbanisation: % of Population in Towns:

	Circa 1870	Circa 1913
Russia (European)	10	15
Germany	36	60
U.K.	55	73

Source: M. Falkus, *The Industrialisation of Russia*, London, 1983, p.34

Table E: Comparative Productivity of Agricultural Labour:

	As at 1900	% growth since 1840
Russia	100	30
Italy	67	50
Spain	83	?
France	172	21
Germany	244	190
U.K.	250	45

Source: C. Trebilcock, *op.cit.*, p.434

Table F: Extent of Private Russian Capital:

Foreign Share of Russian Productive Investment			State Expenditure as % of National Product Circa 1910	
Year	1890	1915	Russia	28.6
	26%	41%	France	11.2
			Germany	6.2
			U.K.	7.1

Sources: M.Falkus, *ibid*, p.72; C. Trebilcock, *ibid*, p.438

Table G: Comparative Literacy: % of Population in Primary Schools (1911):

Russia	5.2
Spain	7.7
Italy	9.7
UK	14.9
France	14.5
Germany	15.9

Source: *ibid*, p.447

Table H: Recent Soviet Economic Performance as compared with selected capitalist countries:

GDP per capita

	1913	c.1988
USSR	100	100
Spain	167	431
Italy	219	702
France	254	827
Germany	314	West 960
UK	487	705
USA	868	964

Source *The Economist Book of Vital World Statistics*, London, 1991, p.34

Table I: Comparative Agricultural Labour Productivity:

	1900	1988
USSR	100	100
USA	?	870
France	177	700
U.K.	250	560
Germany	244	490
Italy	67	480
Spain	83	40

Source: *ibid*, p.56

Table J:

	Life Expectancy		Infant Mortality per 1,000	Maternal Mortality per 100,000
	Men	Women		
USSR	65	74	25	48
UK	72	78	9	9
USA	72	79	10	9
France	72	80	8	14
Germany (W.)	72	78	8	11

Source: *ibid*, p.214

Table K: Comparative Living Standards: Average Labour Time needed to buy commodities, January 15, 1966:

Commodity	Moscow as % of New York
Bread	400
Potatoes	300
Beef	350
Butter	1,000
Milk	500
Cotton Shirt	750
Suit	800
Men's shoes	600
Rayon dress	1,000
Women's shoes	700
Soap	800

Source: *Economic Almanac 1967-1968*, New York, 1967, pp.516-517

APPENDIX III
HOW LEGITIMATE WAS BOLSHEVIK RULE?

Events may well put power in our hands, and then we shall not relinquish it.
V. Lenin

The citizen slept, ignorant of the change from one power to another.
L. Trotsky

The people in mass cannot govern itself.
Robespierre

In the Footsteps of Nechayev

It was entirely fitting that the rise to power of Bolshevism should be consummated as it began – with a rigged Second Congress. The first, in 1903, of the Russian Social Democratic Labour Party, witnessed Lenin's first (and, as it proved, abortive) bid for the 'conductor's baton' of the Russian Marxist movement. The second, the All-Russian Congress of Soviets, held in Petrograd in the November of 1917, also provided Lenin with another not so 'compact' majority, only this time for the purpose of rubber-stamping and legitimising a Bolshevik armed *coup* staged in the Russian capital a matter of hours previously. Lenin, we will recall, asserted (contrary to the facts of the case) that the Congress of 1903 had been called 'on the basis of the fullest representation' ('Collected Works', Vol.8, p.211). No less spuriously, identical claims were made for the Congress of November 1917, obviously with the purpose of lending a covering of legitimacy to what would otherwise have appeared for what it was – a naked act of usurpation of the will and democratic liberties of the Russian peoples. On the night of the *coup*, Lenin declared to its largely sympathetic assembled delegates that they represented 'the will of the vast majority of the workers, soldiers and peasants' ('C. W.', Vol.26, p.247), while Trotsky, his principal executant in the Petrograd putsch, years later ventured an even more extravagant claim that the Second Congress of Soviets was the 'most democratic of all parliaments in the world's history' ('History of the Russian Revolution', p.1147). Just how extravagant, we shall see in due course. But it should be placed on record here that Trotsky's views on the virtues of democracy were not always so positive. On another occasion, he could write that Bolshevik 'theory recognises the utter uselessness of democracy as a way of deciding the conflict between the proletariat and the bourgoisie,' and that 'democracy is only a pseudonym for interest payments' (L. Trotsky: 'How the Revolution Armed', Vol.4, pp.310, 343). Naturally, these and other Bolshevik pronouncements on the deficiencies of democracy were made only after the Bolshevik seizure of power.

In the case of Lenin, his manipulative relationship with the mass movements of 1917 is nowhere better illustrated than in his attitude towards the slogan 'All Power to the Soviets'. Upon his return from Swiss exile in April 1917, Lenin set about converting his party, reared on a decade or more of polemic against first populist, and then Trotskyist ('permanent revolution') short cuts to socialism, to a policy of removing the Provisional Government and an immediate transition to the rule 'of the proletariat and the poorest sections of the peasants' ('C.W.', Vol.24, p.22). Stupified at this *volte face*, one party leader was heard exclaiming that Lenin's new line was 'the raving of a madman', whilst another, with more justice, concluded that by orientating the Bolsheviks a socialist *coup*, Lenin had announced himself as the candidate to the vacant 'throne of Bakunin' (N. Sukhanov, 'The Russian Revolution 1917', pp.286-287).

Yet it is also undeniable that, pending the election of a Constituent Assembly, in April 1917 the only obvious or viable alternative to the recently formed Provisional Government (born of a Duma, the fourth, elected on a grossly unequal franchise) was indeed the Soviets, upon whose support the new regime depended for its functioning, legitimacy and, consequently, survival (the system of shared or 'dual' power). Hence the appeal of the slogan 'All Power to the Soviets' to the ever-increasing numbers of workers, peasants, servicemen and members of the empire's national minorities who grew impatient with the Provisional Government's patent inability to tackle the country's worsening internal and external situation. But events would prove that Lenin's attitude towards the Soviets was fundamentally different from theirs. To the Bolshevik leader, the Soviets were a possible means of achieving and consolidating power for his party, that and nothing more. After all, in the midst of the 1905 revolution which had first given birth to the Soviets, had Lenin not then, as he would in the autumn of 1917, also advocated a policy of 'armed insurrection' independent of the soviets against the tottering autocracy of Nicholas II ('C.W.', Vol.8, pp.368-374)? And ,what is even more to the point, did he not commit his party to just this strategy in provoking the needless tragedy of the Moscow uprising of December? There is no reason, therefore, to assume that because Lenin, on his return to Russia in 1917, saw a tactical advantage in the soviet slogan, that he had abandoned the option of a Jacobin-Bakunist *coup de main*. Already, at the First Congress of Workers' and Soldiers' Soviets in June, Lenin had announced to an incredulous audience (they would have been better advised to take him more seriously) that his pary was ready to assume power, even though it commanded the support of little more than ten per cent of its delegates, and even smaller share of the delegates to a parallel congress of Peasants' Soviets.

Lenin's Blanquist tendencies again surfaced when, in the middle of July, following spontaneous demonstrations and street fighting in Petrograd against the Provisional Government (the 'July Days') Lenin went into hiding and ,from his temporary retreat across the border in Finland, demanded another dramatic reversal of party policy towards the Soviets. Still dominated by the 'compromisers' (the SRs and Mensheviks) their refusal to assume full power rendered the old slogan obsolete. All prospects for a 'peaceful development of the Russian revolution' had 'vanished', and to think otherwise was to indulge in 'constitutional or republican illusions' ('C.W.', Vol.41, p.442). Therefore, the goal now was the preparation of an 'armed uprising', an 'insurrection' (*ibid*, p.443). In other words, a Bolshevik *putsch*! This new turn in Lenin's thinking was reflected in an internal party document dated August 31-September 1. Reprimanding certain party leaders for their supposed constitutional illusions, Lenin avowed that 'should a spontaneous movement break out in Moscow today [i.e. similar to the 'July Days' in Petrograd] the slogan should precisely be to seize power' ('C.W.', Vol.25, p.250). However, while the target remained the same – the Provisional Government – this new policy still left unanswered the obvious and awkward question as to how, and in whose name, the proposed 'armed uprising' was to take place. If not the Soviets, was it to be the Bolshevik party itself? Or perhaps some ostensibly 'non-party' institution captured or maybe even created by the Bolsheviks for the purpose of lending the semblance of a more popular character to the undertaking? Despite the friction this would cause with his co-thinkers back in Petrograd, Lenin wisely chose to keep his options open. For, as it turned out, the Bolshevik *coup* would comprise, both in its technical and political aspects, elements of each option.

However, before examining more closely the various means by which Bolshevism usurped the revolutionary movements and aspirations of 1917, we should first recall that a close colleague of Lenin's, Vladimir Bonch-Bruevich, acknowledged after the revolution that the Bolshevik seizure of power had 'proceeded to a significant degree' according to the conceptions of the most extreme of all Russian Jacobins, Peter Tkachev (see Chapter Three). Yet there are grounds for arguing (as Lenin's Menshevik critics frequently did) that, insofar as they were inspired by a Jesuitical conception of political morality, Lenin's methods owed more to the tradition of Sergei Nechayev than Tkachev. After combining with the gulllible Bakunin in a series of political intrigues and deceptions, culminating in the murder in Russia of a dissident member of his clique, Nechayev was publicly denounced by Marx and Engels, on behalf of the IWA, as a morally degenerate political adventurer, would-be despot and enemy of the working class movement ('C.W.', Vol.23, pp.454-580). Privately, Marx went even further, describing him as 'capable of any infamy' ('C.W.', Vol.44, p.452). *Élitist a la outrance*, the Bakunin-Nechayev plan for a revolutionary party divided membership into a hierarchy of categories, both reminiscent of Peter's fourteen degree 'Table of Ranks' and anticipating the Bolshevik *Nomenklatura*, ranging from the self-selecting, all-seeing and all-knowing few at the core (Lenin's 'dozen wise men'), through various grades of increasing untrustworthiness to the unsuspecting, totally mistrusted and expendable mass at the periphery (see Marx and Engels, 'C.W.', Vol.23).

Lenin's insistence upon a similar system of what he once described as 'organised mistrust', which also required that distinctions be observed between what the party should say to the masses, and its rank and file members, in public, and what could only be discussed amongst and decided upon by the chosen few in secret, obviously followed this model. Yet we have already seen (Chapter Three) how repugnant to Marx and Engels was the idea that the masses had to be excluded from the business of organising their own emancipation, and that it was a task best left to technically more competent professional revolutionaries. Because of their insistance that workers must needs emancipate themselves, they derided the Bakunin-Nechayev- and we should add, Lenin – principle of 'top-down', 'organised mistrust' as one in which only 'to the people elect ... does the prophet dare to speak out openly' (op.cit, p.525). As we have seen, Lenin's views on party organisation in particular, and the the role of leaders in general, led him, early on, to strike out on an altogether different path. From as early as 1902 (and possibly even earlier) Lenin had evolved a hierarchical structure of party organisation, in which, in the manner of Nechayev's 'People's Vengeance' where, according to him one instructions, there should operate a 'whole chain of links' running from 'the centre', 'the handful making up the highly secret and close-knit core of professional revolutionaries' to the 'mass "organisation without members"' ('C.W.', Vol. 34, p.108). The reader will recall that Lenin, some two decades later, employed similarly technocratic terminology – 'cogwheels' and 'transmission belts' – to describe the relationship that had evolved and should operate between the Bolshevik regime and its various mass organisations, principally the by now castrated trade unions. And, as we shall see, although conceived under the Autocracy, and justified by the repressive nature of the Tsarist police state, this two tier system continued to operate after its overthrow in March 1917, especially in the weeks that preceded the Bolshevik coup.

The published record speaks for itself. On September 12, 1917, Lenin dispatched to the Central Committee a letter proposing that the struggle then unfolding against the attempted coup of General Kornilov be harnessed to his own plan for a rival Bolshevik coup against the now disabled Kerensky Provisional Government. He argued (correctly) that the 'development of this war [against Kornilov] alone could lead us to power' ('C.W.', Vol.25, p.289, emphasis in the original). But who exactly was this 'us'? The Soviets perhaps? The 'mass'? Given the context, hardly. 'Us' could only have meant the 'people elect', the 'highly secret close knit core', the 'handful' of the Party élite, or what Lenin described as 'the centre', as is evident from what follows next. He warned that 'we must speak of this [i.e., the intended coup] as little as possible in our propaganda', 'remembering very well that even tomorrow events may well put power into our hands, and then we shall not relinquish it' (ibid). In other words, on no account let slip that behind the screen of a struggle against Kornilov, and under the slogan of 'All Power to the Soviets', the Bolshevik leadership was preparing a putsch that would place all power in its own hands, a power, moreover that, as Lenin makes perfectly clear, it would never relinquish. And, just to make sure there were no misunderstandings on this score, repeatedly Lenin spelt out (again, obviously, only in private letters) how the party's public slogans should be interpreted by the party chiefs when the time came to pass from words to action, and to implement what might today be described as Lenin's 'hidden agenda'. It would, he advised in one letter, be 'naive to wait for a "formal" majority for the Bolsheviks' ('C.W.', Vol. 26, p.21), while in another he candidly explained that 'the slogan "All Power to the Soviets"' was 'nothing but a call for insurrection' and warned that 'whoever uses this slogan without having grasped this and given thought to it will only have himself to blame' (ibid, pp.185, 187). With unconcious understatement, Lenin reminded his colleagues that it was 'probably not quite clear to all comrades' that 'in practice the transfer of power to the Soviets' 'now' meant 'armed uprising' (ibid, p.179).

And understandably so, since the party press, as we shall see, was saying something entirely different. Lenin cautioned that it was important not to be 'blinded' by the way the Soviet slogan had been used in the past. It was now 'equivalent to a call for insurrection' (ibid, p.185). And to compound the cynicism of Lenin's strategy, this 'insurrection' was, moreover, to be carried out by the party behind the backs of these same Soviets, and, if needs be, against their will (Vol.26,pp.185-187)! In other words, as far as the Party chiefs were concerned, for 'Soviet power' they were to read 'Bolshevik insurrection'. But in public, great care was taken to ensure that matters were presented rather differently, very much in the spirit of 'Soviet legality'. For example, in a note to his draft resolution to the Central Committee (written between October 12 and 17) 'On the Slogan "All Power to the Soviets"', which significantly dismissed the Soviets as 'talking shops' and again demanded a more serious and practical attitude towards insurrection, Lenin (understandably) urged that 'not everything' in his Theses 'should be published', and that discussion of its contents should be confined 'within the Party' (*ibid*, p.144: the text was eventually published in 1921). Another private missive, subtitled 'The Mistakes of our Party', chided party leaders for their lack of firmness in the struggle against the moderate socialists. Lenin demanded that the Bolsheviks 'expel them ruthlessly from all revolutionary organisations' (*ibid*, p.57), a call which can only be construed – and this was before the Bolshevik take-over – as an incitement to exclude all other parties from the leading institutions of the Soviets, a policy that was indeed pursued with energy and eventual success after the Bolshevik seizure of power.

Meanwhile, in the party press, Lenin's was the voice of sweet reason and compromise, even waxing enthusiastic on the prospects of an 'alliance of the Bolsheviks with the Socialist-Revolutionaries and Mensheviks' (*ibid*, p.36). Who could have guessed that before the year was out, leaders of the two latter parties would be facing arrest and the suppression of their newspapers? For not a hint of this fate intruded into public Bolshevik propaganda. As before, the Party was prepared to play the role of a peaceful opposition to a Soviet government dominated by the SRs and Mensheviks. What is more, the Bolsheviks would conduct the struggle for the supremacy of their party strictly on the grounds of Soviet legality ('C.W.', Vol.25, pp.305-310, 373; Vol.26, pp.28-54, 59-68). Yet while on October 10, one Bolshevik newspaper carried an article by Lenin advocating 'the peaceful struggle of parties' ('C.W.', Vol.26, p.68), on the *same day*, its author was scolding his own party (in a private letter of course) for '*not* conducting regular work to prepare their *own* military forces for the overthrow of Kerensky' (*ibid*, p.69, emphases in the original). Perhaps only Leninists can show how this Bolshevik doubletalk can be reconciled with the avowal that 'Communists disdain to conceal their views and aims' (Marx and Engels, 'C.W.', Vol.6, p.518). Just how seriously Lenin (and, for that matter, the majority of the Bolshevik *élite*) took their public commitment to the 'peaceful struggle of parties', we know only too well.

Putsch or Revolution?

Given Lenin's understandable concern to confine any knowledge of his real intentions to a tiny circle of party leaders (principally those of the Central Committee) it is easy to appreciate his fury when Zinoviev and Kamenev circulated lower-ranking party organisations (not the public, as is usually alleged) with a statement expressing their doubts as to the wisdom of the Central Committee's intentions (about which, officially at least the latter knew nothing) and then, an even greater crime amongst disciplined Leninists, issued a clarifying statement to Maxim Gorky's *Novaia zhizn* when news of their opposition became public knowledge (A. Bone, *op. cit.*, pp.89-95, 121-122). Despite this latter declaration's loyal denial of all knowledge of a planned Bolshevik *coup*, Lenin demanded their expulsion from the party as 'strike-breakers', and ridiculed their demand that, at the very least, the Bolshevik delegates to the upcoming Second Congress of Soviets (in whose name, it should be remembered, the Bolsheviks were to seize power) be consulted before undertaking any drastic action ('C.W.', Vol.26, p.224). 'Just imagine,' exclaimed Lenin. The decision to stage an insurrection had already been taken in secret by 'the centre' (i.e., the Party Central Committee) in the best traditions, and here were Zinoviev and Kamenev consulting what Lenin refered to, rather scornfully, as the 'rank and file', the Party members who in their humble capacity as delegates to the Second Soviet Congress would, according to the canons of Leninist 'Soviet legality', at the moment chosen for them, convert themselves into Russia's new rulers (*ibid*, p.226-227). Obviously, the less they learned in advance about their allotted role in the proceedings, the better. Truly, this was revolution 'from the top downwards'.

Following Lenin's example, Stalin and Trotsky likewise publicly denied the existence of any plan by the Bolsheviks to stage an insurrection and seize power exclusively for themselves. For example, while Stalin laughably came forward as the proponent of open government, 'exercised in the sight of all, without plots and underhand dealings' ('C.W.', Vol.3, p.395) and Trotsky, as the newly elected Chairman of the Petrograd Soviet, pledged to uphold the 'spirit of justice and of full freedom for all factions' ('Leon Trotsky Speaks', p.55), privately Trotsky plotted the hijacking of the Soviets by their Bolshevik faction, just as Stalin demanded at the Central Committee meeting of October 31 that the Party 'firmly and irrevocably take the path of insurrection' ('C.W.', Vol.3, p.408). But as a classic instance of Leninist duplicity, it would be hard to better the title of an article published by the Bolshevik press on September 28. Penned by Lenin in the midst of his secret campaign inside the party leadership for a *coup* against the Provisional Government, and for a political course that would, if successful, inevitably extinguish Russia's fragile fledgling democracy, it ran: 'How To Guarantee the Success of the Constituent Assembly' ('C.W.', Vol.25, pp.374-379). Does it require an Orwell to translate Lenin's Bolshevik 'Newspeak' into plain English? For 'success', read extinction.

In acting thus, Lenin was yet again following the path charted not only Nechayev but by their shared precursors Blanqui and the Jacobins. Did not Jean-Paul Marat, the original apostle of unlimited 'revolutionary' terror, a full fifteen years before the outbreak of the French Revolution justify the creation of a revolutionary conspiracy and the establishment of a personal despotism on the Rousseauesque, and by now familiar grounds, that the masses could not be permitted to follow their own spontaneous inclinations? 'What can be expected from these unfortunates? ... The measures they take are all ill-conceived, and above all they are incapable of secrecy' (cited in A. Saboul, 'The Revolutionary State 1789-1796', Past and Present, No.65, Nov.1974). Yet, despite their (usually carefully concealed) scorn for the masses, and predeliction for terroristic dictatorship, Lenin still found it possible to revere the Jacobins as the 'most consistent of all bourgeois democrats' ('C.W.', Vol.8, p.432) and advocate, as early as 1906, the emulation of their *coup d'etat* of June 1793 by 'seizing power on the lines of [more accurately, from] the [French] Convention' ('C.W.', Vol.10, p.291). In this at least, he was as good as his word. In July 1917, and with Lenin irrevocably committed to a Bolshevik seizure of power, Jacobinism was again in vogue. Far from being 'obsolete', Lenin found 'the Jacobin example' 'instructive', especially in the manner in which Robespierre's terror had dealt with the so-called 'enemies of the people', 'not just in words' but by employing 'the most revolutionary measures, including the guillotine' ('C.W.', Vol.25, p.57 And, we could add, mass drownings in barges of supposed counter-revolutionaries (including children) in the River Loire at Nantes – R. Palmer, *op. Cit.*, pp.220-223). The example was not invoked idly. Within days of the Bolshevik seizure of power, Lenin could be heard exclaiming; 'how can we accomplish a revolution without shooting?' (L. Trotsky, 'Lenin', p.133), a policy anticipated by his observation, made as early as 1901, that 'in principle, we have never rejected terror and cannot reject terror' ('C.W.', Vol.5, p.19).

But in invoking and then emulating the Jacobin's deployment of the death penalty, what Lenin and his cohorts possiblly overlooked or chose to ignore was that amongst these 'enemies of the people' – a term also employed with no less murderous effect by Bolsheviks from Lenin to Stalin – were not only aristocrats and spies, but the radical and democratic opponents of Jacobin despotism – Chaumette, Cloots, Dubuisson, Desmoulins, Danton, Delacroix, Gobel, Guzman, Hebert, Momoro, Philipeaux, Proli, Ronsin, Roucher, Roux (suicide), Simon, Vincent ... these and many more fell victim to 'consistent' Jacobin 'democracy'; with its proto-Bolshevik, if only partially developed, totalitarian system of demagogy, manipulation, political amalgams, show trials, mass terror, leader cults, bogus internationalism, religious intolerance, cultural regimentation and all-pervading thought control. The revered radical campaigner and pamphleteer Thomas Paine would have been added to the list but for the overthrow of his Jacobin jailers. Initially lionised for his defence of the revolutionary cause in his polemic with Edmund Burke, Paine was elected to the Convention in 1792. But, unlike the Jacobins, his republicanism involved a commitment to individual liberty, the rule of law and toleration, and this divergence soon brought him into conflict with France's new masters, being arrested and imprisoned without trial for his opposition to the Terror and for the mere fact that he happened to share the same nationality as his life long foes, the English aristocracy. In the same manner, the communist pioneer and matyr Gracchus Babeuf enjoyed a temporary deliverance from the blade after his arrest as an opponent of Jacobin dicatorship and betrayal of the Parisian poor. After Robespierre's fall, he launched a journal entitled, with obvious political intent, 'For the Freedom of the Press'.

Despite these many many other evidences of the anti-popular character of the Robespierre regime, Lenin was able to find and uphold in Jacobinism and its terror a 'great example' for those who sought to 'take all state power into their own hands' (ibid, p.58) In fact, Lenin's party learned its Jacobin lessons so well that Trotsky could describe the Bolshevik regime, perfectly truthfully, as a 'dictatorship of the party' (not proletariat) in which 'such a great power is concentrated in the hands of the leadership as was wielded by no single political organization in the history of mankind' ('The Third International After Lenin', p.230). And surely Trotsky could not have forgotten that when he wrote these lines, Bolshevism's 'best pupil' had been in power for nearly eight years!

When we turn to examine Bolshevik claims concerning the democratic credentials of the Second Congress of Soviets which, in their estimation at least, legitimised their seizure of power, we find first of all that Trotsky provides what he describes as 'very incomplete' figures for the attending delegates, adding that 'at the moment of the opening there were 650 delegates with votes', of whom '390 fell to the Bolsheviks' ('History of the Russian Revolution', p.1146). The reader is invited to compare these figures with those in Table A, where it will be noticed that only in column 3 is there to be found a correspondence with Trotsky's data. Also noteworthy are the widely differing estimates of Bolshevik support at the Congress, compared with the two other main parties.

Whatever the exact composition of the Congress, the fact of the matter is that Lenin's majority was not nearly as 'compact' as he would have wished, and depended upon the far from unqualified support the Bolsheviks were able to secure – briefly – from the more leftist delegates of the Socialist Revolutionaries. Balance of parties apart, how did this Congress compare, in terms of its representative nature, with the First, held the previous June? None too favourably, even if we only rely on Trotsky. He relates that at the First Congress, those he describes as 'compromisers' numbered '600 out of the whole number of 832 delegates' (ibid, p.1148; Trotsky is definitely mistaken as to the Bolshevik delegation, which numbered 105 – J. Bunyan and H. Fisher, 'The Bolshevik Revolution', p.11 – but the total number of delegates he gives is correct). So, given that the number of voters in the elections to the June Congress was in excess of 13 million (M. Ferro, 'The Bolshevik Revolution', p.185), and assuming, for the moment, that the individual delegates to the two congresses were elected by equal numbers of voters, then the First Congress, contrary to the protestations of Lenin and Trotsky (and, following their example, every generation of Leninists down to the present day), was undeniably substantially more representative than the Second, upon whose legitimacy the entire Bolshevik claim to power rests.

But would we be right to assume such a parity of voting? Not at all. Recent studies of tactics adopted by the Bolshevik Party to secure for itself the prized 'compact majority' have revealed that Lenin's agents resorted to the very same devices of gerrymandering and fraud that were employed by Iskra to ensure for itself a similar supremacy at the Second Congress of the RSDLP in 1903. Firstly, it should be remembered that the peasant soviets, representing some three quarters or more of the Russian labouring population, played no part whatsoever in the deliberations of the Second Congress of Soviets. Whereas in June, they convened, nationally, as a separate entity from the First Congress of Workers' and Soldiers' Soviets, with the Bolsheviks comprising a mere twenty of the 1115 delegates present (Bunyan and Fisher, op. cit., p.9), in November, they never met at all, rendering Bolshevik claims to represent the peasantry entirely bogus.

Faced with the difficultly that they had, thus far, been unable to rally any significant support in the peasant soviets, the Bolshevik leadership, in the early autumn, set about the task of acquiring, by any means necessary, the semblance of a mandate from those soviets elected mainly by workers and soldiers. Contrary to what one might suppose, this could be done without first securing a majority at the primary level of a city soviet, the so-called 'plenum' where delegates from the various local workplaces gathered to debate policy and elect higher level soviet officials. Studies of city and local soviets have revealed that from its very inception in the heat of the March Revolution, the soviet structure began to exhibit two 'substitutionist' tendencies that eventually rendered it highly vulnerable to its capture by a party skilled, as the Bolsheviks undeniably were, in the arts of political deception and apparatus infighting. The first was its infiltration, usually at the highest executive levels (and, as in the case of Petrograd, there could be as many as four) by party officials, who would then staff, on a full time basis, the apparatus of the soviet machinery (see M. Ferro, *op. cit.*, pp.179-202). The second associated trend, which also worked to the advantage of the Bolsheviks, was for plenum meetings to become less and less frequent, as they yielded to proportionately ever more meetings of the 'professionals', in their capacity as full-time executive officers in the upper echelons of the soviet pyramid. The election of Trotsky, who was neither a factory worker nor (yet) a soldier, as Chairman of the Petrograd Soviet of Workers' and Soldiers' Deputies, exemplified this trend (see Tables B and C).

These two processes of professionalisation and bureaucratisation necessarily coalesced to produce a 'soviet substitutionism' that when deployed by the Bolsheviks, served as an indispensable springboard in their leap for power. So much at home did the Bolsheviks feel in this environment that in all but a few of the key soviets, they were able to capture posts in the upper reaches of the soviet machine on a scale out of all proportion to their real support at the base of the structure (see table D). In the most extreme case, in Samara, the Bolsheviks captured the executive (75%) with support from less than a third of the plenum delegates. After such a *coup*, where would be the incentive for the Bolsheviks to hold anything but meetings of the executive? (See Table B.)

Exploiting these vantage points in the soviet machinery, and riding on a wave of an entirely warranted popular disenchantment with the Provisional Government, the Bolshevik Central Committee urged on in its turn by an ever more impatient Lenin, now in hiding across the border in Finland) set about the manufacturing of the 'compact' majority that Trotsky (and here he differed with Lenin) thought would be required to legitimise, in the eyes of the Soviet masses, the *coup* that Lenin already had in view. In those regions where the Bolsheviks were in a position to do so, they secured the nomination of their supporters or members as delegates by methods that replicated the gerrymandering tactics of used by *Iskra* in the run up to the Second Party Congress of 1903. For example: the rules for the election of delegates to the First Congress of Soviets in June 1917 had stipulated one delegate for every 25,000 soviet members. This was far from being the case in the elections to the Second Congress. Multiple voting and bogus delegating was rife with, in one case, a soviet of 1,500 being represented by five (naturally Bolshevik delegates (that is, one per 300) and another of 500 members by two (a ratio of one to 250, instead of 25,000) (R. Pipes, 'The Russian Revolution', p.476). Of course, all the other parties protested, while the Executive Committee elected at the First Congress of Soviets declared, with total justice, that the Bolsheviks were violating 'all the rules' of soviet democracy (*ibid*). However, since this body was charged with convening the Congress, after registering its protest, the Executive Committee felt it had no choice but to go ahead, Bolshevik gerrymandering or no (*ibid*).

And so there opened, amidst the sound of gunfire, in the early hours of November 8, 1917, the gathering Trotsky would have us believe was the 'most democratic of all parliaments in the world's history'. In truth, when we compare its mandate with that given to the Constituent Assembly elected later the same month (see Table F) it ranks as among its least. Lenin's intentions and double standards in regard to 'Soviet democracy' are well demonstrated by his simultaneously publicly charging his Menshevik and SR opponents with failing to observe 'proportionality' in the representation to the Democratic Conference which preceded the Second Congress of Soviets, while privately criticising Zinoviev for advocating, in the Bolshevik press, 'proportional composition' for the Presidium of the strategic Petrograd Soviet, in which the Bolsheviks had just gained a narrow majority ('C.W.', Vol.26, pp.44, 49). To 'let them in' warned Lenin, 'meant the ruin of Soviet work' (*ibid*, p.49). What Lenin understood as 'Soviet work', and why he wanted them excluded, would become clearer over the next days and weeks.

But the Bolshevik *coup* did not take place in a political vacuum. While the peasants continued to support the Socialist Revolutionaries (although becoming increasingly critical of their prevarications over the land question), amongst the soldiers the continuation of the war encouraged a clear shift either to the party's left, or over to the Bolsheviks. Amongst the workers also, the Bolsheviks gained ground, and in the autumn, definitely won (temporarily) their majority, only this time chiefly at the expense of the Mensheviks, who were identified, in the case of their left wing wrongly so, with the policies of the Kerensky government. But these shifts, though substantial, were nowhere near giving the Bolsheviks a majority in the soviets taken as a whole and, even less so, in any elections held, unlike those within the soviets, on the basis of equal and universal suffrage, as the results of the elections to the Constituent Assembly, conducted in the last two weeks of November 1917, demonstrated. And there is another and no less significant consideration to keep in view. Even in a situation where the Bolsheviks had been able to arrange for themselves, by the means already discussed, something resembling a majority at the Second Congress of Workers' and Soldiers' Soviets, we learn from none other than Trotsky that it was very far from wanting to give a blank cheque to one single party to do with its newly-won power exactly what it liked. Trotsky tells us that a 'straw vote taken amongst delegates [to the Second Congress of Soviets] revealed that 505 soviets stood for the transfer of all power to the soviets, 86 for a government of the "democracy", 55 for a coalition, 21 for a coalition but without the Kadets' (*op. cit.*, p.1148). These figures, which accord very closely with those in Table E, confirm that not only the soviets themselves, but their Bolshevik delegates to the Second Congress, had not the remotest intention of transfering power from the Provisional government headed by Kerensky to an all-Bolshevik government headed by Lenin.

And yet that is exactly what happened!

Trotsky explains the means of its achievement. In order to seize power for themselves, the Bolsheviks would require, as Trotsky aptly puts it, a 'camouflage'(*op. cit.*, p.945) or 'screen' (*ibid*, p.947) to mask the 'preparation for an insurrection' (*ibid*). With Lenin the chief strategist temporarily exiled, Trotsky, as Chairman of the Petrograd Soviet, came forward as the leading party tactician, seeking to 'invent a soviet body' (*ibid*,p.944) that is, an ostensibly non-party institution, which could serve as a means of 'reconciling an instrument of insurrection with an elective and openly functioning Soviet upon whose benches, moreover, sat representatives of the hostile parties' (*ibid*, p.943). What was required, specifically, was an 'authoritative Soviet committee to lead the coming insurrection' (*ibid*) which had access to armed force, and would do the bidding of the Bolsheviks. Such was the 'Military Revolutionary Committee' (MRC) of the Petrograd Soviet which, under Trotsky's direction, served as the 'chief lever of the revolution' (*ibid*). But just how much was the MRC a creation of the masses, or an expression of their will? Let us first record the obvious and important, but often overlooked circumstance, that the MRC was the (belated) offspring of a local, and not national, soviet institution. Consequently, it is difficult to see how any action by the MRC taken in the name of the latter, especially one so momentous as staging an insurrection and assuming the functions (however briefly) of a new national government, could be considered anything other than a violation of that very 'soviet legality' Trotsky especially was so anxious to be seen respecting.

Then there is the matter of timing. Trotsky records that the MRC came into being, on a vote of the Petrograd Soviet, a mere 'five days before the insurrection' (*ibid*, p.961) – so late that even its very existence must surely have remained unknown to the vast majority of the masses on whose behalf it was ostensibly acting. That is why, aware of the precarious nature of the undertaking, the Bolshevik leadership took great care to 'camouflage' the new committee's purpose and party character. To this end, they chose not one of their own number but the Left Socialist Revolutionary, Lazimir, to serve as chairman of the MRC, while ensuring that effective power remained in their own hands (*ibid*, p.945).

Meanwhile, Lenin, still in hiding over the border in Finland, was becoming increasingly alarmed by what he regarded as the party's overly fastidious attitude towards Soviet legitimacy. Ironically, it was an attitude that Lenin had himself helped to encourage, earlier in the year, at a time when he had felt it necessary to restrain the more impatient of his followers from a premature bid for power. As if to warn against a policy he was soon to adopt himself, he reminded party radicals that 'only dreamers and plotters believed that a minority could impose their will on a majority' ('C.W.', Vol.41. p.433). He was, of course, wrong, and he must have known it at the time. After all, had not Engels remarked, in a letter to Vera Zasulich, that if ever such tactics 'had a certain *raison d'etre*' it was 'now in St. Petersburg' ('Selected Correspondence', p.460). Whatever Lenin chose to say for reasons of expediency, his campaign in the party for the November *coup* demonstrated that he was a more skillful exponent of the *coup d'etat* than Blanqui himself. Differences with the party Left over this issue were principally about timing. And, after the failure of General Kornilov's *putsch* on September 14, Lenin was convinced that the moment to act had come. His response was to make his feelings known in a series of letters to the party central committee (see 'C.W.', Vol.26).

Lenin fired his opening shot with a letter written between September 25 and 27 and suitably entitled 'The Bolsheviks Must Assume State Power'. Significantly, in the course of arguing for an insurrection it contradicted itself by claiming in its first section that 'the majority of the people are on our side' and in the last by dismissing as 'naive' the view that it was necessary to 'wait for a "formal" [that is, numerical] majority' ('C.W.', Vol.26, pp.19, 21). Is it necessary to point out that no majority won by Lenin (however transient or gerrymandered) as, for example, the one engineered at the second Congress from which his party took its name, was ever so described? What Lenin meant by a 'formal' majority became clearer in the unpublished (on the author's explicit instructions) section of an article written on September 29 which, entirely contrary to public Bolshevik assertions, insisted that the approaching Second Soviet Congress would 'give nothing' and could 'give nothing' (*ibid*, p.83). That was why it was essential to 'first defeat Kerensky, then call the Congress' (*ibid*).

Such was the unvarying substance of Lenin's strategy. One letter, written late in September, demanded that 'the Bolsheviks' (and not the soviets) 'must take state power into their own hands', 'at this very moment' (*ibid*, pp.19-20); while another, dated October 7, complained of 'notable vacillations' amongst the party leaders that could become 'ruinous' (*ibid*, p.58). Three days later he fumed that the party was 'only passing resolutions' and, consequently, was 'losing time' (*ibid*, p.69). So, instead of playing at what Trotsky described as 'soviet legality' (*op. cit.*, p.944), what should the party have been doing? Lenin did not mince words. To '"wait" for the Congress of Soviets would be utter idiocy' (*op. cit.*, p.83). The Bolsheviks should be 'conducting regular work to prepare their own military forces for the overthrow of Kerensky' (*ibid*, p.69) with the aim of 'an immediate insurrection' (*ibid*, p.82), otherwise the Bolsheviks would be the 'owners of beautiful resolutions and Soviets, but no power' (*ibid*, pp.69-70. No one would dispute the right of the Bolsheviks to own their own resolutions; but surely the Soviets were 'owned' by their creators, the workers?). Neither should the Bolsheviks fear seizing power purely for themselves. In a lengthy essay entitled, significantly, 'Can The Bolsheviks [not the Soviets] Retain State Power?', written in the first two weeks October, Lenin insisted that the 'question of the Bolsheviks taking full state power alone is not only feasible, but urgent' (*ibid*, p.94).

That he had a near-naked putsch by the party in mind is evident from his warning that it was impossible to '"wait" for the Congress of Soviets or for the Constituent Assembly' (*ibid*, p.136). And, in a letter to the Bolshevik Central Committee, dated October 14, Lenin again insisted that the party had 'no right to wait for the Congress of Soviets', it had to 'take power at once'. Delay would be 'criminal' and to 'wait for the Congress of Soviets' was a 'childish game' (*ibid*, pp.140-141).

For once, Lenin's urgings fell on deaf ears. It was one thing to demand a naked party *putsch* from the relative safety of *de facto* independent Finland, but another entirely to actually carry it out in the Russian capital. Convinced that a conspiracy was afoot to prevent his views from receiving a proper hearing in the party, Lenin announced his resignation from the central committee, no doubt hoping that such a drastic move might induce other party leaders to adopt his plan (*ibid*, p.84). As nobody, it seems, took the threat very seriously, the war of words went on. The central committee's 'procrastination' was 'becoming positively criminal' (*ibid*, p.140). Lenin even put in question the very idea of using the soviets as a 'screen' for a Bolshevik take-over. 'To insist on connecting this task [the proposed insurrection] with the [second] congress of soviets, to subordinate it to this congress, means to be merely playing at insurrection' (*ibid*, p.143). Therefore, 'we must not wait for the all-Russia Congress of Soviets' but forestall it by staging the insurrection (*ibid*, p.185). This letter, to party activists of the northern region, was written by Lenin on October 21. (It was typical of Lenin's general style of *Realpolitik* that while he argued inside the central committee for a purely Bolshevik *coup*, in the party press he should demand that 'all power in the country must pass exclusively to the representatives of the Soviets of Workers', Soldiers' and Peasants' Deputies' and a 'government... fully responsible to the Soviets', *ibid*, p.61.)

What Lenin did not (and, removed from the scene, perhaps could not) appreciate was that Trotsky had been pursuing the same goal as himself, the seizure of power by and for their party, but by more indirect tactics. But as the moment of decision approached, the gap narrowed. Even early on, Lenin recognised the need to 'prepare people's minds' (*sic!*) with the slogan 'transfer power now to the Petrograd Soviet which will transfer it to the Congress of Soviets' (*ibid*, p.72) while Trotsky understood that the Congress of Soviets could not be entrusted with the task of removing Kerensky, but only one of rubber-stamping the *fait accompli* of his overthrow by a Bolshevik *coup*. (Perhaps correctly, Trotsky attributed Lenin's relentless advocacy of an open seizure of power by the party as much to his refusal to 'bow down to a "sacred" spontaneousness of the masses' as to his isolation from events, *op. cit.*, p.1022.)

In order to press his case more effectively, Lenin returned to Petrograd on October 23, securing the passing of his resolution, against the objections of Zinoviev and Kamenev, directing the party towards an 'armed uprising', the conditions for which had become 'fully ripe' ('C.W.', p.190). Six days later, at another session of the Central Committe, Lenin continued his offensive against the doubters, principally Zinoviev and Kamenev. Now was not the time for hesitations. 'The party could not be guided by the temper of the masses', as the outcome would not be resolved by votes or majorities, but which side possessed the superior forces. So 'why could not the Central Committee begin?' (*ibid*, pp.191-192). On the very eve of the uprising, Lenin wrote his final letter to the central committee, warning its members against the illusion that the issue could be resolved by 'conferences or congresses'. It demanded 'the struggle of armed people' (*ibid*, p.234).

But still the same question remained unanswered. Which armed people? Who would arm them? In whose name would they fight? To Lenin (though not to Trotsky) these were secondary matters. To the rhetorical question 'who must take power?' he answered: 'That is not important at present. Let the Revolutionary Military Committee [i.e., the MRC] do it, or "some other institution" [!] which will declare that it will relinquish power only to the true representatives of the people.'As if to placate doubters, Lenin explained that in assuming power, the Party would be not be acting against the Soviets, but 'on their behalf'. (ibid, p.235) The 'seizure of power' was 'the business of the uprising', that is, of those who organised it, the Bolsheviks. As for its 'political purpose', that would 'become clear after the seizure' (*ibid*, pp.234-235). It certainly would!

Machiavelli once observed that anyone seeking to 'change the form of government' should 'retain at least the shadow of its ancient customs' ('Discourses', Vol.1, p.272). Knowingly or not, the Bolshevik leadership followed the Florentine's prescription to the letter, applying Trotsky's maxim that 'a revolutionary party is interested in legal coverings' (*op. cit.*, p.1124). Although, as we have seen, the party inner circles knew perfectly well they were seizing power, not for the soviets (or any other popular institution such as the Constituent Assembly, of which more in due course) but for themselves, every attempt was made to disguise, or as Trotsky puts it, 'camouflage' or 'screen' their intentions. Not the least consideration was the Bolsheviks' lack of a majority, as witnessed by the results of the voting to the Constituent Assembly which, since it took place in the last two weeks of November 1917, accurately reflected the balance of political opinion in the immediate aftermath of the Bolshevik *coup*. Always the realist, Trotsky frankly conceded that in so far as Bolshevik strategy was concerned, majority support was 'not understood in a formal sense.' Consequently, there was a 'limit to the application of democratic methods', and had a referendum been conducted on the question of the Bolshevik seizure of power, 'it would have given extremely contradictory and uncertain results' (*ibid*, p.1027). All the more important, then, to adopt Machiavelli's tactic, and to cloak the Bolshevik usurpation of the masses in the guise of empowering their 'ancient customs', the soviets.

In this regard, Trotsky identified three tendencies amongst the popular classes; the first, which supported the Bolsheviks 'on all conditions', the second, 'more numerous, which supported the Bolsheviks in so far as they acted through the soviets', and a third, 'which followed the soviets in spite of the fact that they were dominated by the Bolsheviks' (*ibid*, p.1127). It could not be better put. This balance of forces explained why all 'attempts to lead the insurrection directly through the party nowhere produced results' (*ibid*, p.1129). Exactly. Where they spurned the 'camouflage' of the 'ancient customs', the Bolsheviks invariably exposed themselves as usurpers, and were spurned accordingly. That is why Lenin's initial plan, to conduct the insurrection openly in the name of the party, was 'unthinkable', it would incur the risk of 'set[ting] itself over against the masses' (*ibid*, pp.1131-2). By following Trotsky's tactic, the party was able to 'remain on the ground of soviet legality' (*ibid*, p.1134). Once established, the new regime could then apply, in stages and by increasing degrees of severity, but always in the name of its spurious 'soviet legality', another aphorism of Machiavelli's, namely, 'he who sets out to govern the masses' yet 'does not secure himself against those who are hostile to the new order' would be 'setting up a form of government which will be but short lived' (*op. cit.*, p.254).

It therefore followed that, whatever the Bolshevik chiefs might say behind closed doors or in private letters, on the soviet rostrum and in public pronouncements they took care, especially at the beginning of their rule, to observe the proprieties of their hard won and still-precarious legitimacy. Thus Lenin, who in private had urged a naked party *coup*, on November 7 announced to the world the transfer of power 'into the hands of the organ of the Petrograd Soviet', the 'Revolutionary Military Committee' (*op. cit.*, p.236). Viewed formally (as Trotsky would say) this power was then, in turn, handed over to the Second Congress of Soviets to do with it what it would. Again, Lenin found the 'sovietically correct' formula for this progression. He moved a resolution to the effect that the congress should establish a 'provisional workers' and peasants' government'. But why only 'provisional'? Because, again in accordance with the still-pressing need to respect 'ancient customs', the mandate of the new soviet administration (comprised, incidentally, exclusively of Bolsheviks) was only to 'govern the country until the Constituent Assembly convened' (*ibid*, p.262). Consequently, any policy decisions taken at the Second Congress such as on the land question were, explained Lenin (the head of the new government) likewise provisional, awaiting a 'final decision... by the Constituent Assembly' (*ibid*, p.258). However insincere, this undertaking was given unconditionally, even if the peasants were to 'give this party [that is, the Socialist Revolutionaries] a majority in the Constituent Assembly' (*ibid*, p.261). When the peasants did just that, Lenin closed the assembly down, on the grounds that it had become 'an obstacle in the path of the October Revolution and Soviet power' (*ibid*, p.435).

Democracy Denied

The demand for the convening of a sovereign Constituent Assembly was not just one policy amongst many others. In giving it the prominence they did amongst their party's political slogans, the Bolsheviks were simply continuing a tradition as old as the Russian revolutionary movement itself. Known initially as the *Zemsky Sobor* after the popular assembly that brought to an end the 'Time of the Troubles' at the beginning of the 17th century, the demand for a constituent assembly featured prominently in the programmes of all the radical oppositions to the autocracy from the Decembrists, through the Populists, to the Marxists. And (ironically, in view of his role in its dispersal in January 1918) it was none other than Lenin who drafted the concluding paragraph of the RSDLP programme, adopted at the Second Congress of 1903, which declared that 'complete, consistent and lasting realisation of the political and social changes mentioned' in the programme, were 'attainable only through the overthrow of the autocracy and convocation of a constituent assembly, freely elected by the entire people' ('Second Congress of the RSDLP', p.9, and V. Lenin, 'C.W.', Vol.6, p.33).

And so it it proved to be in the revolutionary year of 1905. From the St. Petersburg workers who marched behind Father Gapon in January and elected the first Soviet in November, to the land-hungry peasants of the villages and the rebellious sailors of the Battleship Potemkin, all movements, parties and classes in revolt against the autocracy did indeed inscribe this demand on their banners, and in each instance, explicitly so (see R. Postgate, 'Revolution 1789-1906', pp.363-383). Despite their varied character, origins and tendency, each found a common language in the demand for an elected assembly that, for the first time in its history, would give Russia individual liberty and a democratic constitution, the means by which its peoples could become the masters of their own destinies. And so it was again in the year 1917 when democracy and liberty were the two goals which united all but a tiny minority of the peoples of the Russian empire.

Little wonder, then, that in the years which followed the split at the Second Congress, the Bolsheviks campaigned for the Constituent Assembly just as vigorously as the Mensheviks, right up to the eve of the Bolshevik seizure of power on November 7-8, 1917. Only after this date did the contours of a new policy towards the Constituent Assembly become visible to the general political public. And even then, not all at once. If we examine the unfolding of this policy we see at work that same Jesuitical, or Machiavellian, method of action which, as we have already observed, characterised his response to issues such as the freedom of the press and the death penalty. Immediately on his return from exile in April 1917, Lenin set the tone for his party's public policy on this issue when he declared to a Bolshevik meeting that he would be 'glad to have the Constituent Assembly convened tomorrow' (ibid, Vol.36, p.440). But then, in a private note, penned in the middle of May 1917, and only published in 1925 (after his death), Lenin revealed his real attitude towards the demand for a Constituent Assembly. It was 'already out of date' (ibid, p.447).

Yet, publicly, the Bolshevik campaign for its convention continued with undiminished vigour. It was presented as the crowning political objective of the entire revolutionary process then underway. Right up to the Bolshevik coup, and even for a while beyond it, the party press faithfully reflected this position. Invariably, the Bolsheviks presented themselves as the most zealous advocates of the Constituent Assembly, and the Provisional Government as its most implacable opponent. Very much in this vein, on August 30 the 'bourgeoisie' was (justly) accused of seeking the 'total sabotage of the Constituent Assembly' and, what was more, 'its replacement by a body in which it can be assured of a majority' (A. Bone [trans.], 'The Bolsheviks and the October Revolution: Central Committee Minutes of the RSDLP, Aug. 1917-Feb.1918', p.14). This was, of course, an ironic 'anticipation' of the Bolsheviks' own response, six months later, to an Assembly in which, like the 'bourgeoisie', they found themselves in a hopeless minority. But that still lay in the future. Meantime, the non-convening of the promised Assembly was a wonderful stick with which to beat the Provisional Government, and an invaluable opportunity to present the Bolsheviks as the advanced guard of a threatened democracy. Very much in this vein, on September 3, the party again accused the 'counter-revolution' of 'skilfully working to get the convocation of the Constituent Assembly put off again and again' (ibid, p.33), and on September 14, demanded its 'immediate convocation' (ibid, p.43). Nor was there any question, despite the party's slogan of 'all power to the soviets', of these institutions usurping the assembly's proper functions, once elected. For example, the land, urged the party, should be 'put under the control of peasants' committees until a decision by the Constituent Assembly' (ibid, p.55).

Just how much respect Lenin harboured for any future decisions of the Assembly was revealed in his remark, at a meeting of the central committee on October 23, that it was 'senseless to wait for the Constituent Assembly', since it would 'obviously not be on our side' (C.W., Vol.26, p.189). Obviously! And he was, of course, right. So while the party chiefs prepared behind closed doors a coup that if successful, doomed the Constituent Assembly to instant extinction, in public the Bolshevik campaign in its support continued with undiminished vigour. On October 20, the party issued the slogan 'on with the Constituent Assembly' (A. Bone, op. cit., p.81), while on the very eve of the coup, Lenin denounced the 'incredible hypocrisy' of those who accused the Bolsheviks of '"frustrating" the Constituent Assembly by transferring power to the Soviets' (op. cit., p.233). The very idea!

Once in power, Lenin prepared to do just that, his public declarations to the contrary merely serving as one more 'camouflage' for one more act of usurpation. His intentions towards the Constituent Assembly were, nevertheless, by this time not hard to divine, as it became clearer that the Bolshevik coup had carried the day not only in Petrograd, but had been emulated in Moscow elsewhere. In fact Trotsky had already captured the spirit of the new policy succinctly with his triumphant declaration to the Second Soviet Congress that its will had been 'anticipated by the tremendous fact of the insurrection', a rising that 'needs no justification' (N Sukhanov, 'The Russian Revolution 1917', pp.630, 639). Neither, it seems, did the formation of an all-Bolshevik government, approved by Lenin and his central committee before being presented to and rubber stamped by the same Congress of Soviets, and composed largely of party professionals who, up to that time, had held no official positions in the Soviet machinery at any level. Again, Trotsky aptly summed up Lenin's policy when he recalled that the 'Central Committee adopted the motion of Lenin as the only thinkable one: to form a government of Bolsheviks only' (L.Trotsky, op. cit., p.1167). To those Central Committee Bolsheviks who, like Zinoviev and Kamenev, favoured a coalition with the other Soviet parties, Lenin replied that 'if you want a split, go ahead'. But he would 'go to the sailors' – presumably to stage another *putsch*, only this time against the Soviets (cited in: L. Trotsky, 'The Stalin School of Falsification', p.111. Ironically, these sailors were in many cases the very men who, after rejecting Bolshevik rule in the so-called Kronstadt 'mutiny' of March 1921, would be ruthlessly crushed as 'counter-revolutionaries'on the orders of Lenin.)

As for socialists and trade unionists who resisted (even if only verbally) Bolshevik single party rule, Lenin's remedy was to 'arrest them all' (*ibid*, p.117). His refusal at this time to share power with any other soviet parties except on his own terms even provoked criticism and open opposition in the upper reaches of his party, most notably from Zinoviev and Kamenev (both opponents of the *coup*) and several resignations from the just-formed all-Bolshevik government. The collective statement of resignation issued by, amongst others, two Bolshevik plebians, Commissars for the Interior Rykov (a former peasant) and for Labour Shliapnikov (once, unlike so many of his central committeee comrades, a factory worker) warned, with rare foresight, that single party rule by the Bolsheviks could only be sustained by 'means of political terror', leading to 'the destruction of the revolution and the country' (A. Bone, op. cit., p.142. In their two cases, as in so many others, it would also lead to their own.) Another independent spirit, Lunacharsky, with a keen sense of foreboding predicted that Lenin's policy of exclusions (or as Trotsky would have once put it, 'substitutions') would continue until in the end, 'only one man remains – a dictator' (cited in L. Trotsky: 'The Stalin School of Falsification', p.114). Even the usually pro-Bolshevik writer Maxim Gorky joined the opposition, protesting that Lenin had been 'poisoned by the slimy venom of power'. But, warned Gorky, it would not be the Bolsheviks who would 'pay for these crimes, but the proletariat itself' (cited in: H. Troyat, 'Gorky', pp.234-235).

Although beset by rebels within his own ranks, Lenin never flinched from a resolution of the challenge to his regime posed by the inevitable election of an anti-Bolshevik majority to the Constituent Assembly. The manner in which the deed was done suggests that the demand for the assembly's convention, like all other democratic planks of the Bolshevik programme, was intended, at least by Lenin, to serve as a Sorelian 'myth' for the purposes of mobilising mass support for quite different objectives than those understood by the masses to whom it was addressed. With the passing of time, the dominant thrust of Bolshevik policy revealed itself as modernising to be sure (like Peter) and in many respects, dynamic, but in ways akin to the 'developmental' tendencies within Italian Fascism and some more recent Third World dictatorships that, like Bolshevism, left no space for the development independent workers' movement or democracy and individual liberty.

Whatever objections Leninists might have to this judgment, Sorel's enthusiasm for Bolshevism is beyond dispute. Engaged as always in his quest for an energising *élite* to supplant 'decadent' and spent liberalism, and still fresh from his infatuation with the proto-fascist anti-semites of *Action Française*, Sorel was totally captivated by Lenin's sense of national mission no less than by his audacity and ruthlessness. So much so, in fact, that in one of his last writings, the (however unwitting) inspirator of fascist 'national syndicalism' lauded Lenin for his 'stupendous effort of intelligence' in accomplishing what traditional Marxism had held to be impossible, namely, the 'forcing of history' after the manner of Peter the Great, for being prepared to to defend the revolution and its regime by 'combatting the instincts which always impel humanity toward the lowest spheres of life' (G. Sorel: 'In Praise of Lenin' in: 'Reflections on Violence', pp.280-281). And was not the Sorelian Mussolini moved by a similar sentiment when, shortly before his 'March on Rome' (staged, supposedly, to save Italy from Bolshevism), he confided to a 'Daily Herald' reporter that of all contemporary politicians, Lenin alone was worthy of his respect? (I. Kirkpatrick: 'Mussolini, a Study in Power', p.120)

Then we have the no less revealing judgment of the young and still essentially 'national Bolshevik' Joseph Goebbels (like Lenin, and the younger Stalin, known to his party associates as 'Robespierre') that Lenin had 'sacrificed Marx and instead given Russia freedom' (R. Reuth: 'Goebbels', pp.64,66). Finally, there was Shaw. Uninhibited by the conventional politician's view of ideology as a spectrum running from left to right, and already the advocate of rule by genetically selected supermen infused with a Nietzschean 'life force', he quickly grasped and embraced the common denominators of all totalitarian movements and doctrines, beginning with Bolshevism. In return, Lenin paid Shaw the compliment of describing him as a 'good man fallen among Fabians'. In view of his subsequent political evolution, it would be more apt to characterise him as a frustrated enlightened despot seduced by, succesively, Bolshevism, fascism and national socialism. For Shaw's adulation of the 'strong man' did not stop at Lenin or even Mussolini. Had not Hitler no less emphatically than Lenin (and Stalin) pronounced the 'receptivity of the broad masses' to be 'very limited' and (again like Lenin) insisted that 'the strength of a party' lay in the ' disciplined obedience with which its members follow the intellectual leadership'. Was this not an arrangement which followed naturally from the conviction, shared by Shaw, that 'the majority of mankind' was 'lazy and cowardly'? How could Shaw (or, in view of the issue over which Lenin and Martov fell out in 1903, any sound Bolshevik for that matter) dispute Hitler's insistance that party membership should be limited 'only to the minority of men', since only 'a small fraction of mankind is by nature energetic and bold' (A. Hitler: 'Mein Kampf', pp.90,457,581). Should we then wonder that Shaw proclaimed Hitler's rambling and racist opus as containing 'a good deal of sound doctrine' (M. Holroyd: 'Bernard Shaw', Vol.3, p.324) After all, had he not already found and praised similar qualities in the thought and actions of Lenin?

Like so many of his ilk, Shaw had concluded by the early nineteen twenties at the latest that salvation would not come through democracy, but from men, like Lenin, with 'iron nerve and fanatical conviction' prepared to carry out the 'necessary shooting' of political opponents (*ibid*, p.224). Mussolini had been right to describe liberty as a 'stinking corpse' and Hitler no less justified in calling British democracy 'Anglo-Semitic plutocracy'. As for Magna Carta, the Petition of Right and the American Constitution, they were 'mere scraps of paper' ('Everybody's Political What's What', p.351). In the light of these and other observations by Shaw on the evils of liberty and democracy, it was only to be expected that the Austrian Socialist leader Victor Adler failed to enlist his support for the victims of fascist repression in Italy. Shaw pronounced 'the campaign of abuse against the Mussolini dictatorship' to be 'just as stupid as the campaign against the Soviet dictatorship in Russia' ('Letters', Vol.4,p.74).

In dispering the Constituent Assembly by armed forced, and then having shot dead on the streets of Petrograd those who protested against the action, Lenin undeniably had established his anti-democratic credentials no less than Mussolini and Hitler after him, and in so doing, furnished proof that in the art of deception, he had acted according to Machiavelli's advice; namely, that a sucessful politician must learn to be a 'great pretender and dissembler' and that 'a wise lord cannot, nor ought he to, keep faith when such observations [such as Lenin's on the Constituent Assembly and press freedom] may be turned against him and when the reasons that caused him to pledge it exist no longer' ('The Prince' p,98).

The other issue which focused internal opposition to Lenin's manipulative and dictatorial policies was that of press freedom. Were there any previous indications that Lenin would so rapidly renege on his many public pledges to honour this most essential of all liberties? Back in 1905, in the heady days that followed the partial (and, as it proved, temporary) capitulation of the autocracy to the demands of the Russian peoples for political freedom and democratic self-government, Lenin sought to stem what he regarded as the resulting dangerous drift towards 'bourgeois literary careerism and individualism' by defining and advocating the adoption of what became known in the Stalin era and beyond as the 'party spirit' in literature ('Party Organisation and Party Literature', 'C.W.', Vol.10, pp.44-49).

To counter the trend towards 'artistic anarchism' (that is, authors writing as they pleased) the party had to ensure that its writers produced literature which could serve as '"a cog and a screw" of one single Social-Democratic mechanism' (ibid, p.45. The reader will no doubt by now find the technocratic imagery familiar.) While conceding (one suspects reluctantly) that by its nature, literature was 'least of all subject to mechanical adjustment' and that 'greater scope must be allowed for personal initiative' than in other areas, Lenin nevertheless demanded that here too, the party must ultimately have its way. 'Publishing and distributing centres, bookshops and reading-room and libraries and similar establishments' were to be 'all under party control'. It was essential to 'keep an eye on all this work', to 'supervise it in its entirety', from 'beginning to end' (ibid, p.46).

Anticipating misunderstandings (if such indeed they were) Lenin made it clear that such a literary regime would be imposed only on party writers. If they found it too restrictive, they could either leave the party, or be expelled by it (ibid, p.47). But by joining the ranks of the 'bourgeois individualists', such writers would discover that the 'freedom of the bourgeois writer, artist or actress' was 'simply masked (or hypocritically masked) dependence on the money bag, on corruption, on prostitution' (ibid, p.48). Far better to spurn this illusory freedom and serve the cause of the party and the revolution. Hence Lenin's battle cry, 'all Social-Democratic literature must become Party literature' (ibid, p.49).

The idea was not new. In the final weeks of Jacobin rule when, chiefly at the instigation of Robespierre and Saint-Just, its conceptions and methods drew ever closer to those of modern totalitarianism, the Committee of Public Safety enjoined poets and writers to 'compose hymns and poems and republican dramas' and to 'inject republican morality into works intended for public instruction' (L. Gershov, 'The Era of the French Revolution', p.161). Only the overthrow of the Robespierrist faction on July 27, 1794 (the ninth of Thermidor by the later discarded revolutionary calendar) frustrated the emergence of a 'Jacobin realist' school of artistic regimentation anticipating its Bolshevik analogue, Stalin's 'socialist realism'.

But to what extent can it be said that Lenin's insistence on 'party literature' paved the way for a cultural army of what the one-time devotee of Trotsky's, Max Eastman, described as 'artists in uniform'? Now, it is perfectly true that in 1905, Lenin's dicta, insofar as they were accepted by his party comrades, were binding on them only, and if they chose to defy them as, for example, Maxim Gorky frequently did, there was little Lenin could have done about it. As for non-Bolshevik RSDLP members in particular and, in so far as they were aware of them, the population of Russia in general, Lenin's views on the functions of 'party literature' must have seemed either absurd or irrelevant. After all, 1905 was the year when an autocracy at bay had granted freedom of the press in the October Manifesto of Nicholas II. Lenin's bid to impose his own version of the pre-October system of political correctness on his fellow Bolsheviks was surely counter to the spirit of the times, and therefore doomed to fail. Yet such a judgment could not have been more mistaken.

Suppose, as twelve years later it proved to be the case, that Lenin's principles of 'party literature' no longer remained the self-imposed and therefore easily discarded straitjacket of a small band of persecuted zealots, but the policy of a party that now not only ruled the state, but used its newly won power to silence dissenters? Of course, it could be argued that censorship in post-Tsarist Russia did not begin with the Bolsheviks. Had not Kerensky's Provisional Government, in the wake of the July Days, acted contrary to their initial pledges to respect press freedom by imposing (largely ineffective) curbs on the Bolshevik press? That is true, and its condemnation is deserved, even though, in the case of the apologists for Bolshevism, tinged with hypocrisy. But, as its founders were often fond of boasting, the Bolsheviks were no ordinary party. Half measures, such as those adopted by Kerensky against their press, were utterly alien to their philosophy. And on coming to power, Lenin's objectives and methods required that, as in other aspects of human activity, so in the realm of ideas, he found himself obliged to bring within his party's grasp the technical and administrative means for producing, censoring and distributing the printed word. What had hitherto been regarded and treated as 'party literature' became, by degrees, state approved literature, beginning with Lenin's censorship decree of November 9, 1917, and culminating, logically and inevitably, in the total thought regulation of the Stalin era. And could it, one wonders, have been by pure chance, or only out economic considerations, that of all Russia's industries in the early years of Bolshevik rule, that of printing should have been alone in being totally state owned, compared to an average for the entire economy (in 1920) of only 65.7%? (S. Malle: 'The Economic Organization of War Communism', p.62).

Just how far Lenin had travelled from his passionate and, quite possibly, totally sincere pre-October commitments to press freedom was nowhere better illustrated than in his clash with a much-respected old Bolshevik proletarian, G. Myasnikov. Taking Lenin at his word, Myasnikov had, at the close of the civil war, published (bravely) a pamphlet in his own name demanding the implementation of his party's pledge, dating back to the Second Congress of 1903, to uphold 'unlimited freedom of speech'. This would, insisted Myasnikov, involve extending press freedom to all political tendencies 'from the monarchists to the anarchists' (cited in Lenin, 'C.W.', Vol.32, p.504). Far from evincing any shame over his policy *volte face*, Lenin's response was to 'deconstruct' his policy of yesteryear and accuse Myasnikov of 'facilitating the enemy's task' by demanding an end to Bolshevik press monopoly. Instead of exposing the failings of the Bolshevik regime, as Myasnikov rightly claimed, Lenin argued that press freedom would simply 'help the force of the world bourgeoisie' (*ibid*, p.505). Diagnosing his mental condition as one of 'panic', Lenin advised Myasnikov (already under investigation by a Party Commission that, with Lenin's encouragement, would shortly culminate in his expulsion for advocating his own party's policy) to abandon his 'anti-proletarian slogan' of press freedom ('a drug that will cause certain death') and 'get down to practical work' (*ibid*, pp.506-509).

And, from his own standpoint, Lenin was right. Allowing freedom of the press in the Russia of 1921 would indeed have been the beginning of death for the Bolshevik regime. In accordance with the objective, defined in 'What is to be Done?', of introducing political correctness 'from without', he sought the establishment of a press regime that would, in the words of one of his more recent disciples in this domain, 'in socialist society develop and bring to perfection the consciousness of its members in the desired direction' (cited in 'Survey', March 1988, p.176).

Understandably then, Lenin accused Myasnikov of planning to found 'a new party' (*ibid*, p.509).

Like Jacques in 'As You Like It' (Act II, Scene vii), his critic was in effect saying:
I must have liberty
Withal, as large a charter as the wind,
To blow on whom I please;
... give me leave
To speak my mind, and I will through and through
Cleanse the foul body of the infected world...[ie]

No wonder that Krupskaya's library purgers, repudiating the entire tradition of the Enlightenment, deemed Shakespeare's works unsuited to the 'mass reader'. And, in the same tradition, surely there can be found no better riposte to the literary *élitism* of the Bolsehvik censors than the republican revolutionary John Milton's 'Areopagitica', with its passionate plea for a press freedom that would allow the 'liberty to know, to utter and to argue freely according to conscience' and its scorn for the Lenins of Milton's day who, out of paternalistic concern for the 'common people', 'dare not trust them with an English pamphlet'.

Some will find these judgments rather harsh. True, they might concede, Lenin had no regard for the traditional correctives of bad government, such as equality before and the rule of law, the separation of powers, the right of dissent and opposition, free trade unions and a free press, and the open competition of rival poltical parties. But they can point to the fact that as a protection against abuses of power under a regime necessarily, if we are to believe its creator, 'unrestricted by any laws' ('C.W.', Vol.28, p.236 – a concept, incedentally, not unlike the 'decisionist' school of constitutional law in the Third Reich) Lenin established a commission for this very purpose, the 'Workers' and Peasant' Inspectorate'. But whom did he place at its head? Need one ask? Thus did Lenin attempt to answer the oldest question in politics – 'who will guard the guardians?'

And, for all his posthumous liberal reputation in such matters, while he held the reins of power, Trotsky was no less concerned than Lenin (and his wife) to extend censorship beyond the overtly political sphere into the world of literature. With this end in view, the Bolshevik cultural police should reserve for itself the right to lay 'its hand on any tendency in art which, no matter how great its achievement in form, threatens to disintegrate the revolutionary environment' (L. Trotsky, 'Literature and Revolution', p.220). The criteria of what could or could not be permitted were 'political, imperative and intolerant' (sic), exercised by a 'watchful revolutionary censorship' (ibid, p.221). In the purest Leninist Newspeak, Trotsky magnanimously promised writers 'complete freedom of self-determination' but only 'after putting before them the categorical standard of being for or against the Revolution' (ibid, p.14). In plainspeak, writers are free to write what we tell them.

It seems never to have entered Trotsky's head until much later that a policy which, in Jacobin fashion, made such mockery of the word freedom could only spell death to artistic creation (and, we should add, to the offending artists). For, as Trotsky frankly conceded, the only matter for debate was not whether, but 'at what point should interference begin, and what should be its limits' (ibid, p.221). One can easily imagine if not sympathise with his dismay and outrage when, following his fall from power, these limits were redefined, and Lenin's successors began to 'interfere' with and 'lay their hands' on Trotsky's own writings, this one included. And it could have been small consolation that the pretext for consigning his entire works to the memory hole were the very same grounds of revolutionary correctness that he had insisted be applied to only non-Bolshevik authors. Only then, and at that cautiously, and without even a hint of self-criticism of his own role in the outcome, did Trotsky attempt to re-define his attitude towards press and artistic freedom under the 'dictatorship of the proletariat'. Entirely contradicting his stance of earlier years, Trotsky insisted in 1933 that there was 'in principle no basis for limiting beforehand' freedom of the press or other liberties 'only to the labouring masses' and, therefore, presumably, to supporters of the revolutionary regime (L. Trotsky, 'Writings 1932-33', p.300). 'No basis'! What would Lenin (post-October) have said to that?

Trotsky's crucial role in the first stages of the transition to the fully developed thought control regime of the Stalin is all the more intriguing in the light of comments which he made on the question of press freedom in the last years of his final exile. Whereas in November 1917, he had argued forcefully, together with Lenin, that press censorship comprised an integral part of the 'maximum' Bolshevik programme, twenty years on (and with his own writings on the same index as the Mensheviks' publications he had earlier suppressed) Trotsky now found that 'banning bourgeois newspapers or censoring them does not in the least constitute a "programme" or a "principle", or an ideal set up' ('Writings, 1937-38, p.418). And as for the possibility that it might be necessary to ban rival socialist papers (as the Bolsheviks did after 1917) Trotsky did not even consider the idea worthy of consideration! Blanking out the years when he, together with Lenin, had imposed a regime of press controls far more effective, ambitious and all-encompassing than any deployed by their Tsarist persecutors, Trotsky heaped scorn on Stalin's 'detestable suppression of speech and of the press that it is now the rule in the Soviet Union' (ibid). Now the rule! – could there be a better example of Bolshevik doublethink?

Lenin's post October policy for the press was not long in revaling itself. Although the ostensible target of the Bolshevik censorship was initially the Cadet press, Menshevik publications were amongst its principal targets and victims. When the central Menshevik organ, the 'Worker's Gazette', was closed down on the orders of the Petrograd Military Revolutionary Committee (forerunner of the CHEKA) in the first days of Bolshevik rule, the Menshevik Central Committee issued a statement denouncing those responsible for having 'disgraced the socialist cause and shown their contempt for the working class' by enforcing a 'regime of arbitrary violence and terror' which made 'the very name of socialism, the salvation of all peoples, hateful to tens of millions of human beings' (A. Ascher (ed.), 'The Mensheviks in the Russian Revolution', p.107). Sadly for the cause of socialism (and, if its programme remains viable, for the human race as a whole) chiefly as a result of seven decades of countless more acts of Leninist duplicity and despotism, the number now has to be reckoned in hundreds of millions, if not billions.

But it should be placed on record that opposition to the Bolshevik censorship was not confined to its victims. Unable to overlook that press freedom had been demanded (without reservations or conditions) in their own party's programme, and perhaps remembering that the specific clause had been drafted by Lenin himself ('C.W.', Vol.6, p.30), not only Left SR but also Bolshevik delegates to the Central Executive Committee of the all-Russian Soviet protested against Lenin's censorship decree of November 9, 1917, which provided for the suppression of publications that 'call[ed] for open opposition or disobedience' to the new regime (Bunyan and Fisher, op. cit., p.220). Trotsky later explained the tactical considerations which led to the Bolsheviks finding themselves in what would have been, for more scrupulous politicians, the embarrassing predicament of opposing after their coup policies and principles which, up to that point, had featured prominently in the party's programme and agitation against the Provisional Government. The Bolshevik regime 'withdrew' what Trotsky described as 'democratic slogans' only when the Soviets 'captured power' and 'clashed, before the eyes of the masses, with the real institutions of democracy [that is to say, above all else, universal civil liberties and the Constituent Assembly]' ('Writings of Leon Trotsky 1929', p.208). In other words, democracy was the 'Sorelian myth' or bait employed both to mobilize the masses and to 'camouflage' the hook of Bolshevik despotism. And Trotsky said as much when he took the floor to defend Lenin's measures against the press, pointing out that whereas under previous regimes, the Bolsheviks had indeed demanded freedom of the press, not least for their own organ 'Pravda', it was because 'at that time we were in a position where we could demand only a minimum programme.' But now, Trotsky explained, the situation had changed. 'We ask [sic] for a maximum' Bunyan and Fisher, op. cit., pp.221-222). And that 'maximum' was, of course, a Bolshevik press monopoly, as subsequent developments rapidly confirmed.

Lenin was only too pleased to endorse the strictures of his recent convert to Bolshevik Jesuitism. 'Earlier on we said that if we took power, we intended to close down bourgeois papers [a term soon to be so broadly interpreted as to cover all but Bolshevik publications]. To tolerate the existence of these papers is to cease being a socialist' (C.W., Vol.26, p.285). Quite apart from Lenin's extraordinary definition of a socialist, his (and Trotsky's) claim that the Bolsheviks had been envisaged adopting this policy while publicly advocating its direct opposite surely confronts their apologists and epigones with a fundamental question: how much credibility should be accorded to any policy statements or pledges by any organisation subsribing to Leninist principles? Because nowhere in the entire published writings, letters and speeches of Lenin prior to November 8, 1917, can there be found even a hint of, or allusion to, the possibility that the Bolsheviks might, after assuming power, impose statutory limits on the freedom of the press. Indeed, fears amongst Bolsheviks as to the implications of crossing this particular rubicon were reflected in the voting on Lenin's measure. It was carried by only 34 votes to 24, with several prominent Bolsheviks voting against (Bunyan and Fisher, op. cit., p.222).

These and other related differences within the Bolshevik leadership greatly troubled Lenin and his supporters on the party central committee, and gave hope to the left Mensheviks that a coalition might still be achievable with the more moderate Bolsheviks such as Kamenev. But Lenin held firm. Then, finding themselves isolated from the party apparatus, and the rubicon, despite their doubts, having been crossed without serious mishap, the rebels came to heel. In the cases of Zinoviev and Kamenev, their surrender, against their better judgments, to the fait accompli of Lenin's coup marked the first of a series of capitulations which, under Stalin, would lead them on, step by step, to their final and tragic self-abasement at the first Moscow Trial of August 1936.

With internal party unity restored, Lenin could now move with more confidence against the Constituent Assembly. Correctly divining Lenin's intentions in this respect, the Mensheviks had already warned that the Bolsheviks were preparing to disperse the just elected body, with a view to 'prolong[ing] their dictatorship' (A. Ascher, op. cit., p.108). And indeed, when the subject first came up on the central committee agenda on December 12, Bukharin had recommended 'beat[ing] it bit by bit', a strategy which involved 'driving out' , if necessary, arresting, all the Bolsheviks' opponents, and then having the rump proclaim itself (presumably after the manner of the Jacobin purge of the Girondins in June 1793) a 'revolutionary convention' (ibid, p.154). Interestingly, in view of the use his party had made of the issue of the Constituent Assembly it the campaign against Kerensky, Bukharin let slip the comment that before the party took any action, 'an explanation [was] needed for the masses', not least because the party had been 'working and trumpeting about getting the Constituent Assembly convened for one and a half months' (*ibid*, pp.155-156). Indeed it had. Predictably, Stalin favoured a more radical solution, which was simply to 'finish off' the Cadets (*ibid*, p.155). Who at that meeting could have imagined that the time would come when Stalin would be 'finishing off' not the party's opponents, but its most illustrious leaders? Yet it is hard to deny that once the struggle for a Bolshevik political monopoly was begun, it would set in motion processes and release forces that could only culminate, as Trotsky (and not he alone) had once predicted, in total power being concetrated in the hands of a single despot.

This shift of line was now reflected publicly, with Lenin warning, only two days later, that although there was no 'more perfect institution for determining the will of the people than the Constituent Assembly', this judgment did not apply in the prevailing situation of 'class war which has developed into civil war' (*op. cit.*, p.353. Of course, it can be persuasively argued that it was the Bolshevik's own *coup*, and their subsequent onslaught on democracy and civil liberties, that precipitated the ensuing civil war.).

The long-prepared and fateful blow to Russian democracy was delivered on January 18, 1918. Its possibility was, it will be remembered, debated as far back as 1903 at the Second Congress of the RSDLP. Now Lenin, with ample justification, took the opportunity to remind Plekhanov that on that occasion, as Lenin's ally, he had advocated the dispersal of parliament should its election not give the revolutionaries the desired majority (Lenin, 'C.W.', Vol.42, p.48). Having refused, in the words of Marx and Engels, by an 'immense majority' to endorse the Bolshevik *putsch* of November 8, the Constituent Assembly was dispersed by armed force in accordance with a decree drafted by Lenin personally, in his capacity as the Chairman of the Council of People's Commissars. The grounds given were that its non-Bolshevik delegates with the exception of a small group of Left S.R.s, whom the Bolsheviks had meanwhile enticed, briefly, into an uneasy coalition) were serving as a 'screen for the struggle of the counter-revolution to overthrow Soviet power' (*ibid*, p.436). The former public Bolshevik policy of the soviets serving as the stepping-stone to the election, convening and assumption of power by the Constituent Assembly, and involving the transfer of a mandate from a body, the Second Congress of Soviets, elected (indirectly and unequally) by certainly no more than ten million voters (and, for the reasons enumerated above, probably far less) to one elected directly and equally by over thirty-nine million, now yielded to another. The Constituent Assembly was, pronounced Lenin, a 'step backwards', and would 'cause the collapse of the October workers' and peasants' revolution' (*ibid*, p.435). Instead, it was to be forward, to rule by terror, by one party, one central committee, one faction, and, finally, one tyrant, just as Lenin's comrades from yesteryear had predicted. And, as on so many other occasions, Lenin had acted according to an axiom of Machiavelli's; namely, 'he who becomes master of a city accustomed to freedom and does not destroy it may expect to be destroyed by it' ('The Prince', p.26).

And yet, as in the case of press freedom, in the years before 1917, Lenin had in his published writings invariably adhered to the traditional Marxist position on the relationship between democracy and socialism. Even as late as 1916, the future architect of the one party state was still insisting that socialism was 'impossible without democracy' ('C.W.', Vol.23, p.74) and that 'victorious socialism must necessarily establish a full democracy' ('C.W.', Vol.22, p.43). Must... and necessarily!. Whether this perspective could be realised in Russia after 1917 would depend not only on objective circumstances, but also upon Lenin's capacity to radically re-cast the traditional Marxist concept of democray (as did the Jacobins, following Rousseau, with liberty) no less than upon the manner in which Bolshevism resolved the obvious contradiction between the rule of the 'immense majority' and the supremacy of a single vanguard party enjoying the at best qualified support of a minority.

Certainly, following Lenin's return from Swiss exile in April 1917, he gave few if any public hints that a new policy was in the making. Russia, he declared, was now, with the overthrow of the autocracy, the 'freest and most progressive country in the world' (*op. cit.*, Vol.36, p.437). And, as he later explained, until the seizure of power, the Bolsheviks 'had been for democracy'. But since democracy was in reality nothing but 'heartless oppression of the working people by the bourgeoisie,' a 'form of bourgeois state championed by all traitors to genuine socialism' (including, we should add, Marx and Engels themselves), it followed that after the revolution, the Bolsheviks were obliged to take a 'firm and resolute stand for the dictatorship of the proletariat' (*ibid*, Vol.26, p.473).

Scorning as it did, and as a matter of principle, any constitutional devices which took into account the need for the 'checks and balances' of the now superceded and despised liberal democracy, Bolshevik rule demanded not only the primacy of Soviet organs over the Constituent Assembly, but of Commissars over the Soviets and, naturally no less than finally, leading Party bodies over the Commissars. Twenty years after the creation of this system, Trotsky did indeed confirm, in response to a question on this very point, that it was not the Soviets, but 'the policies of the [Bolshevik Party] Central Committee or the Politburo' that would have 'controlled the action of the Commissars' ('The Case of Leon Trotsky', p.354). And yet Trotsky's description of the real distribution and organisation of power within the Bolshevik regime is totally at odds with the official legend of the time, not to speak of the already cited (by Trotsky) intentions of the delegates to the Second Congress of Soviets. According to a decree passed at that Congress (obviously with Bolshevik, and therefore Trotsky's, support), 'control over the People's Commissars and the right of [their] recall belong[ed] to the All-Russian Congress of Soviets of Workers', Soldiers' and Peasants' Deputies and its Central Executive Committee' (cited in Bunyan and Fisher, *op. cit.*, p.133). This constitutional arrangement was endorsed by the newly elected (and predominantly Bolshevik) Central Executive Committee of the All-Russian Soviet on November 30, 1917, in a resolution which declared the 'Soviet of People's Commissars' to be 'wholly responsible to the Central Executive Committee' (*ibid*, p.189). As for the powers of the Bolshevik Party and its Central Committee, they were not so much as mentioned, let alone defined, in either resolution! But despite this omission (or perhaps because of it) they proved infinitely more insidious and enduring.

It is hard to deny that Lenin's *élitist* principles of (party) organisation came to triumph, in a matter of months, over those of the Soviet, which initially operated in the spirit of the broadest democracy and free participation. Trotsky, as we have seen, certainly did not contest the point. And, what is more, the system of rule described by Trotsky conformed precisely to the principles of party organisation first enunciated by Lenin as far back as 1903-04; namely those of building 'from the top downward' ('C.W.', Vol.7, p.397), of 'bureaucracy versus democracy' and 'centralism versus autonomism' (*ibid*, p.396), of exercising the grip of an 'iron glove' (*ibid*, p.75). Interestingly, even at this early date, and for someone who (like almost the entirety of the Bolshevik leadership) had never performed a single day's paid manual labour in his entire life, let alone worked in a factory, Lenin took as his model for the party regime an 'immense factory headed by a director in the shape of the Central Committee' (*ibid*, p.391).

The idea proved, for some, highly attractive. Seventeen years later, on December 1, 1921, and with Fascism on the road to establishing its own version of the one-party state, Mussolini complimented the Communist deputies in the Italian parliament on the fact that like his own party, they 'consider[ed] necessary a centralised and unitary state which imposes iron discipline on all individuals' (G. Urban, *op. cit.*, p.153) and, at about the same time, expressed his admiration for Lenin's 'brutal energy' (R. Pipes: 'Russia Under the Bolshevik Regime, 1919-1924,p.252). But what else would we expect from Bolshevism's 'best pupil'? In earning the Duce's praises, Italy's Bolsheviks were simply acting on principles established by their Russian tutors. Had not Lenin, in his quest for the discipline of the factory, at the Tenth Party Congress that year successfully insisted that his party dispense with the 'impermissible luxury' of 'studying shades of opinion' and instead, after the manner of the Jacobins, 'pull together with a single will' ('C.W.', Vol.32, pp.176-178)? And to what extent, if any, did Lenin's 'top down', 'factory'conception of party discipline differ from Hermann Goering's definition of Nazi rule as one in which authority was 'exercised from above downwards and responsibility from below upwards' (cited in: M. Raeder, 'No Compromise', p.184)?

These congruities were readily acknowledged not only by Trotsky, who conceded that 'Mussolini stole from the Bolsheviks' and that 'Hitler imitated the Bolsheviks and Mussolini' ('Stalin', p.412) but by Bukharin. In a speech to the 12th (1923) Congress of the Bolshevik Party, he demonstrated how Italian fascism had 'adopted and applied in practice the experiences of the Russian revolution' and had carried out a 'complete application of

Bolshevik tactics' (R. Pipes, *op. cit.*, p.253). Surely this acknowledged -on both sides it should be noted – similarity of the two movements derived at least in part from their shared belief in the primacy of party leaders and institutions over all other spheres of society, including even those of the state, no matter what the official constitutional provisions asserted to the contrary.

For example, in answering (entirely warranted) charges that Russia was ruled by an 'oligarchy'. Lenin conceded that it was indeed the case that 'no important political or organisational question' was 'decided by any state institution in our republic without the direct guidance [*sic*] of the Party's Central Committee' ('C.W.', Vol.31, pp.47-48). In other words, just as Engels had predicted, the same political clique which had created the regime reserved to itself the exclusive right to rule it. As Trotsky put it, 'the party created the state apparatus and can rebuild it anew ... from the party you can get the state, but not the party from the state' ('Leon Trotsky Speaks', p.161). But surely the state apparatus had its origins in the Soviets, which were created by the masses, first in 1905, and again in 1917? Trotsky's assertion to the contrary indicated just how far the Bolshevik regime had succeeded in separating itself, in the space of a few years, not only in fact but also in doctrine from the classes and institutions in whose name it claimed to rule. And the Bolsheviks were not alone in claiming for their party (in defiance of the most elementary principles of Marxism) the capacity to create states. Adolf Hitler informed the Nazi faithful at the Nuremberg rally of 1934 that it was 'not the state that has created us; it is we that make a state for ourselves' (cited in: A. Kolnai, 'The War Against the West', p.159).

But this does not exhaust the list of constitutional difficulties confronted by the Bolsheviks after their seizure of power. What of their oft repeated claim to represent the peasants? It has already been noted that only 20 of the 1,115 delegates attending the June 1917 First All-Russian Congress of Peasant's Soviets were Bolsheviks, and that no recognised body of peasants met at the time of the Bolshevik *coup* of November 7-8. Russia's new rulers attempted to remedy this obvious deficiency in their mandate to govern a predominately peasant country by securing endorsement for their regime from a 'Special Congress of Peasant Soviets', which met in Petrograd from November 23 to December 8. Not the least problem for the Bolsheviks was that they had felt obliged, for obvious tactical reasons, to entrust the convening of this Congress to their temporary, but not wholly trusted or trusting allies, the Left Socialist Revolutionaries. Greatly reduced in representation when compared with the First Peasant Congress of the previous June (and this in itself was significant), its main party delegations were composed of 195 Left SRs, 65 of the Right, and only 37 Bolsheviks (*ibid*, p.210). This Congress, despite relentless pressure from the Bolsheviks (with Zinoviev, perhaps to compensate for his earlier vacillations, absurdly playing a leading part in an assembly of peasants) then gave its support, by 175 votes to 22, to a resolution calling for a coalition of all socialist parties 'from the [moderate] Socialist-Populists to the Bolsheviks inclusive', a policy that was, of course, anathema to Lenin and Trotsky (*ibid*, p.214).

In view of the lack of a genuine mandate for Bolshevik rule from any substantial section of the population, it was inevitable that within days of Lenin's *putsch*, there would begin a series of popular challenges to the new regime. Amongst the most humiliating must have been that of the workers of the giant Putilov factory in Petrograd who, under the guns of Bolshevik *élite* guards, voted by 10,000 votes to 2 for a resolution repudiating Bolshevik claims to represent the will of the working class (R. Abramovich, 'The Soviet Revolution', p.154). In fact, the counter-attack from amongst Russia's supposed new rulers was so vigorous and widespread that in the elections to the city soviets in the first six months of 1918 – some 19 in all – the Bolsheviks were defeated in every contest! Only the disbanding of these Soviets (often by terror) and the exclusion of anti-Bolshevik candidates at new 'elections' enabled the regime to sustain even the illusion of its slogan of 'all power to the Soviets' of the previous year (V. Brovkin, 'The Mensheviks After October', pp.126-160). Even in the hitherto Bolshevik stronghold of Petrograd, the by now customary gerrymandering devices had to be deployed to convert a minority of 127 Bolshevik factory delegates out of a total of 260 into an overall majority of 424 out of 677, chiefly by swamping the Soviet plenum with nominees from newly created Bolshevik-created or dominated bodies or organisations (S. Smith, 'Petrograd Workers and the First Phase of Soviet Power', Appendix II).

This re-alignment in the Soviets not only went some way to restoring the political balance between Menshevism and Bolshevism to what it had been a year previously. It also put in question yet another unproven, but broadly accepted assumption of Leninist orthodoxy that the 'immense majority' of the Russian working class became irrevocably 'Bolshevised' in the weeks that preceded Lenin's November *coup*. In truth, all the indicators show that during 1917, as distinct from a small committed core, the mass of the Russian workers (many being recently arrived in the cities and therefore new to the world of urban politics) constantly swung between and through the radical parties and their subfactions (Mensheviks, Bolsheviks, S.Rs, Anarchists and Syndicalists) without ever settling in one specific political location. And if one considers the comparative youthfulness of the Russian workers' movement, its lack of experience under the autocracy of open political activity, and the all-pervading turbulence of 1917, could it have been otherwise?

It said very little for the perspicacity of the Russian masses to argue that purely on the strength of radical slogans and promises, they were prepared to submit themselves once and for all, unconditionally, to the tutelage of any party, least of all one that in 1905 had been so unresponsive to their demands and modes of combat. The fact is that these oscillations amongst the popular classes were brought to an end, not by the proletariat's opting for Bolshevism in November 1917, but by the subsequent Bolshevik elimination of all political alternatives to its own rule. So much so, that by the summer of 1921 at the very latest, Russia had become (and, according to Trotsky, necessarily so – see Appendix One) in all but name, the first one-party totalitarian state in the history of the world, a prototype that others would soon imitate.

As we have already noted (Appendix Two) Engels once observed, astutely as it turned out, that usurping radical parties can only sustain their rule by 'feeding' their supporters 'with talk and promises, and with the asseveration that the interests of that class are their own interests' ('C.W.', Vol.10, p.470). But more than mere talk and promises were required to keep Lenin's regime in power. It also demanded, as we have seen, the deployment of naked terror. And this too Lenin had foreseen, reminding a more squeamish comrade, a full year before the Bolshevik *coup*, that his party was 'not at all opposed to political killing' (*op. cit.*, Vol.35, p.238). But perhaps it was Aristotle, pupil and then critic of Plato, who best understood the mechanics of early Bolshevik rule when he observed more than 2,000 years before the event, that 'conspirators sometimes beguile men at the very start to acquiesce in a change of constitution and then, despite opposition, hold on by force to the advantage they have won' ('Politics', p.142).

l] *Menshevism Vindicated*

From the birth of Bolshevism through its rise to eventual victory, the record shows that, standing clearly on the ground of 'classic' Marxism, and for the most part adhering to or sympathising with one or other of the tendencies within Menshevism, Lenin's first opponents had also proved the most perspicacious. As early as December 1903, Paul Axelrod, who knew Lenin better than most, had already detected in an as yet still infant Bolshevism a 'fetish of centralisation' that would lead to the party being staffed by a 'hierarchy of professional and semi-professional revolutionaries with the proper ranks of departmental head, clerk, sergeant-major, NCO, private, constable, foreman of whatever it may be' (A. Ascher, *op. cit.*, p.49-50). Inevitably, this barracks-like regime converted humbler party members into 'so many cog-wheels, nuts and bolts, all functioning as the centre decides' (*ibid*, p.50). By 1906, and with the example of the Bolsheviks' adventurist tactics during the 1905 revolution clearly in mind, Axelrod had arrived at the firm conclusion that Lenin's faction was a 'conspiratorial mixture of anarchist and Blanquist tendencies, dressed up in the terminology of Marxism or Social Democracy' (*ibid*, p.60). Soon he would go even further, denouncing (perhaps with the already notorious Stalin in mind) the 'Leninists' as a 'Black Hundred gang of double-dyed criminals within the Social Democratic party' (*ibid*, p.132) – a judgment which, however severe, proved in the light of later events to be closer to the truth than the descriptions Bolshevism has, over the decades, offered of itself.

And yet, for all its accuracy and foresight, the Menshevik critique of Bolshevism found little sympathy or echo beyond the borders of Russia, either before the revolution or afterwards. Before 1917, the general tendency amongst leaders of western socialism was to dismiss the dispute between the two factions as either a classic *émigré* quarrel between typically Russian fanatics or, if of more substance, concerned with issues of little or no import to more civilised countries than Russia. Much to the discredit of those involved, this myopic attitude prevailed even after the Bolshevik seizure of power. In vain did Axelrod and Martov attempt to secure a sympathetic, even neutral, hearing, for their measured and factually grounded, if unseasonal, indictment of Lenin's regime. They addressed an audience in the western socialist parties of the Second International, and more generally, amongst the radical intelligentsia, (for example Shaw) which either believed Bolshevism to be the wave of the future everywhere, or the ideal form of socialism for the supposedly more primitive peoples of Russia and the East. Undeterred, Axelrod took his mesmerised western comrades to task for having failed to 'analyse Bolshevism on the basis of actual facts, or to inform themselves and others from unimpeachable sources of the nature and consequences of the Bolshevik dictatorship' (*ibid*, p.128). Instead of listening to Axelrod, like so many radicals over the decades, they preferred either to believe Bolshevik accounts of their own activity, or reject out of hand hostile reports on the grounds that they emanated from tainted anti-socialist sources. Consequently, western socialists 'had no conception' that Bolshevism was 'nothing but a savage and pernicious throwback to Bakuninism, Nechayevism and Blanquism'(*ibid*).

Whatever the other failings of Menshevism – and they were many – its leading representatives did their very best to bring to the attention of western socialists the crimes perpetrated in the name of Marxism by the Bolshevik regime, while at the same time defending what they regarded as the positive achievements of 1917 against the counter-attacks of reaction. (See Martov in *ibid*, pp.125-127, where he advocates 'combating the revival of Utopian socialism, Jacobinical and anarcho-communist tendencies' 'in the name and spirit of revolutionary Marxism', with the object of leading the proletariat onward from Bolshevism towards true socialism.')

Ironically, the only one of the original critics of Leninism who lived to witness the culmination of the process they had predicted and which he, as far back as 1904, had analysed as substitutionism, was more than a little bashful in claiming any credit for such a remarkable wisdom before the event. Obviously concerned to dispel any suspicion of a lingering regard for his former Menshevik allies in the struggle against Leninism Trotsky, in his final years, went to absurd and and it must be said humiliating extremes in what proved in the event to be a futile attempt to establish his Bolshevik *bona fides*. Following his expulsion from the party at the end of 1927, and now guided by the maxim, 'with Stalin against Bukharin? Yes, with Bukharin against Stalin? Never!' (S. Cohen, *op. cit.*, p.269) Trotsky and his co-thinkers threw their weight behind Stalin's drive to crush the newly emerging 'Right Opposition' of Bukharin, Rykov and Tomsky. Their resistance to Stalin's onslaught against the peasants (which culminated in the enforced 'collectivisation' launched in December 1929) was denounced by Trotsky (here echoing Stalin) as a 'right danger' to the USSR. For good measure, Rykov, on account of his defiance of Stalin, was charged by Trotsky with having 'thrown down the gauntlet to the October Revolution' and of 'openly beginning to surrender the October Revolution to the enemy classes' ('Challenge of the Left Opposition 1928-29', pp.139, 173, 175). Stalin could not have put it better. And indeed, such proved to be the political substance of the indictment brought against Rykov, together with all the other victims of Stalin's 'show trials', a decade later.

Nor was this all. After Bukharin secretly visited the still disgraced Kamenev in July 1928 to seek an alliance against Stalin Trotsky, having acquired a report of the encounter, had the text published in his own opposition press in January 1929. Thus informed of the consipracy against him, Stalin raised the matter on the party Politburo as a means of further discrediting and isolating the Bukharin opposition. Learning of Stalin's strategem, Trotsky claimed triumphantly that his pamphlet 'had been published by the Central Committee' and had 'spoiled the game of combinations by Zinoviev and Bukharin' ('Writings of Leon Trotsky, 1929', p.67). Almost gleefully, Trotsky related how, as a result of his own complicity, 'the

Stalin faction decided to eliminate Bukharin' (*ibid*). In 1938, at the Third Moscow Trial, Stalin did exactly that, Trotsky following another two years later.

Stalin presented Trotsky with another opportunity to prove his loyalty when, in March 1931, he staged a 'show trial' of former Mensheviks turned 'specialists'. No less bogus than the charges brought against himself and other oppositionists at the trials of 1936-7-8, Trotsky nevertheless found the accusations of plotting 'armed insurrection' and 'armed intervention from without' to be 'irrefutably confirmed by the confessions of the members of the Menshevik centre' ('Writings of Leon Trotsky, 1930-31', pp.198-199). Just as were, according to Stalinist jurisprudence, the charges against the defendants in the Trotsky treason trials of 1936-38.

Incredibly, even as late as 1936, Trosky was was still insisting that, faced with a choice between the continued rule of Stalin (with all that that entailed) and the coming to power of the Mensheviks, he would 'obviously have to pick the Stalinists', since a Menshevik administration would serve as a 'stepladder' for the installation of a 'typically Russian fascism' ('Writings of Leon Trotsky, Supplement, 1934-40', p.672). Some would argue, far more persuasively, that Stalinism itself was a 'typically Russian fascism' and, moreover, that it was recognised as such by the fascists themselves. And, and as we have seen, to give him his due, Trotsky in his last writings likewise did indeed concede that Stalinism and fascism shared many similar features. But this recognition, radical though it was, never persuaded him to reconsider the totalitarian consequences of the Bolshevik seizure of power, or the legitimacy of the regime that issued out of it, even when under Stalin it entered the phase of unprecedented, all-pervading terror.

So as Lenin's 'marvellous Georgian' clambered to the summit of absolute personal power over a mountain of butchered fellow Bolsheviks and on the backs of an empire of enslaved workers, expropriated peasants and Russified national minorities, Trotsky felt obliged to undertake the daunting theoretical task of reconciling Stalin's Byzantine tyranny with the power of the Soviets. Repudiating the entire tradition of Marxism, not to speak of his own (pre-Bolshevik) writings on the subject, Trotsky now argued in the manner of the most doctrinaire 'substitutionist' that the 'rule of the proletariat' could be sustained not only through 'an open struggle of parties' or a 'monopoly of one party' but, after Marat, by 'a factual concentration of power in the hands of a single person' ('Writings of Leon Trotsky, 1937-38, p.61). In other words, a Bolshevik Robespierre – or a Bonaparte. To which Stalin could only say 'Amen'. But not Stalin alone. When Bukharin argued, in his 1920 work, 'The Economy of the Transition Period' , for the recognition of the necessity of a Bonapartist 'personal regime', Lenin commented: 'It is true...but the word is not to be used' (Cited in A. Ciliga, 'The Russian Enigma' p.287). So the reader is left asking:...if this indeed be Marxism, why did its founders insist that to emancipate themselves, the working classes had, in their 'immense majority', to win 'the battle of democracy'? How can Caesarism...call it proletarian if you will... be reconciled with the Communist Manifesto's definition of working class rule as 'the proletariat organised as the ruling class'?

For all his lip serive to Marxism, Lenin's political inspiration obviously derived from an altogether different source. Let us once again recall how the Jacobins, riding on the crest of a growing disenchantment with the Kerenskys of their day, the Girondins (though also, like the Bolsheviks, never enjoying majority support) by dint of superior organisation and skillful propaganda planned and carried through, at the beginning of June 1793, their classically prototypical radical *coup d'etat*, overthrowing the 'conciliationists' of the Convention. But what followed was no more 'all power to the sans culottes' than 'all power to the soviets' after the removal of Kerensky. Having arrested (and later executed) its moderate opponents on trumped up charges of treason, former lawyer Robespierre's Committee of Public Safety (numbering, ironically, former lawyer Lenin's 'dozen wise men') then rounded on the excluded and discontented groupings to its left, and the popular institutions on which they thrived and depended. On October 10, 1793, at the instigation of Saint-Just, the purged and cowed Convention suspended the newly adopted Constitution, with all its protection of civil liberties, for the duration of the Revolution, on the identical grounds to those advanced by Lenin for the suppression of the Constituent Assembly.

As in 1918, so in 1794, the popular mood became more mistrusting and even hostile, provoking yet more repression, the pretext as always being the threat of counter-revolution masked by popular radicalism. The Parisian sectional committees, clubs and societies suffered the same fate as the Soviets, trade unions and rival parties under Bolshevism, being either suppressed or purged and absorbed into the Jacobin machinery of rule under a batch of new emergency decrees emanating from the Committee of Public Safety. The intention, according to a Jacobin document of the time, was to 'maintain the unity of the Republic' (Rousseau again) by ensuring that 'there should be no new societies except those affiliated to the [Jacobin] Society of the Friends of Liberty [sic] and Equality' (A. Saboul, op. Cit.). So energetically did the Jacobins pursue this goal that in the period between March 21 and June 18 1794 alone, thirty-nine offending organisations were closed down, creating, in Paris at least, what amounted to a one-party police state.

Nor does the similarity with Bolshevik rule end there. Lenin, the reader will recall, sanctioned bounty hanging as a means of 'political cleansing' in conquered territory during the invasion of Poland in the summer of 1920 (see Chapter Eight). Here, too, there were Jacobin precedents. In a report submitted to the Convention dated June 12-13, 1793, two government agents proposed that overcoming popular resistance in western France demanded 'deporting the present generation to different parts of France and resettling it with new men' (cited in H. Mitchell, 'Resistance to the Revolution in Western France', 'Past and Present', May 1974). The time would come when, towards the end of the Second World War, Stalin would do precisely that, only now the victims of what should more properly be termed ethnic cleansing were entire nations accused of treason to the USSR.

Trotsky Testifies

The principal focus throughout this book is upon Lenin, and rightly so. But Trotsky's own role in the Bolshevik seizure of power, for decades written out of history by Stalinists, needs to be given its due. By virtue of his close involvement with the preparation of the November *coup*, in his capacities as both Chairman of the Petrograd Soviet and, after Lenin, the most commanding figure of the Bolshevik Central Committee, Trotsky's recollections of the period, scattered through several of his writings, have a special interest. Leaving aside their other aspects, they do indeed confirm a 'Nechayevist' dimension to Lenin's politics that is already suggested by his own writings, letters and speeches. Let us recall that it was this ally of Bakunin in the latter's campaign against the IWA who, of all pre-Bolshevik Russian radicals, most consistently and fanatically advocated, and then put into practice, the Jesuitical principle 'everything is moral that favours the triumph of the revolution' (cited in Marx and Engels, 'C.W.', Vol.23, p.545). Lenin unashamedly endorsed this axiom in a speech to Soviet youth leaders in October 1921, when he defined 'communist morality' as 'entirely subordinated to the interests of the proletariat's class struggle' ('C.W.', Vol.31, p.291). And, applying the principles of 'What Is To Be Done?', who would be best qualified to define those 'interests', and the morality that is to further them, if not the party and, above all, its leaders and, eventually, leader? Not to be outdone (and with his usual frankness) Trotsky even took upon himself a vigorous defence of Jesuit morality, claiming not only that it had been 'maliciously' slandered by its critics, but that 'the Bolsheviks appear in relation to the democrats and social-democrats of all hues as did the Jesuits in relation to the ecclesiastical hierarchy' ('Their Morals and Ours', pp.10-11). And, since commitment to the goal of the liberation of the oppressed is, from this standpoint, entirely compatible with total indifference as to the means which can be employed to achieve it, deceiving the masses can become a routine operation. And in fact Trotsky describes how such methods were adopted, chiefly at Lenin's instigation, in the course of the Bolshevik seizure of power.

A leading participant in the session of the Central Committee meeting of October 23 which voted to prepare the insurrection, he recalled how vehemently Lenin attacked the very idea of connecting the action in any way with the Congress of Soviets. 'The question of the Second Congress, he said, was of no interest to him; what meaning did the Congress have? ... We must seize the power, but not bind it to the Congress. ... It would be the best thing to let the 25th October [7 Nov.] be a masquerade, but the rising must be begun absolutely before and independent of the Congress. The Party [n.b.] must seize the power with armed hand and then we would discuss [*sic*] the Congress' ('Lenin', p.93). The Second Congress of Soviets (already partially rigged by the Bolsheviks) a 'masquerade'! So much for 'All Power to the Soviets', even Bolshevik Soviets! For Lenin was far from sanguine about the willingness of even Bolshevik delegates to sanction the planned *coup*. They were, he warned in a private letter to the Central Committee on the very eve of the insurrection, quite capable of 'wavering' ('C.W.', Vol.26, p.235). What Lenin evidently had in mind was not Soviet power at all, save in name, but power seized by and for his own party and, what is more, specifically its Central Committee. Trotsky, for one, never made any attempt to deny it. Three years after the Bolshevik *coup*, Trotsky recalled how on its eve Lenin had taken the party leadership to task for not 'attributing sufficient importance to the elements of military complot' and had gone so far in the direction of naked *putschism* as to advocate the 'surrounding of the Alexandrine Theatre where the Democratic Conference was in session and the proclamation of the dictatorship of the Central Committee of the party' ('Lessons of the Paris Commune' in 'Leon Trotsky on the Paris Commune', p.58).

In another account of the same dispute, Trotsky again related how, after a heated discussion (and against Trotsky's objections) Lenin still insisted that 'at all events ... the conquest of power must precede the Congress of Soviets' (*ibid*, p.95). Here Trotsky comments, revealingly, that it was at this (enlarged) October 23 meeting of the CC (attended by two dozen or so) that 'the fate of the revolution was decided' (*ibid*, p.96). A 'revolution' decided thus is surely better described as a *putsch*, whatever name its instigators might prefer to give it. And, as Engels once observed, a clique of leaders who conducted their business in such a manner before they seize power could hardly be expected to mend their ways once power had been won. Trotsky next describes how Lenin's attitude towards the problem of the Constituent Assembly was no less Jesuitical or Machiavellian than it had been towards the Second Congress of Soviets. He relates how 'a few days, if not a few hours' after the seizure of power, Lenin had insisted that the new regime 'postpone the elections' to the promised Assembly whilst steps were taken to ensure a more favourable outcome ('Lenin', p.119). Significantly, one such measure involved the outlawing of the Cadet Party (*ibid*). Already, evidently, the structure of the future one party state was taking shape in Lenin's mind. And when fellow party leaders justifiably objected that yet another postponement would this time rebound against the Bolsheviks, and not the deposed Kerensky, Lenin brushed these arguments aside, retorting that to permit the Assembly to meet at all would mean taking 'a step backwards', an 'open mistake' that 'may cost us dear' (*ibid*, p.120). So, when the scale of the Bolshevik set-back became obvious (just under 25% of the total vote), Lenin felt vindicated. He demanded that 'naturally we must break up the Constituent Assembly', its dispersal serving as a 'good lesson' as to the distinction between 'formal democracy' and 'revolutionary dictatorship' (*ibid*, pp.120-123). This it most certainly did.

Not that Trotsky was any the less cynical in his advocacy of the exploitation of the trust which the masses placed in their own Soviet institutions. Trotsky always insisted (correctly) that his differences with Lenin in the Autumn of 1917 revolved around purely tactical questions. He freely acknowledged that Lenin had been 'undeniably right in demanding that power be seized before the convening of the Congress of Soviets' while protesting a little too much that Lenin's plan to proclaim a dictatorship of the Bolshevik Central Committee had nothing in common with Blanquism ('The Challenge of the Left Opposition 1923-25', pp.283, 281). And, recalling his own role in the preparations for the Petrograd *coup*, Trotsky explained, some seven years after the event how, under his direction, 'we covered up the actual insurrection of the Petrograd garrison with the traditions and methods of dual power' (i.e., the device of exploiting 'ancient customs'). By 'formally adapting our agitation on the question of power to the opening of the Second Soviet Congress, we developed and deepened the already existing traditions of dual power and prepared the framework for the Bolshevik [n.b.] insurrection on an All-Russian scale' ('Lessons of October', in 'The Essential Trotsky', p.159). Very much in the same vein, Trotsky recounted how, by a variety of stratagems, the Bolshevik leadership succeeded in 'luring our enemies, the conciliationists, into the trap of Soviet legality' (*ibid*, p.159). What was more, 'our "trickery" proved 100 per cent successful ...

Our opponents ... were inclined to accept the Soviet cover at its face value. They yearned to be deceived, and we provided them with ample opportunity to gratify their desire' (*ibid*, p.160).

The unsuspecting or uninformed reader could be forgiven for believing that only the 'conciliationists', that is, a handful of Menshevik and S.R. leaders, were thus 'tricked' into granting the Bolsheviks power, while the masses, presumably not accepting the 'Soviet cover' at its 'face value', not only divined the real meaning of the entire enterprise, but also desired and then approved of its outcome, which was to place all power in the hands of the Bolshevik Central Committee. Yet although Trotsky accuses these same 'conciliationists' of attempting to use the mechanisms and influence of the Soviets to 'catch the revolution with the bait of Soviet legality' so as to 'drag it into the channel of bourgeois parliamentarianism', he frankly admits that the Bolsheviks were employing similar tactics to secure, by deception, power for their own party. For, as he explains, 'it is one thing to prepare an armed insurrection under the naked slogan of the seizure of power by the party, and quite another thing to prepare, and then carry out an insurrection under the slogan of defending the rights of the Congress of Soviets' (*ibid*, pp.160-161). That is indeed the case. But, even so, as Trotsky himself relates, the prime mover was still the Party (more accurately, its Central Committee) and not the Soviets, whose Congress was anyway being derided by Lenin as a 'masquerade'.

Finally, in his biography of Stalin, Trotsky avers without any qualification that it was the Bolshevik Central Committee which 'directly launched the insurrection' at its session of November 6, 1917 ('Stalin', p.233); that is, one day before the Second Congress was due to convene. Even though involving only a discrepancy of hours, the question of timing is all-important, for it bears directly upon the validity of Bolshevik claims to legitimacy. Since the Bolshevik *coup* was set in motion (by a secret meeting of the Party Central Committee) and in fact had accomplished its initial objective (the arrest of all the Provisional Government ministers in the Winter Palace) before the Second Congress was allowed to begin its proceedings, it follows that the Bolshevik *élite* were prepared to risk an insurrection even if its endorsement by the Congress was not forthcoming. Lenin, as we have seen, had considered just such a possibility. So had Trotsky. After the event, he recalled how the all-seeing Party leaders – Bakunin's 'general staff' – had, unlike the masses, entertained 'no naive hopes that the Congress itself could settle the question of power'. After all, 'such a fetishism of the Soviet form' was 'entirely alien to Bolshevism'. Indeed so. What the Soviet provided was a 'legal cover' for decisions and for actions taken elsewhere, a device enabling the Bolsheviks to ensure that their opponents were 'completely hooked with the bait of Soviet legality' (*ibid*, pp.161, 163). As the reader will observe, this tactic dovetailed neatly with Lenin's 'hidden agenda' discussed previously. But, in so far as the masses desired the rule of the Soviets and not the domination of a single (minority) party (and elsewhere Trotsky concedes that such was the case) they were hooked with the very same bait used to dupe the 'conciliationists'. For it surely follows that a conspiracy to seize power (and that is what Trotsky is describing) must, by its nature, be the work of a select few, in the tradition of Bakunin's 'secret pilots'; an operation which necessarily conceals its true objectives and even very existence from the masses it purports to be liberating no less than from the political rivals it seeks to outwit. And was it not this same consideration which led Marx and Engels to reject the *élitist* methods of utopianism, Jacobinist Blanquism and Bakuninism, in all their guises and manifestations, and to instead insist that the 'emancipation of the working classes', constituting the 'immense majority', 'must be conquered by the working classes themselves'? There was a period in Trotsky's political career when he thought so too. Assessing the significance of the revolution of 1905, at a time when, although no longer a Menshevik, he continued to share their hostility towards Leninist 'substitutionism', Trotsky not only lauded the Soviets as 'unconditional democratic institutions' but saw as their principal virtue their not being 'previously prepared conspiratorial organisations which have seized power over the proletarian mass in a time of unrest' ('Thirty Five Years After' in 'Leon Trotsky on the Paris Commune', p.25). As for the sins and shortcomings of Soviet 'formal democracy', not a word. That had to await Trotsky's belated (and possibly only partial) conversion to Bolshevism.

Trotsky's numerous and, for the most part, frank post facto justifications for the tactics adopted by the Bolsheviks in their struggle for power are all the more piquant when one recalls just how severe a critic he had been of Lenin's Jacobin principles and methods over the previous thirteen years. In his anti-substitutionist polemic, 'Our Political Tasks', of 1904, Trotsky tellingly demonstrates how Lenin's *élitist* and militarised system of party organisation was inspired by the same all-pervading paranoia that had motivated Robespierre's 'total distrust towards real [as distinct from ideal] men' in the period of the Terror (*ibid*, p.122). In counterposing itself to traditional Marxism, Leninism, like Jacobinism, found itself at war with the objective trends of society, and therefore with 'the fact that the development of bourgeois society leads the proletariat spontaneously to take shape politically' (*ibid*, p.123). Convinced that he was 'surrounded on all sides by intrigues and traps', 'Maximilien Lenin' found it necessary (and let us at once concede that it was for the best of motives) to 'theoretically terrorise' the party as the only means of ensuring their ideological orthodoxy (*ibid*, p.125). Where Trotsky erred in his early analysis of Bolshevism (and this he shared with Axelrod, but not Luxemburg) was his belief that in Lenin's identification of Jacobinism with Marxism, he was deviating in the direction of ultra-radical bourgeois democracy. Trotsky arrived at this false conclusion because he, in his turn, regarded the original Jacobinism as a 'particular', 'left wing variety of liberalism' (*ibid*, p.127), and failed to detect within it those tendencies which would later be understood as totalitarian. But, however mistaken Trotsky may have been over this aspect of the matter, surely he was right to insist that classical Marxism and self-proclaimed Jacobinist Leninism were 'separated by an abyss' (*ibid*, p.123). Nevertheless, in 1917, Trotsky chose to leap across it, without ever subsequently finding convincing theoretical grounds for having done so.

THE GREAT EXAMPLE

Leninists will doubtless object that what actually occurred under the rule of Bolshevism in his life-time was, in many respects, far from Lenin's previous intentions, even as late as the summer of 1917, when he wrote his uncompleted essay, 'The State and Revolution' ('C.W.', Vol.25, pp.383-492). There, they will claim, can be found the authentic voice of Bolshevik 'proletarian democracy', with Lenin's prediction that, with the overthrow of bourgeois rule (and here he invoked Engels) 'the state begins to wither away' (*ibid*, p.419). True, 'simultaneously with an immense expansion of democracy' there would be exercised, for a while, 'a series of restrictions on the freedom of the oppressors, the exploiters and the capitalists' (*ibid*, p.461). But of the denial of freedom to the socialist opponents of the Bolsheviks ... not a word. Yet could it be that the idea had not yet occurred to him? Hardly, since Lenin's first measures against the opposition socialist press were, as we have seen, justified (with Trotsky's endorsement) not on the grounds of expediency, but those of principle. Again, there was something of the *deja vue* about all this.

Before assuming the leading position in the Jacobin Committee of Public Safety, Robespierre had waxed lyrical on the anticipated new republican order, a world in which the law would 'always afford peoples the purest model of reason and justice' (G. Rude, 'Robespierre', p.26) and where, like Lenin's no less mythical 'Soviet democracy', 'the people may change its government and recall its representatives when it pleases' (*ibid*, p.55). But what if it does not please their wise rulers? Both Lenin and Robespierre had their answer. The people, though (as Rousseau would say) being good, are also simple, and therefore easily misled. To serve them is not to yield to their every whim and fancy. Only the 'vanguard' (Lenin) or the 'magistrate' (Robespierre) perceives, embodies and can realise their true 'general will'. And the result? Terror, against the masses, for the good of the masses. As Robespierre put it, 'the people are sublime, but individuals are weak.' And, since the people was comprised of nothing but these 'weak individuals', it followed that 'the people in mass cannot govern itself' (R. Palmer, 'Twelve Who Ruled', p.33). Perhaps no-one captured either the essence or the contradictions of Jacobin *élitism* so succinctly as Saint-Just, with his exasperated comment that 'everyone wants to govern, no one to be just a citizen' (*ibid*, p.290). In view of the incapacities of the masses for self-government, the people needed a 'rallying point' (*ibid*, p.33), happily provided for them in 1793 by Robespierre's Committee of Public Safety, and in 1917 by Lenin's Bolshevik Central Committee. Like most of his fellow Jacobins, the austere Saint-Just followed Rousseau in preferring the barracks society of Sparta, 'ever made to conquer', to democratic and free-thinking Athens, whose 'blabbering' citizens 'feared their words as much as their bodies' (C. Blum, 'Rousseau and the Republic of Virtue', p.188). Like the rulers of Sparta and Plato's ideal Republic, the Jacobins believed that conformity of thought and unity of action were part of the natural order of things, being not only the means of victory but comprising the very goal itself. And therefore it followed that, like Lenin's Bolshevik's after March 1921, 'free [sic] Frenchmen' could 'have no internal dissensions' (ibid, p.201).

Finally, Robespierre no less than Lenin was repeatedly warned by his colleagues of the inevitable outcome of his bid to seize the 'conductor's baton' and, as the self-annointed high priest of his absurd cult of the Supreme Being, impose a 'despotism of liberty' on all of France. One fellow Jacobin predicted that of the 750 members of the Convention, 'only 200 will survive', while another forecast that of the Jacobins and their allies, 'there will not be twenty members of the Mountain left' (ibid, p.224). And they were both to be proved right, if not in the exact magnitudes, then in the substance of the process, no less than were the equally scorned Cassandras in Lenin's day. Guided by their maxim that 'all is permitted to those who act in the revolutionary direction', (Palmer, op.cit., p.167) the Jacobin Terror, like the Bolshevik, struck down critics and opponents on its Left just as readily as those on its Right. Thus, following the capture of Lyons and the massacre of at least two thousand of its (mainly plebian) citizens, the city's 60,000 textile workers, being supposedly infected with 'Federalism' (the Menshevism of its day) and having refused to submit to Jacobin rule, were to be deported and dispersed to more loyal regions of France, there to be 'watched' and to learn to 'follow the lead of those who march beside them'. Otherwise, united, 'they would long be a dangerous nucleus, always favourable to enemies of true principles' (ibid, p.165).

As if in conscious imitation of its prototype, Lenin's regime routinely employed identical methods against the erring masses, usually striking factory workers and rebellious peasants and national minorities. But the most notorious instance followed the suppression of the Kronstadt 'mutiny', with the execution or despatch to labour camps of its leading spirits and the dispersal of the bulk of the remainder of the participants to other fleets of the Red Navy (cf Avrich, op.cit., Getzler, 'Kronstadt: The Fate of a Soviet Democracy'). Here at least we can concur with Lenin in his oft-repeated claim that of all previous revolutionary movements, his revered and resembled above all others Jesuitical, terroristic and totalitarian Jacobinism.

And, for all Lenin's claims that Jacobinism represented the interests of the oppressed classes, a mere one year of their rule sufficed to so alienate the masses that the fall and execution of Lenin's exemplar aroused no popular protest. Quite the contrary in fact. Only a matter of days previously, an ever more strict enforcement of the 'Maximum' limit on worker's wages had precipitated a wave of (naturally illegal) strikes in Paris and, more generally, strengthened the conviction amongst the Parisian poor that they had been used as a street army to fight the battles of the Jacobin élite (G. Williams, 'Artisans and Sans-Culottes', p.88, R. Palmer op.cit., p.379). Robespierre, denounced as a 'cannibal' on a workers' anti-Jacobin demonstration, responded in the Convention that his plebian critics were accomplices of 'a general plan of conspiracy' against the revolution (G. Williams, op.cit., p.85, G. Rude, op.cit., p.75). Shades of Kronstadt! But at least the workers of Paris had the last word. As the 'Incorruptible's' severed head fell into the basket, they were heard to exclaim, 'There goes the Maximum!'' (G. Williams, op.cit., p.89).

Not that the peasants were treated any more favourably by the Jacobins than by the Bolsheviks. As the rural counterpart to the 'Loi Chapalier' outlawing trades unions and strikes, the Jacobins no less ruthlessly enforced the law of March 18, 1793, which punished by death the mere advocacy of an equal division of the land (C. Jones, op.cit., p.27). As for women, they fell victim to legislation inspired by Rousseau's teachings on the inate superiority of men. On October 30, 1793, the Committee of Public Safety declared dissolved all women's political societies, no matter how radical, and then, over the next few months, extended its crusade against feminism to the harrassing, arrest and, in at least one instance, execution of advocates of women's rights (ibid, pp.35, 175, 351, and C. Blum, op.cit., pp.204-219). Obviously, the August 1789 Declaration on the Rights of Man was intended to be taken literally. And could not the fate of feminism under Jacobin rule help us to place in its broader historical and ideological context not only Lenin's conduct in the 'Bauman Affair', but his opinion that Bolshevism represented the masculine line of Russian social democracy, and the conspicuous absence of women from the summits of the Bolshevik hierarchy, except in the capacity of dutiful wife (Krupskaya) or mistress (Inessa Armand)?

More generally, it is certainly reasonable to assume that, judging by his conduct during and after 1917, Lenin had learned much from the fall of the Jacobins. Unlike Robespierre, who stumbled as much as conspired his way to the top, Lenin, as we have seen, knew from the outset exactly 'what had to be done' to secure and maintain his party's monopoly of political power. It required, amongst other measures, firstly either the destruction, as in the case of the Constituent Assembly or, as in that of the Soviets and trades unions, the 'Bolshevisation' (the Nazis later described their own similar undertaking as 'co-ordination') of non-party institutions and, secondly, the total discrediting, isolation and elimination of all potential opponents, so that when the popular mood turned hostile, it could find no rallying points or means of legal expression. As an avid student of the French Revolution, Lenin knew full well how in July 1794, utilising the residual independence of the Convention, and rashly forewarned by Robespierre of his intention to 'crush all the factions' (G. Rude, op.cit., p.78) the disparate threatened groups and individuals had combined forces to launch their pre-emptive blow. Such was the genesis of the 9th of Thermidor (July 27, 1794), exactly one year to the day after Robespierre's appointment to the Committee of Public Safety.

And even in this event, there are striking parallels with the history of Bolshevism. Departing from previous practice, the already Jacobin-dominated Committee endorsed Robespierre's selection without first seeking the approval of the (largely non-Jacobin) Convention, to which, in theory at least (as in the case of the Bolshevik Commissars) the Committee was constitutionally subordinate (C. Jones, op.cit., p.90) Trotsky relates how Stalin had his entrée into the upper echelons of the RSDLP similarly facilitated by Lenin behind the backs of and against the wishes of his own party comrades. When Stalin's initial nomination to the Central Committee was rejected, on grounds which were to be fulsomely and tragically vindicated, by delegates to the Prague all-Bolshevik conference of January 1912, Lenin, 'after preliminary negotiations with delegates', had 'apparently deemed it wiser not to advance Koba's candidacy'. And when an insistent Lenin subsequently arranged the future tyrant's co-option, fellow Bolsheviks 'gave vent to their indignation among themselves' ('Stalin'. p.137). And this, remember, is Trotsky's asccount.

But the sad chronicle of Lenin's advancement of Stalin does not end there. Ten years on, at another Bolshevik convention (the 11th Party Congress of March 1922) Lenin encountered and again overcame no less vehement objections to Stalin's continued rise when, after having already secured his appointment to the Orgburo (the immensely strategic organ responsible for the deployment of party officals) Lenin came under attack for his defence of Stalin's shortcomings as Chairman of the Workers' and Peasants' Inspection, a body charged with, of all things, the task of combatting bureaucratic practices in the state administration. Stung by claims that Stalin was ill suited to his posts of responsibility (to which he would soon add the ultimate prize of Party General Secretary) Lenin challenged his critics to 'suggest any better candidate than Comrade Stalin', a 'man who enjoys high prestige' ('C.W.', Vol.33, p.316). With Lenin, evidently, But not with everyone. Even so, as in 1912, Lenin had his way. He paid no more heed to his comrades' warnings about Stalin (until it was too late) than he had some twenty years previously concerning his plan for a 'vanguard' party, in each case with consequences which were to leave their tragic marks on the entire subsequent course of world history.

So, we are led to conclude that not only according to the known facts but, what is even more persuasive, putting to one side the accounts and objections of opponents and victims, and relying exclusively upon primary sources, specifically the testimony of the principal architects and executants, neither the Bolshevik seizure of power nor regime conformed in respect of their degree of popular support or modus operandi to the classic Marxist conception of a genuine socialist revolution. 'Merrie Leninist' legend has it that the technique of engineering a near unanimous (usually 99% plus) electoral self-endorsement of the Bolshevik regime belongs properly to the Stalinist era. Once again, a closer inspection of the facts establishes that this totalitarian practice had become a routine operation as early as 1922, a full year before the final illness of Lenin and the onset of the eclipse of Trotsky. In that year, of all the delegates 'elected' to Soviet bodies, at the district level a mere 0.1% were representatives of other parties, while at the higher provincial level, the percentage was zero (O. Anweiler: 'The Soviets', p.261). Are we seriously expected to believe that these figures remotely reflected the real political preferences of the Soviet public?

The truth of the matter is that 'Soviet' Russia had become totalitarian Bolshevik Russia, a one party state in fact if not in law. And, as such, its masters were busy excluding even token proletarians from their deliberations. Although composing but a tiny proportion of the country's population (let us generously place their share at 5%) the catagory of white collar worker comprised, in the early 1920s, an average of around 50% of the executive bodies of the same soviet institutions. Just as Engels had predicted, the core of former professional revolutionaries (those whom Lenin had specifically and explicitly defined as the 'wise men' of the party – 'C.W.', Vol.5, p.464) were now apace transforming themselves into the professional and no less indispensable rulers and organisers of the new post-revolutionary order. And this, the Trotskyists will still assure us, was what they choose to call a 'healthy workers' state'.

Since we are considering yet again the process of 'substitutionism', just one last question needs to be considered. Is it possible for a class to conquer political power in its sleep? According to Trotsky, yes. As he relates it, the Kerensky government was deposed, and the soviets assumed state power, in the early hours of November 8, 1917 (op. cit., p.1158). By virtue of the nocturnal activities of the Bolsheviks, 'the capital awoke under a new power' (ibid, p.1163). What was this new power? Presumably, the power of the class which, in its 'immense majority', not only in Petrograd, but throughout Russia, had slept, unlike its professional leaders, throughout the entire proceedings.

And yet, whatever one's views on the outcome, it is hard to deny the world-historic significance of what Lenin had accomplished. Beginning with an idea – the vangard party – a book – 'What Is To Be Done?' – and the slenderest of majorities at a gathering of itinerant Russian radicals in a dingy London church hall, Lenin had designed, assembled and drilled a political machine whose leaders, in less than two decades, had 'placed themselves at the head of a country which occupies one sixth of the surface of the globe' ('In Defence of the Russian Revolution' (1932) in 'Leon Trotsky Speaks', p.259).

It is a story without parallel in the history of the modern world. Let it not be said of our and future generations that in the necessary attempt to make a better world than this one, we neglected to heed the warning of George Santayana and, by failing to understand history, were condemned to repeat it.

Table A: Representation by Party at the Second Congress of Soviets, November 1917 (Column 1 is based upon newspaper accounts of the Congress, column 2 on reports made by Congress officials, while column 3 is the parties own estimates of their support):

	1	2	3
Bolsheviks	250	300	390
Mensheviks	74	92	92
Socialist Revolutionaries	165	193	160
Others	28	85	7
Total	517	670	649

Source: J. Bunyan and H. Fisher, The Bolshevik Revolution, 1961, p.110

Table B: Frequency of Soviet meetings in Saratov:

Month	Plenum Level	Exec. Level	Other Organs
March	15	19	–
April	4	16	–
May	2	17	–
June	2	12	3
July	–	15	–
August	1	10	1
September	–	12	1
October	1	12	4

Source: J. Keep, *The Russian Revolution*, London, 1976, p.125

Table C: Frequency of meetings at Petrograd Peterhof district:

Month	Plenum	Executive
March	20	0
April	11	2
May	18	3
June	15	6
August	11	6
September	6	6
October	4	4

Source: M. Ferro, *The Bolshevik Revolution*, 1985, p.195

Table D: Bolshevik Representation in Soviety Hierarchy (Spring):

Soviet	Plenum (% of Dels.)	Executive (% of Dels.)
Petrograd	2.4	16.5
Moscow	22.8	30.6
Saratov	11.3	50
Samara	25.9	75
Kiev	14.0	16.2
Kharkov	12.8	7

Table E: Political Intentions of Delegates to Second Congress of Soviets:

Policy	Number	%
All Power to Soviets	505	75
All Power to Democracy	86	13
All Power to Democracy, but without Cadets (Liberals)	21	3
A Coalition	58	8.6
No Answer	3	0.4

Source: R. Pipes, *The Russian Revolution*, London, 1990, p.508

Table F: Results of Elections to Constituent Assembly, November 1917:

Party	Total votes	% of Total vote
Socialist Parties:		
Bolsheviks	10,661,000	24.0
Mensheviks	1,806,000	4.1
Socialist Revolutionaries	21,376,000	48.1
Left S.R.	451,000	1.0
Total Socialist Vote:	34,294,000	77.2
Nationalist Parties:		
Mussavat (Azerbaijan)	616,000	1.4
Dashnaktsutium (Armenia)	506,000	1.3
Alash Orda (Kazakhstan)	262,000	0.6
Others	407,000	0.9
Total Nationalist Vote:	1,781,000	4.2
Right Wing Parties:		
Constitutional Democrats	2,088,000	4.7
Others	1,261,000	2.8
Total Right Wing Vote:	3,349,000	7.5
Total Votes Cast	39,434,000	

Source: R. Pipes, *ibid*, p.542

AFTERWORD
LENIN'S RUSSIAN DOLLS

'The Bolshevik Party was created by Lenin. Stalin grew out of its political machine and remained inseparable from it.'

L. Trotsky

More than once, George Orwell asked why it was that leftist intellectuals found it so difficult to confront the truth about the nature of the regime created by the Bolshevik revolution of 1917. Even when – often very late in the day – they found the crimes of Stalin too much to digest, they would seek comfort – as they do even now – in the thought that the rot began after the death of Lenin and the fall of Trotsky. Orwell would have none of it. The 'seeds of evil were there from the start' and, what is more, 'things would not have been substantially different if Lenin or Trotsky had remained in control' ('Collected Essays', Vol.4, p.35). But seeds need time and the right conditions in order to grow and flower. Moreover, even though the seed contains the plant, it never resembles it, any more than a caterpillar does the butterfly. For similar reasons, generations of leftists have found it hard, or even impossible, to accept that someone so urbane, rational, and lacking in personal ambition or malice as Lenin could have fathered such a monster as Stalin. And yet, that is what happened. Our inquiry into the origins of Bolshevik doctrine and practice has repeatedly touched upon one of the most central and characteristic features of Leninism, namely, its unique, chameleon-like ability to assume a variety of political guises, the better to equip itself for its strategy of manipulating and subverting ideals, movements and institutions on its march to total power.

But what is true of the movement is no less true of the human material which it attracted, fashioned and utilised in various ways. Retrospectively, it is now possible to understand more fully than in their lifetimes the relationship that evolved between the always clinical Lenin, the founder of Bolshevism, and the butcher Stalin, its indispensible executant. At the very least, two facts concerning this relationship are surely beyond dispute: firstly, that Stalin owed his elevation in the Bolshevik hierarchy to Lenin's persistent patronage and, secondly, that those qualities which Lenin appreciated in Stalin were not only precisely those that had served the founder of Bolshevism so well in his struggle for the 'conductor's baton' of the revolutionary movement in Russia, but which his 'marvellous Georgian' deployed to such devestating effect in his rise from comparative obscurity to total mastery of the Bolshevik party and state.

The Second Party Congress provided Lenin with his first serious opportunity to display these skills, bringing off (but only with the indispensable support of Plekhanov) his remarkable *coup*, seizing, with a majority of no more than two votes, all the leading positions in the Party apparatus. True, Lenin's bid for the 'conductor's baton' proved premature. But in raising the banner of the 'hards', Lenin ensured that he would attract to his side precisely those who, like Stalin, saw in Lenin's methods the most effective means to secure the Party's still shared goals. With the sole exception of the initially 'soft' Trotsky, this new 'hard' generation of party professionals became the general staff that, under Lenin's supervision, executed – this time with total success – the Bolshevik *coup* of November 1917. The method, however, remained essentially the same as that pioneered in 1903. And, fittingly, it resembled nothing so much as a sequence of traditional Russian dolls.

Lenin's revolutionary strategy in 1917 progressed in the following manner. Realist enough to recognise that the demand which unified all the desires or struggles of the various movements of that year (urban workers, peasants, soldiers, national and religious minorities) was not the rule of the Bolshevik central committee, but the establishment of an authoritative national parliament, the Bolsheviks, as we have seen, outbid all other parties in urging the rapid convening of the promised (but delayed) Constituent Assembly. This, the universally popular demand (save amongst the old ruling classes) for Russia's first ever truly free election, served as Lenin's outer democratic doll.

Next came the Soviets. The Constituent Assembly, so the Bolshevik argument ran, could only be elected if the Soviets deposed the Provisional Government of Kerensky and temporarily (this condition was repeatedly stressed) assumed power until the Assembly convened. Hence the slogan 'all power to the Soviets', a demand which, up until the Bolshevik *coup*, and even for a time after, few outside the inner circle of the Bolshevik *élite* believed would pose a threat to the sovereignty of an assembly elected on the basis of free and equal universal suffrage. Rather, it was seen (and intended to be seen) as the means for its realisation.

Next came doll number three – the Military Revolutionary Committee of the Petrograd Soviet. Inside the leading organs of the Bolshevik Party, principally its central committee, Lenin campaigned for the idea that even a rigged and Bolshevik-dominated Second Congress of Soviets could not be relied upon to administer the death blow to the Provisional Government. After all, remember what happened at the no less-rigged Second Congress of the RSDLP! Better that the Party itself, harnessing a hastily and belatedly contrived military apparatus of a compliant and strategically placed local Soviet – Petrograd – seize power, and then transfer it formally to the Soviets once the Bolsheviks had clearly demonstrated as a *fait accompli* their removal of the old regime.

Doll number four was the Party or, more precisely, its central committee. The decision to overthrow Kerensky and seize power in the name of the Soviets (initially, the Military Revolutionary Committee of the Petrograd Soviet) was taken by a body that had no formal connection with the MRC, and at the instigation of a professional politician who up to that point had never held office in any Soviet institution. But Lenin, as we have had occasion to observe, was totally uninterested in such niceties. He was his own doll, driving forward the machine he had so painstakingly and selflessly built for just this moment, and just this purpose – the seizure of power and the creation of a socialist society – by whatever means necessary. But there still remained hidden within the fifth, a sixth doll, the last in the chain of 'substitutions' predicted by Leon Trotsky, Rosa Luxemburg and George Plekhanov in the wake of Lenin's first *coup* at the Second Congress of the RSDLP. On that heady night in November 1917, no-one amongst the Bolshevik *élite* could have possibly guessed its name. It was Stalin.

BIBLIOGRAPHY

WORKS REFERRED TO IN THE TEXT

R. Abramovitch, *The Soviet Revolution*, London, 1962
A. Antonov-Ovseyenko, *The Time of Stalin*, New York, 1983
Aristotle, *Politics*, London, 1961
O. Anweiler, *The Soviets*, New York, 1974
A. Ascher (ed.), *The Mensheviks in the Russian Revolution*, London, 1976
M. Bakunin, *On Anarchism*, Montreal, 1980
S. Baron, *Plekhanov: The Father of Russian Marxism*, Stanford, 1963
E. Bernstein, *Evolutionary Socialism*, New York, 1963
S. Bernstein, *August Blanqui and the Art of Insurrection*, London, 1971
R. Black, *Fascism in Germany*, Vol.1, London, 1975
A. Bone (trans.), *The Bolsheviks and the October Revolution*, London, 1974
C. Blum, *Rousseau and the Republic of Virtue*, Cornell, 1990
A. Bramwell, *Blood and Soil*, Bourne End, 1985
R. Breitman, *The Architect of Genocide*, London, 1991
J. Brennan, *The Origins, Development and Failure of Russian Social Democratic Economism*,
    Berkeley, 1963
M. Brinton, *The Bolsheviks and Workers' Control*, London, 1970
V. Brovkin, The Mensheviks After October, London, 1991
R. Brym, *The Jewish Intelligentsia and Russian Marxism*, London, 1978
J. Bunyan and H. Fisher, *The Bolshevik Revolution*, Stanford, 1961
E. Carr, *The Bolshevik Revolution*, Vol.1, London, 1950
A. Ciliga, *The Russian Enigma*, London, 1978
R. Clark, *Lenin*, London, 1988
S. Cohen, *Bukharin and the Bolshevik Revolution*, London, 1974
T. Dan, *The Origins of Bolshevism*, London, 1962
J. Degras (ed.), *The Communist International, Documents*, 3 vols, Oxford, 1956-1965
Dictionary of Quotations, London, 1990
Documents of the First International, 5 vols, Moscow, n.d.
Documents of the Fourth International, New York, 1973
S. Duff, *A German Protectorate*, London, 1970
F. Engels, *On Britain*, Moscow, 1962
L. Engelstein, *Moscow in the 1905 Revolution*, Stanford, 1976
M. Ferro, *The Bolshevik Revolution*, London, 1980
First Decrees of Soviet Power, London, 1970
J. Fishman, *The Insurrectionists*, London, 1970
C. Floud, *Hitler: The Path to Power*, Boston, 1989
J. Frankel, *Vladimir Akimov on the Dilemmas of Russian Marxism*, Cambridge, 1969
M. Futrell, *Northern Underground*, London, 1963
L. Gershov, *The Era of the French Revolution*, New York, 1957
I. Getzler, *Martov*, Cambridge, 1967
I. Getzler, Kronstadt 1917-1921, London, 1983
Hague Congress of the First International, Moscow, 1978
D. Hardy, *The Critic as Jacobin*, London, 1977
V. Haynes and O. Semyonova, *Workers Against the Gulag*, London, 1979
G. Higler and A. Meyer, *The Incompatible Allies*, London, 1953
History of the CPSU ('Short Course'), Moscow, 1941
History of the CPSU, Moscow, 1960
A. Hitler, *Mein Kampf*, Boston, 1943
H. Hoehne, *The Order of the Death's Head*, London, 1972
M. Holroyd, *Bernard Shaw*, Vol.3, London, 1991
C. Jones, *The Longman Companion to the French Revolution*, London, 1990
A. De Jonge, *Stalin*, Glasgow, 1987
K. Kautsky, *Communism Versus Social Democracy*, New York, 1946

K. Kautsky, *Selected Political Writings*, London, 1983
J. Keep, *The Rise of Social Democracy in Russia*, Oxford, 1963
A. Kelly, *Mikhail Bakunin*, London, 1987
Samir Al Khail, *Republic of Fear*, London, 1989
I. Kirkpatrick, *Mussolini: A Study in Power*, Westport, 1976
A. Kolnai, *The War Against The West*, London, 1938
N. Krupskaya, *Reminiscences of Lenin*, Moscow, 1959
D. Laurence (ed.), *Bernard Shaw: Collected Letters*, Vol.4, 1926-1950, London, 1988
G. Legett, *The Cheka*, Oxford, 1989
V. Lenin, *Collected Works*, 47 vols, Moscow, 1960-1980
Lenin: A Biography, Moscow, 1965
J. Loomis, *Paris in the Terror*, New York, 1986
R. Luxemburg, *Rosa Luxemburg Speaks*, New York, 1970
A. Lyttleton, *The Seizure of Power*, London, 1987
A. McBriar, *Fabian Socialism and English Politics 1884-1918*, Cambridge, 1966
N. Machiavelli, *The Prince*, London, 1958
N. Machiavelli, *The Discourses*, Vol.1, London, 1950
S. Malle, *The Economic Organization of War Communism*, Cambridge, 1985
K. Marx and F. Engels, *Collected Works*, 50 vols, Moscow, 1975-?
K. Marx and F. Engels, *Selected Correspondence*, Moscow, n.d.
K. Marx, *A Contribution to the Critique of Political Economy*, London, 1971
G. Meaker, *The Revolutionary Left in Spain 1914-1923*, Stanford, 1974
J. Meijer (ed.), *The Trotsky Papers*, Vol. II, The Hague, 1971
R. Michels, *Political Parties*, New York, 1959
H. Mitchell, 'Resistance to the Revolution in Western France', *Past and Present*, Jan. 1974
B. Mitchell, *European Historical Statistics*, London, 1987
G. Mosca, *The Ruling Class*, New York, 1939
J. Noakes and G. Pridham (eds.), *Documents on Nazism 1919-1945*, London, 1974
E. Nolte, *Three Faces of Fascism*, New York, 1969
G. Orwell, *The Collected Essays, Journalism and Letters*, Vol.4, Harmondsworth, 1980
R. Palmer, *Twelve Who Ruled*, Princeton, 1941
S. Payne, *Falange: A History of Spanish Fascism*, London, 1962
M. Pearson, *The Sealed Train*, London, 1975
R. Pipes, *Social Democracy and the St. Petersburg Labour Movement 1886-1897*, Harvard, 1963
R. Pipes, *The Russian Revolution*, London, 1990
R. Pipes, *Russia Under the Bolshevik Regime 1919-1924*, London, 1994
Plato, *The Republic*, New York, 1960
G. Plekhanov, *Selected Philosophical Works*, Vol.1, London, 1961
R. Postgate (ed.), *Revolution from 1789 to 1906*, New York, 1962
J. Primo De Rivera, *Selected Writings*, London, 1972
M. Rader, *No Comprise*, London, 1937
R. Reuth, *Goebbels*, London, 1993
J.-J. Rousseau, *The Social Contract*, London, 1948
G. Rude (ed.), *Robespierre*, New Jersey, 1967
A. Saboul, 'The Revolutionary State 1789-1796', *Past and Present*, No.65, Jan. 1974
L. Schapiro, *The Communist Party of the Soviet Union*, London, 1962
M. Shachtman, *The Bureaucratic Revolution*, New York, 1962
Second Congress of the RSDLP, London, 1978
G.B. Shaw (ed.), *Fabian Essays in Socialism*, London, 1931
G.B. Shaw, *Everybody's Political What's What?*, London, 1944
R. Skidelsky, *Oswald Mosley*, London, 1975
M. Smith-Morris (ed.), *The Economist Book of Vital World Statstics*, London, 1991
G. Sorel, *Reflections on Violence*, New York, 1961
B. Souvarine, *Stalin*, London, n.d.
A. Spencer, 'National Bolshevism' in: *Survey*, 44-45, Oct. 1963

J. Stalin, *Collected Works*, 13 vols, Moscow, 1954-1955

M. Stieg, 'The Second World War and the Public Libraries of Nazi Germany' in: *Journal of Contemporary History*, Vol.27, No.1, Jan. 1992

N. Sukhanov, *The Russian Revolution 1917*, London, 1917

J. Talmon, *The Origins of Totalitarian Democracy*, London, 1961

C. Trebilcock, *The Industrialisation of the Continental Powers*, London, 1990

H. Trevor-Roper (ed.), *Hitler's Table Talk*, Oxford, 1988

L. Trotsky, *The Challenge of the Left Opposition*, New York, 1975

L. Trotsky, *Communism and Terrorism*, New York, 1961

L. Trotsky, *The Essential Trotsky*, London, 1963

L. Trotsky, *History of the Russian Revolution*, London, 1934

L. Trotsky, *How The Revolution Armed*, London, 1980

L. Trotsky, *Lenin*, New York, 1962

L. Trotsky, *Leon Trotsky Speaks*, New York, 1972

L. Trotsky, *My Life*, New York, 1960

L. Trotsky, *On the Paris Commune*, New York, 1970

L. Trotsky, *Our Political Tasks*, London, n.d.

L. Trotsky, *Report of the Siberian Delegation*, London, n.d.

L. Trotsky, *The Revolution Betrayed*, New York, 1957

L. Trotsky, *Stalin*, London, 1947

L. Trotsky, *The Essential Trotsky*, London, 1963

L. Trotsky, *Their Morals and Ours*, London, 1968

L. Trotsky, *The Third International After Lenin*, London, 1974

L. Trotsky, *Writings of Leon Trotsky, 1929*, New York, 1975

L. Trotsky, *Writings of Leon Trotsky, 1932-33*, New York, 1972

L. Trotsky, *Writings of Leon Trotsky, 1937-38*, New York, 1976

L. Trotsky, *Writings of Leon Trotsky, Supplement 1934-40*, New York, 1979

G. Urban, *European Communism*, London, 1978

A. Valentinov, *Encounters with Lenin*, London, 1968

A. Weeks, 'The First Bolshevik' in: *Problems of Communism*, Nov./Dec. 1967

A. Weeks, *The First Bolshevik: A Political Biography of Peter Tkachev*, New York, 1968

A. Westoby and R. Blick, 'Early Soviet Designs on Poland' in: *Survey*, Vol.26, No.4 (117), Autumn 1982

G. Williams, *Artisans and Sans-Culottes*, London, 1968

B. Wolfe, *Marxism: 100 Years in the Life of a Doctrine*, London, 1967

B. Wolfe, 'Krupskaya Purges The People's Libraries' in: *Survey*, Summer, 1969, No.72

Z. Zeman, *Germany and the Revolution in Russia*, London, 1958

G. Zinoviev, *Lenin*, London, 1966

SUGGESTED FURTHER READING

On the French Revolution and Jacobinism

F. Aftalion, *The French Revolution: An Economic Interpretation*, Cambridge, 1990

R. Bienvenu (ed.), *The Ninth Thermidor: The Fall of Robespierre*, London, 1968

J. Bosher, *The French Revolution*, London, 1989

P. Kropotkin, *The Great French Revolution*, Montreal, 1989

G. Lefebvre, *The Thermidorians*, London, 1965

G. Rude, *The Crowd in the French Revolution*, London, 1965

J. Sole, *Questions of the French Revolution*, New York, 1989

A. Saboul, *The Parisian Sans-Culottes and the French Revolution 1793-94*, London, 1964

An Overall History of Modern Russia

A. Westwood, *Endurance and Endeavour: Russian History 1812-1986*, Oxford, 1990

On pre-revolutionary Russia

M. Falkus, *The Industrialisation of Russia*, London, 1983
P. Gatrell, *The Tsarist Economy 1850-1917*, London, 1986
B. Mitchell, *European Historical Statistics*, London, 1987
R. Pipes, *Russia Under the Old Regime*, London, 1990

On Russian populism

E. Lampert, *Sons Against Fathers*, Oxford, 1965
O. Radkey, *The Sickle Under the Hammer*, London, 1963
F. Venturi, *Roots of Revolution*, London, 1960
A. Yarmolinsky, *Road to Revolution*, London, 1957

On Marx

F. Mehring, *Karl Marx: The Story of His Life*, London, 1951
L. Schwarzschild, *The Red Prussian: The Life and Legend of Karl Marx*, London, 1986

On early Russian Marxism

A. Ascher, *Pavel Axelrod and the Development of Menshevism*, Cambridge, 1972
L. Haimson, *The Russian Marxists and the Origins of Bolshevism*, Cambridge, 1955
R. Kindersley, *The First Russian Revisionists*, London, 1962
D. Lane, *The Roots of Russian Communism*, Assen, 1975
A. Wildman, *The Making of a Workers' Revolution*, Chicago, 1967
G. Zinoviev, *History of the Bolshevik Party*, London, 1983

On Lenin

D. Shub, *Lenin*, London, 1966
A. Ulam, *Lenin and the Bolsheviks*, London, 1966
B. Wolfe, *Three Who Made a Revolution*, London,1956

On the history of the Internationals

F. Borkenau, *World Communism*, Michigan, 1962
F. Borkenau, *European Communism*, London, n.d.
J. Braunthal, *The History of the International*, 2 vols, London, 1966-67
G. Cole, *A History of Socialist Thought*, 7 vols, London, 1953-61
M. Drachkovitch and B. Lazitch (eds.), *The Comintern: Historical Highlights*, London, 1966
C. James, *World Revolution 1917-1936*, London, 1937
A. Westoby, *The Evolution of Communism*, Oxford, 1989
Ypsilon, *Pattern for World Revolution*, New York, 1947

On more recent trends

A. Westoby, *Communism Since World War Two*, Brighton, 1981

On Stalin

A. Bullock, *Hitler and Stalin: Parallel Lives*, London, 1991
I. Deutscher, *Stalin*, London, 1961
D. Volkognonov, *Stalin: Triumph and Tragedy*, London, 1991

On Trotsky

I. Deutscher, *The Trotsky Trilogy*, London, 1954-63
B. Knei-Paz, *The Social and Political Thought of Leon Trotsky*, Oxford, 1979

On the 1905 Revolution

S. Schwarz, *The Russian Revolution of 1905*, London, 1967
T. Shanin, *Russia 1905-07*, London, 1986
L. Trotsky, *1905*, London, 1972

On the year 1917 and the Bolshevik seizure of power

J. Basil, *The Mensheviks in the Revolution of 1917*, Columbus, 1984
G. Katkov, *Russia 1917: The February Revolution*, London, 1967
J. Keep, The Debate on Soviet Power, Oxford, 1979
D. Mandel, *The Petrograd Workers and the Fall of the Old Regime*, New York, 1983
D. Mandel, *The Petrograd Workers and the Seizure of Power*, London, 1984
R. Mckean, *St Petersburg Between the Revolutions*, London, 1990
A. Rabinowitch, *Prelude to Revolution*, Indiana, 1991

On the Revolution and the early Soviet Years

W. Chamberlain, *The Russian Revolution*, New York, 1963
L. Haimson (ed.) *The Mensheviks*, London, 1974
L. Schapiro, *The Origin of the Communist Autocracy*, London, 1977
J. Spargo, *Bolshevism: The Enemy of Political and Industrial Democracy*, London, 1919
J. Spargo, *The Greatest Failure in All History: A Critical Examination of the Actual Workings of Bolshevism in Russia*, New York, 1920

On the Bolshevik terror, the fate of the oppositions and Stalin's purges

P. Avrich, *Kronstadt 1921*, Princeton, 1970
A. Avtorkhanov, *Stalin and the Soviet Communist Party*, Munich, 1959
F. Beal, *Word From Nowhere*, London, 1938
A. Berkman, *The Bolshevik Myth*, London, 1989
A. Berkman, *The Russian Tragedy*, Orkney, 1976
V. Broido, *Lenin and the Mensheviks*, Aldershot, 1987
V. Brovkin, *The Mensheviks After October*, London, 1991
R. Conquest, *The Great Terror*, London, 1968
R. Conquest, *Inside Stalin's Secret Police*, London, 1985
R. Daniels, *Conscience of the Revolution*, London, 1960
I. Getzler, *Kronstadt: The Fate of a Soviet Democracy*, Cambridge, 1983
E. Goldman, *My Disillusionment in Russia*, London, 1925
E. Lyons, *Assignment in Utopia*, London, n.d.
G. Maximoff, *The Guillotine at Work: Vol.1 The Leninist Counter-Revolution*, Orkney, 1979
A. Orlov, *The Secret History of Stalin's Crimes*, London, 1954
W. Reswick, *I Dreamt Revolution*, Chicago, 1952
V. Serge, *Destiny of a Revolution*, London, 1982
A. Smith, *I Was a Soviet Worker*, London, 1937
A. Solzhenitsyn, *The Gulag Archipelago*, London, 1982
A. Vaksberg, *The Prosecutor and the Prey: Vyshinsky and the 1930s Show Trials*, London, 1990
Voline, *The Unknown Revolution*, Detroit, 1974

THE SEEDS OF EVIL

On the Soviet Economy

J. Chapman, *Real Wages in Soviet Russia Since 1928*, Cambridge, 1963
D. Dallin and B. Nicolaevsky, *Forced Labour in Soviet Russia*, London, 1948
D. Filtzer, *Soviet Workers and Stalinist Industrialisation*, London, 1986
M. Lewin, Russian Peasants and Soviet Power, London, 1968
A. Nove, *An Economic History of the USSR*, London, 1969
E. Preobrazhensky, *The New Economics*, London, 1965

On the Stalin-Hitler Pact and related matters

R. Black, *Fascism in Germany*, 2 vols, London, 1975
J. Degras, *Soviet Documents on Foreign Policy*, Vol.III, London, 1953
W. Leonhard, *Betrayal*, New York, 1989
G. Roberts, *The Unholy Alliance*, London, 1989
A. Rossi, *The Russo-German Alliance*, London, 1950
Z. Sheinis, *Maxim Litvinov*, Moscow, 1990
Sikorski Institute, *Documents on Polish-Soviet Relations 1939-45, Vol.I 1939-43*
R. Sontag and J. Beddie (eds.), *Nazi-Soviet Relations*, Washington, 1948
E. Wollenburg, *The Red Army: A Study in the Growth of Soviet Imperialism*, London, 1940

117

CHRONOLOGY

1758	Maximillien Robespierre born (executed 1794)
1760	Camille Desmoulins born (executed 1794)
1762	Publication of *The Social Contract* by Jean-Jacques Rousseau (1712-78)
1767	Louis Antoine Saint-Just born (executed 1794)
1789 July	French Revolution begins
1792 Aug.	King Louis XVI overthrown, republic proclaimed
1793 Jan.	Louis tried, executed for treason
1793 June	Jacobins seize power, Reign of Terror begins
1794 March	Robespierre purges Left (Hebert)
1794 April	Robespierre purges moderates (Danton)
1794 July	Overthrow and execution of Robespierre, Saint-Just
1799 Dec.	Coup by Napoleon, proclaims revolution over
1805	Auguste Blanqui (socialist Jacobin) born (d.1881)
1814	Mikhail Bakunin born (d.1876)
1818 May	Karl Marx born (d.1883)
1820 Nov.	Frederick Engels born (d.1895)
1825	Ferdinand Lassalle born (d. in duel 1864)
1825	Decembrist revolt in Russia (fails)
1830	July Revolution in France
1839 May	Failed *coup* by Blanqui in Paris
1844	Peter Tkachev (Russian Jacobin) born (d.1886)
1848 Jan.	Marx and Engels publish *Communist Manifesto*
1848	Year of Revolutions throughout Europe (except Russia)
1850	Paul Axelrod born (d.1928)
1852	Vera Zasulich born (d.1919)
1853	Crimean War begins
1855	Alexander II becomes Tsar
1856	Crimean War ends in defeat for Russia
1857	George Plekhanov born (d.1918)
1861	Tsar Alexander II abolishes serfdom
1863	Lassalle founds forerunner of German Social-Democratic Party (SPD)
1864	International Workingmen's Association (I.W.A.) founded ('First International')
1867	First volume of Marx's *Das Kapital* published in Germany
1869	Alexander Potresov born (d.1934)
1869	Nadezdha Krupskaya born (d.1939)
1869	Bakunin translates *Communist Manifesto* into Russian
1870 April	Vladimir Ilyich Ulyanov (Lenin) born (d.1924)
1870	Rosa Luxemburg born (murdered 1919)
1870	Italy completes unification
1870	Franco-Prussian war begins
1870 (circa)	Beginnings of populist movement in Russia
1871	Franco-Prussian war ends, Germany unified
1871 Spring	Paris Commune
1871	Vladimir Akimov born (d.1921)
1872	*Das Kapital* translated into Russian
1872	Hague Congress of I.W.A. expels Bakunin
1873	Yuri Martov born (d.1923)
1876	Bakunin dies
1876	'Land and Liberty' (Russian populist movement) founded
1877	Russo-Turkish war (ends 1878)
1878	German Chancellor Bismark bans SPD
1879	'Land and Liberty' splits into 'People's Will' (Jacobin-terrorist) and Plekhanov's 'Black Partition'

1879 Nov.	Leon Trotsky born (assassinated 1940)
1879 Dec.	Joseph Stalin born (d.1953)
1880	Plekhanov leaves Russia, becomes a Marxist
1881	Alexander Kerensky born (d.1970)
1881 Jan.	Blanqui dies
1881 March	Assassination of Alexander II by 'People's Will'
1883 March	Marx dies
1883	Benito Mussolini born (executed 1945)
1883	'Emancipation of Labour Group' founded by Plekhanov, Axelrod, Zasulich in Switzerland
1883	Grigori Zinoviev, Lev Kamenev born (both executed 1936)
1886	Tkachev dies
1887 May	Lenin's elder brother Alexander executed for failed plot against Tsar Alexander III
1887 Dec.	Lenin expelled from Kazan University
1889	Socialist (Second) International founded in Paris
1889 April	Adolf Hitler born (suicide 1945)
1890	Chancellor Bismark dismissed by Kaiser Wilhelm II, SPD legalised
1892	Lenin graduates in law
1893	Lenin settles in St Petersburg and joins illegal Marxist circle
1894	Nicholas II becomes Tsar
1895 Spring	Lenin visits Plekhanov, Axelrod in Switzerland
1895 Aug.	Engels dies
1895 Autumn	Lenin meets Martov for first time, they found 'St Petersburg League of Struggle for the Emancipation of the Working Class'
1895	Lenin, Martov, Potresov under arrest
1897	(Jewish) Bund founded
1897 Feb.	Lenin, Martov, Potresov sentenced to three years' Siberian exile
1898	Russian Social-Democratic Labour Party (Marxist) founded at Minsk, first Congress of RSDLP
1898	Lenin marries Krupskaya in Siberia
1899	Struggle against 'Economism' begins
1900 Spring	Lenin, Martov, Potresov end exile
1900 Autumn	Lenin, Martov, Potresov join with Plekhanov, Axelrod, Zasulich to form *Iskra*
1902 March	Lenin publishes *What Is To Be Done?* in Stuttgart
1902 April	Lenin leaves Munich for London, where he produces *Iskra* with Martov and Zasulich
1902 Oct.	Trotsky escapes from Siberia, arrives in London to join *Iskra*
1903 Aug.	Second Congress of RSDLP, Lenin (Bolsheviks) and Martov (Mensheviks) fall out over rules
1904	Russo-Japanese war begins
1905 Jan.	Workers' march on Winter Palace (opposed by Bolsheviks), massacre ('Bloody Sunday')
1905	Revolution in Russia, first Soviets formed, boycotted by Bolsheviks
1905 April	Bolsheviks hold Third RSDLP Congress (London)
1905 May	Russia cedes victory to Japan
1905 June	Mutiny on battleship 'Potempkin' in Black Sea
1905 Oct.	General strike in St Petersburg, Tsar Nicholas II grants constitution and civil liberties, parties legalised; 'Black Hundreds' (anti-semitic) launched
1905 Nov.	Lenin returns to Russia, Trotsky elected chair of St Petersburg Soviet, second general strike fails, Soviet dispersed, Trotsky arrested
1905 Dec.	Bolsheviks launch insurrection in Moscow, crushed
1906 Spring	Elections to first Duma (parliament), boycotted by Bolsheviks
1906 April	Fourth ('Unity') Congress of RSDLP (Stockholm)
1906 July	First Duma (oppositional) dissolved

1907 March	Second Duma elected
1907 May	Fifth RSDLP Congress (London)
1907 June	Second Duma (even more oppositional) dissolved by Tsar, third Duma elected on restricted (propertied) franchise, monarchist majority
1908-1910	Years of reaction
1912 Jan.	All-Bolshevik conference in Prague, Stalin later (Feb.) co-opted to Central Committee by Lenin
1912 April	Massacre of workers (200) at Lena gold fields, protest strikes throughout Russia
1912 May	'Pravda' (Bolshevik) begins daily publication, Stalin editor
1912 Oct.	Elections to fourth Duma, swing to Left, Kerensky leads liberal opposition ('Progressive Bloc')
1912-1913	Balkan wars
1914 July	Strikes, street fighting in St Petersburg
1914 Aug.	First World War begins, Lenin moves from Austrian Poland to Switzerland, issues call for new International
1915 Sept.	Lenin, Martov, Trotsky, Axelrod, Zinoviev attend anti-war conference in Zimmerwald (Switzerland), it adopts (unanimously) Trotsky's anti-war manifesto
1917 March	Revolution in Russia, Tsar Nicholas II abdicates, provisional government formed (Kerensky prominent), Soviets elected in towns, villages and army
1917 April	Lenin and other revolutionaries return from Switzerland to Russia in German 'sealed train', Lenin changes policy and aims for power, serious German funding of Bolsheviks begins
1917 June	First Congress of Soviets, Lenin (12% of delegates) says Bolsheviks ready to take power
1917 July	'July Days', Kerensky becomes Prime Minister, Lenin and Zinoviev accused of treason, go into hiding, Trotsky and Kamenev arrested
1917 Aug.	Bolsheviks hold seventh RSDLP Congress, Trotsky elected to Central Committee
1917 Sept.	General Kornilov coup fails, Bolsheviks win majority in Petrograd Soviet, Trotsky becomes Chair
1917 Nov.7-8	Bolsheviks seize power on eve of Second Congress of Soviets, which then approves by narrow majority, all-Bolshevik government formed, press censorship introduced, first arrests of opponents
1917 Nov.	Elections to Constituent Assembly
1917 Dec.	Bolshevik political police (Cheka) established
1918 Jan.	Bolsheviks dissolve Constituent Assembly on second day after losing elections (10m. votes out of 40m.)
1918 Spring	Bolsheviks step up repression of opponents, dissolve 19 Soviets (out of 20) after losing elections to Mensheviks and allies, first arrests of anarchists
1918 March	Soviet Russia signs Treaty of Brest Litovsk with Central Powers, German funding ends, Germans transfer troops to Western front
1918 May	George Plekhanov dies
1918 July	Final German push to Paris fails
1918 Nov.	War ends, revolutions in Austria and Germany, Kaiser Wilhelm II abdicates, republic proclaimed, SPD government formed, repression of revolutionaries begins, 'Free Corps' formed
1918 Dec.	Communist Party of Germany (KPD – 'Spartacists') formed
1919 Jan.	Communist leaders Liebknecht and Luxemburg murdered by 'Free Corps'
1919 Feb.	First Soviet concentration camps
1919 March	Communist (Third) International ('Comintern') founded, Zinoviev Chairman
1919-1920	Civil war and intervention in Russia
1920 Jan.	Secret agreement between Trotsky (Red Army) and von Seeckt (Reichswehr) to re-partition Poland

THE SEEDS OF EVIL

1920-1921	Famine in Russia
1920 Aug.	Red Army fails in bid to take Warsaw
1920 Sept.	Martov leaves Russia for Germany
1921 March	Tenth (Bolshevik) Party Congress bans factions, abandons 'War Communism' and adopts temporary return to market (New Economic Policy – NEP), repression of: peasant rebellions (Tambov), strikes in Petrograd and Kronstadt naval 'mutiny'
1921 end	All opposition driven underground or into exile, Russia now first one-party state in history
1922	Secret collaboration begins between Red Army and Reichswehr for German re-armament
1922 April	Stalin appointed Party General Secretary
1922 Oct.	Mussolini stages 'March on Rome', Fascist regime begins in Italy
1922 Dec.	Lenin writes 'Testament' attacking Stalin
1923 March	Lenin proposes alliance with Trotsky against Stalin, Trotsky temporises, Lenin incapacitated by final stroke until death in Jan. 1924
1923 April	Martov dies in Berlin
1923 Nov.	Hitler putsch in Munich fails
1923-1924	Trotsky isolated by alliance of Stalin, Zinoviev and Kamenev ('Troika'), Trotsky belatedly demands more liberal party regime, is accused of Menshevism
1924 Jan.	Lenin dies
1924 Summer	5th Comintern Congress, Zinoviev and Stalin call social democrats 'social fascists'
1924 Autumn	Stalin first advocates 'socialism in one country'
1925 April	Trotsky, still isolated, removed as head of Red Army
1925 Dec.	14th Party Congress, Zinoviev and Kamenev ('New Opposition') break with Stalin over his regime, 'socialism in one country' and his opposition to industrialisation
1926 Spring	Kamenev, Zinoviev and Krupskaya join with Trotsky to form 'United Opposition' ('Left Opposition')
1926	Stalin forms new bloc with Bukharin, Rykov, Tomsky on right, Zinoviev removed as head of Comintern, replaced by Bukharin
1926	Mussolini bans trade unions, rival parties, creates one-party state
1927 Dec.	15th Party Congress approves expulsion of United Opposition, Zinoviev and Kamenev capitulate
1928 Jan.	Trotsky exiled to Alma Ata
1928	Stalin demands end to NEP, launches first Five Year Plan (stolen from Trotsky), rift with Bukharin, Stalin installs own faction (Molotov, Voroshilov, Kirov, Kalinin, Rudzutak, Kuibyshev)
1928 Summer	Sixth Congress of Comintern declares main enemy to be social democrats ('social fascists')
1929	Collectivisation of farming begins, Bukharin capitulates, removed as head of Comintern, replaced by Molotov, Trotsky deported to Turkey
1929 Oct.	Wall Street Crash
1930 June	16th Party Congress, first without open opposition
1930 Sept.	Nazis win 18% of vote in Reichstag elections, Trotsky demands united front of SPD and KPD against Nazis, branded 'social fascist'
1931 Aug.	KPD joins with Nazis in referendum against Prussian SPD government
1932	Famine in USSR
1932 July	Nazis win 37% of vote in Reichstag elections, KPD says 'social fascists' still main enemy
1933 Jan.	Hitler appointed Chancellor
1933 Feb.	Reichstag fire, Nazis ban KPD, introduce press censorship, brown terror begins
1933 May	Nazis ban trade unions

1933 July	Nazis ban SPD, create one-party state
1933 Summer	Trotsky calls for new (Fourth) International
1934 June	'Night of the Long Knives', Hitler purges brown-shirt radicals (Roehm)
1934 Dec.	Stalin has Party rival Kirov murdered, used as pretext for new purge
1935	Stalin purge begins, Zinoviev and Kamenev tried and jailed over Kirov murder
1936 July	Civil war in Spain begins
1936 Aug.	First Moscow 'show trial', execution of Zinoviev and Kamenev
1937-1938	Continued trials, purges, Red Army chiefs and Bukharin executed
1938 March	Hitler seizes Austria
1938 Autumn	Czech crisis, Hitler given Sudetenland at Munich
1939 March	Hitler seizes rest of Czechoslovakia
1939 March	At 18th Party Congress Stalin begins overtures to Hitler
1939 April	Franco wins Spanish civil war
1939 Aug.	Stalin-Hitler pact signed in Moscow
1939 Sept.	Hitler, Stalin invade/partition Poland, Second World War begins
1939 Winter	Stalin invades Finland
1940 April	Hitler invades western Europe
1940 June	Stalin congratulates Hitler on capture of Paris, fall of France
1940 June	Stalin seizes Baltic states with Hitler's approval
1940 Aug.	Trotsky assassinated in Mexico by an agent of Stalin
1941 June	Hitler invades USSR
1941 Dec.	Japan attacks Pearl Harbour
1943 March	Comintern wound up by Stalin
1945 May	War ends in Europe
1945 Aug.	Stalin's rule in Europe extended by Potsdam agreement
1945 Aug.	US drops two atom bombs on Japan, war ends in Asia
1947	Communist Information Bureau ('Cominform') established to replace Comintern
1948 Spring	Tito (Yugoslavia) defies Stalin, expelled from Cominform
1948-1953	Purges, trials, executions in East Europe, Stalin launches campaign against Jews
1949 Oct.	Mao wins civil war in China, 'People's Republic' proclaimed
1950-1953	Korean War
1953 March	Stalin dies
1953 June	Workers' revolt in East Germany crushed by Red Army
1953 Summer	Revolt in Soviet slave camp (Vorkuta) crushed, camp later closed
1953 Nov.	Nikita Khrushchev appointed party General Secretary
1956 Feb.	Khrushchev denounces Stalin in 'Secret Speech' to 20th Party Congress
1956 June	Workers' revolt in Poznan (Poland) crushed by security forces
1956 Oct.	Workers' revolt in Hungary crushed by Red Army
1961 Aug.	Berlin Wall erected
1962 June	Workers' revolt in Novocherkassk (USSR) crushed by Red Army
1964 Oct.	Khrushchev replaced by Leonid Brezhnev as Party General Secretary
1968	'Prague Spring' (Dubcek) in Czechoslovakia, crushed by Red Army
1970 Dec.	Workers' revolt on Polish Baltic crushed by security forces
1976 June	Workers' revolt in central Poland crushed by security forces
1979 Dec.	Red Army invades Afghanistan
1980-1981	'Solidarity' trade union formed in Poland, crushed after military *coup* installs Gen. Jaruzelski (Dec. 1981)
1982 Nov.	Brezhnev dies, replaced as Party General Secretary by Yuri Andropov
1984 Feb.	Andropov dies, replaced in March by Konstantin Chernenko
1985 March	Chernenko dies, replaced by Mikhail Gorbachev
1989-1991	Revolts throughout Eastern Europe and China (crushed in China), Berlin Wall comes down, Germany unifies, free elections in eastern Europe, Red Army leaves Afghanistan
1991 Aug.	Failed military-KGB *coup* in USSR leads to collapse of system, USSR breaks up